To Mike,
all My Best #23

6/14/8

# The People's Champion
## ◆◇ Willie Horton ◇◆

# The People's Champion
## ◆◆ Willie Horton ◆◆

## With Kevin Allen
## Foreword by Al Kaline

Published by
Immortal Investments Publishing
www.immortalinvestments.com
35122 W. Michigan Avenue, Wayne, Michigan 48184
1-800-475-2066


**Publisher's Cataloging-in-Publication**
*(Provided by Quality Books, Inc.)*




Allen, Kevin M.
    The people's champion : Willie Horton / by Kevin M.
Allen. – 2nd ed.
    p. cm.
    LCCN 2005920407
    ISBN 0-9723637-5-0

    1. Horton, Willie, 1942-  I. Title.

GV865.H63A55 2005                    796.357'092
                                     QBI05-800202

I dedicate this book to my mom and dad, my wife, my children, my grandkids, and my entire family for being my backbone.

I'd also like to dedicate it to Coach Strong, Coach Thompson, Coach Bishop, Charlie Dressen, Mr. [Jim] Campbell, and Judge [Damon] Keith for my development and for being there for me. I must also include Mr. [Mike] Ilitch and the Detroit Tigers organization for giving me the opportunity to be back in baseball.

Finally, I want to dedicate this book to the fans. You are my extended family. Thanks for allowing me to come into your homes, workplaces, yards, and playgrounds. You have always treated me like family.

—Willie Horton

# CONTENTS

# ◈◈ FOREWORD ◈◈

**WHILE IT IS THE STRENGTH OF WILLIE** Horton's character that has bonded our friendship for more than 40 years, it was the strength of his hands and arms that apparently saved my life on May 30, 1970.

Truthfully, I have no memory of what happened that day in Milwaukee. But what I'm told is that center fielder Jim Northrup and I collided as we were chasing down a drive hit by Brewers infielder Roberto Pena. On impact, I swallowed my tongue, and when Willie came galloping over from left field, he found me turning purple and gasping for air.

In those situations, the jaw is tight and difficult to open, and I'm thankful Willie has incredible strength, because although others came to my aid, he was the only one who could pry my jaw open.

But Willie and I had connected long before that episode. In some ways, we were a lot alike. Like me, Willie never said much in the clubhouse. We weren't the kind of players who yelled and screamed. We went out and did our jobs. We were also alike because we both loved Detroit. We both loved the Tigers, and we both loved playing the game of baseball. We didn't have to talk about that. We just looked at each other and understood that's how we felt.

When Willie came to the Tigers, I was already a veteran player. He wanted to get better, and he came to me and we talked about improving his overall game. What I told him was what I had learned: You can't just think of yourself as a hitter. If you strike out with the bases loaded, you can't take that out in the field with you. You have to forget about that at-bat, and then you go out and play good defense and win the ballgame that way.

We also talked about how I believed you should never show fear to any pitcher. When a pitcher knocked me down, it became a grudge match between that pitcher and me. I wanted to take the next pitch up the middle and beat that pitcher. Willie developed that same attitude.

When Willie Horton was on a roll, he could carry a ballclub like few players I've seen. Particularly in 1967 and 1968, it was almost as if we were in a constant countdown to one of his offensive explosions.

When Willie was hot, it was always just a matter of time before he was going to launch one out of the ballpark. We won many games coming from behind in 1968, and Willie was involved in many of them.

With 53 years logged with the same organization, I view myself as a lifelong Detroit Tiger. And I view Willie the same way, even though he played for other teams. He was always a Tiger at heart. And it's been a real joy to be working together in the Tigers front office after all these years.

Willie's done amazing things in Detroit, and he's a focal point in this town. Detroiters love him because he's one of them. He symbolizes what Detroit is all about. Whether you're black or white, you appreciate what Willie has accomplished because he's shown that with a lot of hard work and determination, you can make it.

*Al Kaline*
*Baseball Hall of Fame, Class of 1980*

# ❖❖ INTRODUCTION ❖❖

WHEN FANS EXCAVATE MEMORIES OF Willie Horton, they remember the fire in his eyes and the thunder of his bat. When "Willie the Wonder" stepped to the plate in the 1960s, it was a happening in Motown. You didn't mow the lawn or wipe the kitchen countertop during a Willie Horton at-bat. You put your life on hold just long enough to turn up the volume on Ernie Harwell on your radio, or to adjust your rabbit-ear antennae to get a clearer view of what Willie would do.

When Willie swung the bat, it was not to be missed. He was baseball's most marvelous physics exhibit. When the force of Willie's swing connected with a baseball traveling at high velocity, there was a reaction the likes of which most of us had never witnessed. The impact was explosive enough that it could be heard from Detroit to Traverse City to Port Huron to Ishpeming. His home runs seemed almost nuclear-powered, like they could be more accurately analyzed with a seismograph than with a tape measure. When Willie launched a hardball into orbit, you could hear people gushing on every street in every city in Michigan.

The 1960s were troubling times in America, as society struggled through a civil rights battle that was long overdue. Not everyone had made their peace with racial issues, but the people of Michigan knew where they stood on Willie Horton. He was the Detroit Tigers' first black star, developed on Detroit's inner-city playgrounds. But his stardom was not divided along racial lines. Like all black athletes of his generation, Willie received his share of hate mail, but he was clearly just as revered by white fans as he was by black fans.

Fans loved Willie because he played baseball with boyish passion, and maybe because he symbolized the American dream that a child can rise up from a poor neighborhood to become an idol. Fans loved Willie because he entered the batter's box with a menacing stare that could melt the confidence of the heartiest of hurlers, and yet he wore a smile everywhere else on the diamond.

The curious aspect of fans' allegiance to Willie Horton was that they fell in love with him without ever really knowing that he was a better man than he was a ballplayer. The truth is that Willie is as much about people and family as he is about baseball. He loved the game because he loved its people. He loved his teammates like they were his brothers, and he always had time for the fans. Some athletes see a fan seeking an autograph as an imposition, but Horton sees it as an honor. When Willie makes reference to his family, you can't be sure if he's going to be talking about his wife and seven children, his former teammates, or members of the Tigers' grounds crew. They're all family to Willie.

This is a man who wakes up at five o'clock every morning to read the Bible, and who spends hours on the phone talking to friends and family. During the course of a day, he has a kind word for everyone he meets and a hug for many of them. He is a 63-year-old sports icon and yet he refers to Tigers owner Mike Ilitch as "Mr. Ilitch." And he pays similar respect to many others in his life. But if people call him "Mr. Horton," he begs them to call him "Willie" instead. And he punctuates every goodbye with a reminder to give his best to your family.

The worst criticism his friends can lay on Willie is that he has a hard time saying "no" to anyone for any reason. Imagine what a pleasant world this would be if that were the worst of all of our faults.

The reflection of a man's character is often revealed in the company he keeps, and it's noteworthy that many of Horton's closest chums are the same friends he possessed a half century ago when he was living in the Jeffries projects. They were all there at Tiger Stadium in 1959 when Horton, then a sophomore at Northwestern High School, hit the light tower in right-center field with a monumental home run clout. They were there the night in 1963 when Willie hit a home run in his first Tiger Stadium plate appearance wearing a Tigers uniform. They were at Comerica Park in 2000 when his No. 23 was officially retired and his impact was immortalized with a statue. And they were all there at his home, in October 2004, when his family hosted a gathering to celebrate the state of Michigan's passage of a resolution annually recognizing Horton's birthday, October 18, as Willie Horton Day throughout the state.

As friends and family told stories about Willie's life of giving, his former Northwestern teammate and close friend Walt Terrell (who shares his name with a former Tigers pitcher) allowed his love of Willie to bubble up in an emotional testimony.

"I can't hold this in any longer," Walt said. "I have to say this—Willie Horton lives Detroit. Willie Horton *is* Detroit."

"Amen," the crowd murmured, nodding their heads in agreement. At that moment, spirituality circulated in the room to the point that it felt like a Baptist revival. My regret is that I didn't step forward and testify to my belief that Willie is the single most important homegrown athlete to play for a Detroit sports team.

In terms of impact in his community, Willie Horton is as important as Joe Louis is to the Detroit community.

What I also should have said to the gathering that day is that I asked Willie to tell his story because it was a story that needed to be told. There needed to be a historical record of the life of one of Detroit's most important athletes. Before this book was written I had never met Willie. But it would not be an exaggeration to suggest that he has played a role in my development as a person and—maybe even as a writer.

It was confusing to grow up in the 1960s, particularly if you were poor and unsure of where you fit in a world that was in the midst of dramatic change. You tried to develop your self-esteem by idolizing those who had an abundance of it. In that era, you longed to be as proud and defiant as Muhammad Ali and as strong and confident as Jim Brown or Johnny Unitas. But it was allegiance to our hometown baseball teams that got us through the difficult summers when we had too much time to think about what might lie ahead. Back then, adults didn't know to allay children's fears about the Cold War, and race relation discussions were never held at the dinner table. We popped Good & Plenty, not antidepressant pills. We didn't have counseling; we just had baseball.

And Willie Horton was great therapy. There was something about Willie the Wonder's aura that I wanted to rub off on me. It was his attitude. He put his talent and his soul into every swing he took. Willie was never cheated on his cuts. When he rolled his wrists at the pitch, he swung with gale force. Sometimes when he missed, his helmet would spin off his head, and I was sure he was going to corkscrew himself all the way to the center of the earth. Even when Willie failed, he walked from the plate with pride in his gait, comfortable knowing that he had given the game his best effort at that particular moment.

He was just a kid in the neighborhood who escaped poverty to live his dream. Maybe some of us who watched him started to believe we could do that in our own lives, in our own way. Through Willie, I began to know that I was not going to allow myself to be cheated on my swings, no matter what I did with my life. Willie taught us to swing for the fences with all of our being.

Fans have told Willie similar stories for years, but he's such a humble man that he's only now starting to understand the impact he made on his community. He's told me the interview process for this book has reminded him how blessed he's been during his career. What I should have told him is that Fridays with Willie have been as therapeutic for me as his at-bats were years ago.

Walt Terrell was right when he said Willie is Detroit. But Willie belongs to all of us in the state of Michigan, regardless of whether we're rich, impoverished, well-connected, disenfranchised, white, or a person of color.

He is The People's Champion. And I hope you enjoy his story.

*Kevin M. Allen*

# Chapter 1

## THE COWARD'S CALL

EVERY BASEBALL PLAYER HAS ENDURED a hitting slump where it feels as though he doesn't even know which end of the bat to grip.

It feels like you've never held a bat in your hands before. Your stance seems unnatural. You can't get comfortable in the batter's box. And every pitch seems impossible to hit. It's either just out of your reach on the outside corner of the plate, or it's burrowing in on your hands like a laser-guided missile. When you're in a slump, borderline pitches are always called strikes. When you are in a slump, you swing at bad pitches and foul-off good pitches.

When I was playing Triple-A baseball in Syracuse in 1963, I went through one of those slumps. I was 20 years old and maybe I doubted myself. I was probably homesick. I don't remember exactly what I told my mother when I called home to Detroit, but I remember that she was pouring her love through that phone line. Lillian Horton, called "Sis" by almost everyone who knew her, might have been the best listener God ever put on earth. If you had troubles, she had buckets of sympathy. And she believed that if she could get you to her supper table, she could solve all your problems. She had given birth to 21 children, and yet she always acted as if she didn't have nearly enough people at her table for meals. She was always bringing someone home to eat. She would whip up some biscuits and homemade syrup, and whatever troubles you had seemed far less bothersome. When I told Mom that I was wondering if I was good enough to play in the major leagues, she was sympathetic and caring. She didn't even flinch when I told her I was thinking of quitting.

"Baby," she said, "if you decide baseball's not for you, don't you feel bad. You just c'mon home. This will always be your home, and I'll be here to take care of you."

Papa must have figured out what the conversation was about. I could hear him stomping across the room, saying, "Sis, give me the phone…give me the damn phone!"

James Thomas Clinton Horton was not a man to mince words, and he certainly didn't on that night.

"You aren't going to jump up and leave the job you've been given," he said sternly. "You aren't going to give up this opportunity the Tigers have given you. You're not going let down Judge (Damon) Keith. And you're *not* going to let down your family. You have responsibilities, Willie, and you're going to live up to those responsibilities. What are you going to do if you come home—work in an auto plant?"

As I tried to explain the self-doubt that was dancing through my mind, Papa didn't want to hear it.

"What do you have to complain about? You're nothing but a damn coward," he said, and slammed down the receiver.

His words were like a knockdown pitch, and it was a struggle for me to dust myself off. Papa shocked me. And it was the worst feeling I'd ever had.

Immediately, I called my oldest brother in West Virginia.

"James, did Papa ever call you a coward?" I asked.

"Nope," he said. "You must have done something bad. What did you do?"

That didn't help me so I called Ray. Same question. Same answer. Papa had never called him a coward.

Next up was Frank, and that was a mistake because he was the brother most like my father.

"Frank, did Papa ever call you a coward?" I asked.

"No," he said. "You must've really messed up if Papa called you a coward."

As one of 21 children of Lillian and Clinton Horton, I had plenty of folks to call. And I called them all. When I ran out of brothers, I called my sisters, and none of them had ever been called a coward. I even called my brother-in-law George, who had helped raise me in Kentucky. We looked up to him almost as a parent.

"Papa said what?" George said, incredulous.

When I wouldn't tell him what I had said to warrant Papa's wrath, George would only say, "You must've done something very wrong for him to say that."

That night might've been the turning point of my career. Maybe it turned my life around because it was the first time I really thought about accepting my responsibility as a man. By that time, I was already married, and I had my first son, Darryl William.

That night, it occurred to me that my dad was telling me that baseball wasn't just my hobby anymore. It was also my job. And if my job wasn't going well, I had to figure out a way to perform better.

He really shouldn't have had to say that to me because I saw my parents live that philosophy every day of their lives. My father was working in a coal mine in Virginia when I was born, and when the mine closed, he came to Detroit because that's where he thought he had the best opportunity to find work. He accepted his responsibility and he did whatever he could to help us survive. He did what he had to do to feed his family. He always had two or three odd jobs, and my mother always ironed our clothes.

And even though we didn't have much, my mother always wanted to share what we had. Today, we have reunions to bring families together, but back then, we had reunions every weekend. My parents believed in family and community.

That night, my dad made me realize that I'd been blessed with a gift to play baseball, and that it would've been a sin not to use that gift to the best of my ability. I never called home to complain again—and I didn't need to. Everything started to fall into place that night. I stopped worrying about what had gone wrong and started to concentrate on how to improve my game every day.

Although I was demoted to AA Knoxville that season, I ended up batting .333 with 20 doubles, nine triples, 14 home runs, and 70 RBI's down there. And in September, the Tigers called me up to the majors. In 15 games with Detroit in 1963, I batted .348. And by the end of that season, my confidence was soaring.

If I would've listened to my mom, I might've come home that night. And who knows what would've happened after that? To be honest, I'm not a quitter. I loved baseball, and it's hard for me to believe that I would've quit the game. But I can't be sure.

All I know is that I've carried Papa's powerful words with me for more than 40 years. The lesson he taught me that night wasn't just about baseball. It was about life.

# Chapter 2

## PAPA'S RULES

CONSIDERING HOW MUCH RESPECT MY DAD had for Negro League baseball, it's funny to recall that the first time he met Negro League legend Buck O'Neil, he chased poor Buck out of our house.

O'Neil was in the Negro Leagues from 1937–'55 as a player and a manager, and he was credited with helping prepare George Altman, Ernie Banks, Elston Howard, and several others for the major leagues. By 1957, O'Neil was working as a scout for the Chicago Cubs, and one day, he showed up at our door with a plan to sign me as a 15-year-old.

At the time, the Cubs were aggressively trying to sign underage Latin American players because, apparently, there were no age restrictions on foreign players. O'Neil told my dad that we just needed to say that that was I was Puerto Rican or Latino, and the Cubs could sign me. That's when my dad told O'Neil to leave our house. I still tease Buck about that when I see him today.

To this day, I'm still not sure why Papa was so upset with Buck. Maybe he was insulted because Buck wanted him to lie about our ethnicity. Or maybe he believed that Buck shouldn't be trying to sign a 15-year-old boy. Or maybe the money he offered was too low for Papa. I can't be sure because Papa never discussed those things with me. What I do know is that O'Neil's arrival at our house was my first indication that I might be able to play in the majors.

Papa was working in a coal mine in Arno, Virginia when I was born in 1942. I was their 21st and youngest child. By then, my dad was 43, and my mother was almost 40. My brother would tease me about being the "accident baby" long before I knew what that meant. In fact, some of my brothers and sisters were so much older than me, they seemed kind of like surrogate parents. And their children seemed more like my brothers and sisters. We were a close-knit family, and it was commonplace that I would spend weeks, or even months, living with one of my siblings.

During my major-league career, I had several nicknames. Willie the Wonder. Boomer. The Ancient Mariner. And Mull Digger, a southern term passed down from my grandfather to my father to me. But the one nickname some of relatives still call me today is "Boozie."

Even some of my nieces and nephews call me "Uncle Boozie." When I was just a boy, I was big for my age and a little uncoordinated, too. My relatives said I looked "kind of boozy" when I walked. And even before that, I had several adventures as a toddler. One day, I was exploring our cupboards and discovered some canisters of lard and flour. By the time adults found me, I had already been eating it by the handful. Apparently I was enjoying it so much that I looked tipsy, and they stuck me with the nickname "Boozie."

Although I feel as if I'm a Detroiter, the roots of my baseball career are actually in the south. In fact, my family roots are in the south. My brother Billy and I were the only two sons of Clinton Horton who didn't work in the mine at some point. And in 1954, when I was just 11, we were living in Stonega, Virginia, a small town in the midst of a mining area. I had heard that there were tryouts for a baseball team in Appalachia, which was about four or five miles down the road.

My dad said I could try out for the team, but I couldn't convince any of my friends to walk to Appalachia with me. I was upset, and I started walking down the tracks with tears rolling down my cheeks. After awhile, I stumbled across a boy named Larry Munsey, who was fishing. Sure enough, he said he'd go with me to the tryout.

When we got there, there must've been 60 or 70 kids at the tryout. Former pro ballplayer Junior Strong was one of the coaches. Junior took charge and essentially loaded his team with the best players. I was the only black player on that squad, and we were sponsored by Wolfe Hardware store. It was the first uniform I ever wore, and I don't think any of us took off those uniforms for a few days.

The year before, I'd actually played a half-season of youth baseball in Tennessee when I was living with my brother Ray and his wife, Pinkie. I actually used my brother Billy's name to play, and even today, some folks still think I'm Billy, who was also a talented athlete. But that Wolfe team seems more memorable, maybe because of Larry Munsey, or maybe because I really started to develop as a player.

Years later, Coach Strong told me he saw my potential, and that's why he wouldn't let me bat against other kids in batting practice. He insisted on pitching to me himself. He wanted me to face a higher caliber pitch to help me improve. Coach Strong had a decent knuckleball, and today, Munsey likes to remind me that Coach couldn't sneak it past me even when I was 11.

After I moved to Detroit, I didn't see Munsey for more than 35 years. But not long ago, my niece organized a charity outing in Kingsport, Virginia, where—unbeknownst to me—Munsey was serving as vice mayor. Just as I was about to go on the air at a local radio station, Munsey showed up and surprised me. We hugged and cried and talked as if we'd just played a game together that morning.

Looking back on my youth down south, I can honestly say that my family situation wasn't crystal clear to me. Having more than 20 years between the youngest and oldest child was rather confusing. We always had relatives and friends over at our house, and it didn't seem all that important to me to sort out who was who.

The summer that I played baseball in Appalachia, Munsey and I would often stop at the store and buy a Moon Pie or some other treat.

One day, a man that I recognized—we called him James—drove alongside us and offered us a ride.

"Noooooo," I said, because Papa had warned me never to hitchhike. He'd always told me to walk the tracks home, and that's what I was going to do.

"Suit yourself," the man said, "I have to stop by to get some fish for Mom."

As we were walking, it occurred to me that his mom was *my* mom. When I got home, everyone laughed because I didn't even know my oldest brother.

Even though I was the only black player on a team in the south in the 1950s, I really didn't grasp the concept of racism. Even today, Munsey and I both recall that I was treated like every other kid on the team. If kids were passing around a Coke, I got my swig. My parents always taught us to be colorblind, and they always had both black and white friends around the house. My father's mother was actually white, but again, our family was so large and continually coming and going, I didn't even know she was my grandmother until I was older. I just thought she was some white lady that hung around the house.

My sister Helen and her husband, George, were almost like parents to me, because I would frequently stay with them in Kentucky. When the mines closed for good, I stayed with them in Kentucky while my parents relocated to Detroit. My parents lived on Canfield and Avery with my two nephews, Mike and Joe. A year later, I rejoined them. We moved to Sixth and Forest in a duplex with a shared bathroom. My sister Faye lived on the eleventh floor in the Jeffries projects, and I would spend as much time over there as I did at my parents' house. My buddy Walt Terrell lived on the sixth floor in the projects, and he used to joke that by living on the eleventh floor, I was "in the penthouse."

Once I finally moved to Detroit, my baseball career began to blossom. The late Ron Thompson, the legendary football coach at St. Martin DePorres, was attending Wayne State University back then, and he organized a neighborhood youth team of black and white players out of Poe School on Canfield. He managed the team out of the back of his station wagon, and we began to think in terms of leagues and finding the highest level of competition. We named ourselves the Ravens. Mr. Thompson taught us about teamwork and about the fundamentals of baseball.

Whatever lessons Mr. Thompson taught us about sticking together as a team must have taken root, because when the Detroit Amateur Baseball Federation told us we couldn't bring an integrated team into its league, we voted to play another year of recreation baseball rather than split up. At that time, black players were supposed to go to the black teams, and white players were supposed to go to the white teams.

As kids, many of us would frequently be down at Tiger Stadium playing "strikeout" against the stadium's outside walls. To play "strikeout," you draw a box on the wall, and if the pitcher hits the box and you miss, you're out. If you hit it a certain distance, it's a home run. People always ask me if I want anything if they tear down Tiger Stadium. I tell them that I want that piece of wall where we played so I can peel off the paint to find the spot where we scratched out that box.

But it was also strategic for us to play "strikeout" at Tiger Stadium because we often tried to sneak into ballgames without paying. When the delivery trucks would show up, we'd follow behind them and then climb into the dumpster. Near game time, we'd simply climb out and watch the game for free.

It seemed like a foolproof plan. But one day, we miscalculated and came out of the dumpster too early and were apprehended by the security guards. Just as we were being hauled away, the Cleveland Indians walked by. Rocky Colavito and Don Mossi—I remember him specifically because he had those gigantic ears—came over to see what the trouble was all about.

Once the Cleveland players were told of our crimes, Colavito asked if we could be released into his custody. The security guards obliged, and Colavito took us down to the visiting clubhouse and asked the visiting clubhouse attendant, Rip Collins, to give us jobs.

I've never forgotten the kindness that Rocky showed us that day. Years later, when Rocky and I were teammates, I discovered his big heart wasn't just a one-day event. That's just Rocky's way.

Money was always an issue for those of us growing up in the Jeffries projects. That's why my buddy James Slate was revered because he figured out we could earn money by carrying people's groceries home from the store. That's how we bought our bats and baseballs.

Slate was the only one in our group who didn't actually play sports, but I don't think he ever missed one of my games or my boxing matches when we were growing up.

Believe it or not, I made my big money as an actor when I was a kid. In those years in Detroit, there was a locally produced television series called *Juvenile Court*. Local kids were paid $25 to portray the troubled youths who were supposed to be showing up in court. Now that I think about it, it was a great way to keep us all out of trouble. First, it kept us busy all day. It gave us some much-needed cash. And by acting as kids going to juvenile court, we all understood that we didn't want to go there in real life.

But mostly every waking hour was reserved for playing baseball. Mr. Thompson's Ravens were a very good team. We had a shortstop named Al Melvin who we used to call "Little Al Kaline." This was probably about the time that Papa began to realize I had some natural baseball ability. Although my dad never talked about it, I found out later that he had played some baseball in Negro leagues in the south, particularly around Birmingham, Alabama, and in Tennessee. He was an infielder. Papa understood the game, but he didn't pressure me the way some kids are pressured.

He was a tough, principled man—not the kind of dad who played catch with his son. He believed that I should learn to do things on my own. He taught me to find a wall, and to bounce a few hundred balls off it to improve my catching skills.

Papa never praised me, and he was always quick to point out if I messed up in a game. "Willie, you need to practice more," he'd say. "You just aren't concentrating enough."

My father always stressed respecting the coaches and the opposition. If I wasn't listening to my coaches, I was in trouble with Papa. My father didn't drive, but I remember he made it to all of my games anyhow. We'd play all over the city, but somehow, he always managed to be there by game time.

My mom, meanwhile, heaped out praise as if she was doling out mashed potatoes. Everybody received a second helping of praise from her. There was just something about Mama that made everyone feel better. And she could make a meal out of nothing. She would make her own syrup on the stove better than anything you could find at any store in town. She'd cook up some bacon and a pan of biscuits, and you would have yourself one fine meal. Some of the food that people think of as dinner food—pork chops, gravy, etc.—was breakfast food in my mother's kitchen. And I used to love to watch her eat because she enjoyed her food so much. My good friend Reggie Chapman said he still fixes greens the way my mother taught him 40 years ago.

Although my dad was tough, he was also a thinker when it came to my baseball career. The best move he made was to let me to play for more than one team at once. I would play with the Ravens at my age level, and then I'd play with older players on different nights.

That's how I ended up playing against Bill Freehan and Dennis Ribant, both of whom would later become my teammates with the Detroit Tigers.

Freehan was from Florida, but he lived with his grandparents in the Detroit area in the summer so he could play baseball for Lundquist Insurance. One season, the Lundquist team qualified for the inter-city sandlot World Series in Altoona, Pennsylvania. The team was permitted to add local players, and I was one of the players they chose, along with Ribant and Alex Johnson. I think I made only three or four outs that entire tournament.

Detroit's sandlot team ended up beating Cincinnati's that year, and Cincinnati boasted Eddie Brinkman, who would one day play with Freehan and me on the Tigers. John Havlicek, who would eventually play in the NBA for the Boston Celtics, also played on that team. I was told that the year before, Pete Rose played with Brinkman, and believe it or not, Brinkman, who was a light-hitting major-leaguer, was the better player back then.

One memory of my childhood illustrates the difference between how my mom and dad approached parenting.

In the mid 1950s, they were still building the Lodge Freeway near the Jeffries project, and for some reason, I started trying to hit bottle tops over the highway with a broom handle. Soon, I was able to hit a bottle top all the way over the freeway. I was pretty excited about it, and I went home to brag to my parents.

My dad didn't believe me. "Quit lying," he said, "or I'm going to spank your behind."

But Mama didn't doubt me. "You keep doing that, baby. You keep hitting 'em over the highway."

If I got myself in trouble, the consequences were severe, such as the time I swiped a $1.98 baseball cap from Cunningham's drug store on Trumbull Avenue. It was an Ivy League cap with pinstripes, and I didn't have money for it. So I just walked out of the store with it.

That night, Papa saw me wearing it. "That's a nice cap," he said.

"Thank you, sir," I said, knowing this probably wasn't going to go well for me.

Once he determined the cap had come from Cunningham's, he had a few more questions for me.

"Did you work for Cunningham's to pay for that cap?"

"No, sir."

"How did you pay for it?"

"I didn't. I just walked out of the store with it."

Lying about it only would've made it worse, although I don't know how it could have been. Papa whipped me from our house on Sixth and Forest all the way to Cunningham's. Once we got there, my dad told the manager that I would be working there all summer to pay for that $1.98 cap. That meant I was going to miss baseball games, but Papa didn't care. He wouldn't even budge when Mr. Thompson appealed on my behalf, and on behalf of the team.

It was a harsh penalty but it taught me a valuable lesson. My dad wasn't shy about passing out the whippings, but he was a wise man. He was sure he could teach me the lessons of life, but he also felt that I needed more help than even he could provide me.

Before I headed off to Northwestern High School, my dad told me that he'd decided to make Judge Damon Keith my legal guardian.

That kind of news is shocking to a teenager who doesn't quite comprehend the legal system.

"You aren't giving me away, are you, Papa?" I asked.

"Nah," he said. "But I think Judge Keith can help you."

Papa didn't elaborate then, but now I know that he just wanted me to understand both sides of the tracks. We were living in the Jeffries projects with my sister Faye, and Judge Keith was a successful African-American man and a good role model. Sometimes I'd spend the night at his house, and even today, he still says I have a room at his house. Legally, Judge Keith may have been my guardian, but in reality, he was becoming my mentor and adviser, too.

When I started spending time with Judge Keith, I began to dream of a better future. The judge didn't counsel me about being a better baseball player; he led me down a path to be a better person. When I thought about being a professional baseball player, I really did think in terms of what it would mean for my parents.

Essentially, I was recruited to go to Northwestern to play for their coach and athletic director, Sam Bishop. Coach Thompson was an alumnus of Northwestern, and he clearly had an influence. Judge Keith supported the idea. Based on my address in the Jeffries projects, Northwestern would not have been my school. So in order to enroll there, I moved in with my sister Virginia during the week so I had the right address.

Coach Bishop knew who I was before I arrived at Northwestern, but I didn't know who he was. On the first day of classes, my buddies Sam Blue and James Slate and I were leaning against the cannon that stood guard in front of the school. Out of the school came a man dressed in a white suit, and he was heading directly toward us. With the way he was dressed, I thought he was with the janitorial service.

He told us to get off the cannon, but we refused. The next thing I knew, he was chasing us down Grand River Avenue.

A few weeks later, we all lined up in the hallway to sign up for sports. Soon I noticed that the man taking down information at the front of the line was the man who wore the white suit. I was looking for somewhere, anywhere to hide, but Coach Bishop just shook his head at me. Coach Bishop to me was like General George Patton; he could be hard on you to keep you disciplined. But he might also hug you, too.

At Northwestern, I started out as an outfielder/third baseman, but after two games, I was moved to catcher, where I played for the rest of my prep career.

As it turned out, the distance between Northwestern and Tiger Stadium wasn't very far, both literally and figuratively.

Word seemed to spread quickly that I could be a major-league prospect. Northwestern Field, located along Grand River near the junction of West Grand Boulevard near Northwestern High School, had six diamonds back then, and scouts were always around. Detroit scout Louie D'Annunzio told me years later that he had a scouting report on me that dated back to my days playing in Virginia. Apparently, he had seen me play there as an 11-year-old when he was visiting there with a Detroit team.

With good grass and a spiffy infield, the Northwestern Field was the best in the city. Sandlot and high school baseball was a bigger event in those days, and the games always drew a crowd. There were no home run fences, so the outfielders played deep. But they weren't allowed to leave the outfield grass. They were forbidden from positioning themselves on Grand River Avenue, and that was important because I began to hit the ball onto Grand River and beyond. According to the ground rules, anything hit onto Grand River was a home run.

The other field where I began to draw some notice was Manz Field, near the corner of Conner and Mack Avenue. One day, I hit a ball that cleared the fence, crossed the street, and broke a window in an employment office on the other side of the road. After that, word spread quickly.

Northwestern had a strong athletic tradition, and I was just one of several athletes getting media attention for their exploits. Henry Carr was a three-sport star at Northwestern when I was there, and he went on to win two gold medals in the 200 meters and the 1,600-meter relay at the 1964 Olympics. He also played in the NFL for the New York Giants. We called him "The Ghost" because when he ran, he was there and then he was gone. He just disappeared right in front of you.

Future American League batting champion Alex Johnson was on my baseball team. Alex's brother is former Michigan and NFL running back Ron Johnson. The crazy thing is that Ron might've been a better baseball player, and Alex might've been a better football player. Matt Snorton also played on my baseball team, and he later played football at Michigan State and signed with the Denver Broncos. And much of the Motown explosion came out of Northwestern High. Singer Mary Wells, and Elbridge Bryant and Melvin Franklin of the Temptations were also from our school. And big John Mayberry, who played in the major leagues with Houston, Toronto, and Kansas City, went to Northwestern, too.

Plenty of Northwestern students enjoyed their moment in the spotlight back then. Mine came on June 9, 1959, when I was a 16-year-old sophomore playing in the Public School League championship game at Briggs Stadium, which later became Tiger Stadium. It was Cass Tech vs. Northwestern, and in the first inning, I hit a home run that people still talk about nearly fifty years later.

My opposite-field shot, hit off right-handed pitcher George Cojocari, landed on the stadium's right-center field roof, struck a light tower, and fell into the stands. It's the same light tower that Reggie Jackson—a left-handed hitter—hit in the 1971 major league All-Star game. It's been estimated that my drive traveled more than 450 feet.

Alex Johnson played with me on that Northwestern team, and he tells me what he remembers most about my home run was that my dad was standing behind the dugout, yelling, "Dammit, that's my son! That's my son!"

The *Detroit Free Press* has called my home run "one of the greatest individual baseball accomplishments in state high school history." The ball exploded off my bat, and it kind of shocked me. I had never hit a ball quite that hard before. I just stood there. In fact, the home plate umpire had to remind me to run the bases.

To be honest, not many people in the stands cheered when I hit my blast because in the early innings, the fans were mostly Cass Tech supporters. Northwestern's principal wouldn't let students out of school early to see the game, so our fans didn't show up until the middle innings.

We were actually down 6–1 to Cass Tech after two innings, but we came back with three runs in the third, six in the fifth, one in the sixth, and two in the seventh to win 13–10 for Coach Bishop's third PSL crown. I think that once our fans got to the park, we suddenly found some energy.

In the third inning, I just missed another home run when I hit a long drive to the upper deck in left field—just a few feet foul. I ended up 2-for-4 with a double, a home run, three runs scored, and three RBIs. Snorton also homered in that game, and Johnson was 1-for-3.

Talk about a game overflowing with talent. Carmen Fanzone hit a home run for Cass Tech, and went on to play five seasons with the Boston Red Sox and Chicago Cubs before joining the "Tonight Show" orchestra as a trumpet player during the Johnny Carson era.

Curiously, after our three home runs in that 1959 game, no high school player hit another homer in a championship game at Tiger Stadium until 1980. Detroit St. Andrew's first baseman Mark Gniewek hit a two-run homer into the lower deck in right field on May 28, 1980, against Detroit St. Hedwig. The next time a high school player reached the upper deck was in 1998 when Casey Rogowski of Redford Catholic Central launched a one into the upper deck in right field in the Catholic League title game.

Not long after that game, there was talk of me turning pro. But Judge Keith and my father decided to wait until just before I turned 18—then it was time for me to sign as a hardship case. Many teams were interested, and I couldn't have guessed where I was going to sign because I had tryouts with several teams, including the Boston Red Sox and the Cincinnati Reds. The New York Yankees mailed me a catcher's glove, and I assumed I would sign with them. But my dad came in and told me I was going to sign with the Detroit Tigers.

D'Annunzio had pushed aggressively for the Tigers to sign me. What was interesting is that was that he had only recently joined the Tigers. Before then, he'd worked for the Orioles and had signed Milt Pappas out of the Detroit area. Had D'Annunzio still worked for the Orioles, I could have wound up in Baltimore.

In the 1960s, clubs would negotiate with your parents. I was still a minor, and no one told me precisely what kind of deal I got. But from what I was able to piece together later, I believe I received a signing bonus of $50,000–$70,000 and a car. With the bonus money, I bought a new house and furnishings for my parents, and the rest went into a 10-year pension for my parents.

On August 7, 1961, right before I signed my contract, my dad offered me some words of wisdom:

"Don't sign that contract unless you're willing to make a commitment to the people," he said firmly. "You have to promise that you'll serve the community as a player for the Detroit Tigers."

The purchase of the house was primarily for my mother. She had always liked a certain house, once owned by the Henry Ford family, at 112 Edison. At first, we didn't tell her about the Tigers buying it. Instead, we told her we were going to look at some houses. We went out for a drive, and when we turned down Edison, her eyes lit up. There was her favorite house—all wrapped up with a big bow. Mama couldn't have been happier.

The house had five or six bedrooms, and people wondered why my mom wanted such a big house. But we knew she had visions of grandchildren running all over that house and yard. She wanted a big house, like she'd owned down south.

Along with the furnishings came a new, modern stove. But Mama wanted no part of it. She wanted her old gas stove. Papa and I were worried to death because once we moved all of their belongings to the new house, we left the old stove out on the street. Usually the junkman or someone from the neighborhood would swoop in and pick up something like that in a matter of hours. But when we got back to our old place, her stove was still sitting out by the road. So the new stove went into the garage, and Mama's old stove went into her new home—just the way she wanted it.

I always tell my kids that out of my original signing bonus, I probably didn't spend $200. I didn't even receive the car. Papa sold it, saying, "You don't need a car until you're 21 years old."

Shortly after I turned pro, the Tigers were paying me to play winter ball, and my dad was still giving me about $50 every two weeks to live on. The first time I met Gates Brown and told him that, he started laughing. He insisted that I tell my dad that I needed a raise.

"I can't be telling my dad I need a hundred dollars," I said. "No, no, no."

When I finally made it to the big leagues, I had to live by Papa's rules when I was home. Back then, Ford Motor Company was supplying players with cars, and when pitcher Dick Egan was demoted to Triple-A, I got his car. After the season was over, I bought it. I was so afraid to tell Papa about it, I parked it at my buddy James Slate's house.

But in retrospect, I wouldn't change anything about how we handled my first contract because what I really wanted most was to help my parents. The best bonus I received from the Tigers was to see the smile on my mother's face when we drove her to her new house.

The Tigers sent me to winter ball with the sole purpose of converting me from a catcher to an outfielder. To be honest, the Tigers never told me why they wanted me to make the switch. However, logic suggests that they had spent a bundle of money—reportedly over $100,000—to sign Bill Freehan out of the University of Michigan. They probably figured that by the time I was ready for the big leagues, Bill would already be the team's starting catcher.

The Tigers' winter league team played at Al Lang Field in Tampa, Florida, and I played for manager Phil Cavaretta, who had played in the major leagues, mostly with the Cubs, from 1934–1955. Actually, it's hard to say that I played for him, because I only got one at-bat. Primarily, Phil's son, Corky, and I were used to chase balls during the games. Then they'd work us out after the game. We played the role of waterboy and batboy, and did whatever chore they wanted done. But the funny thing is, the lessons I learned there I carried with me for the rest of my career.

My dad told me to go down to Florida and learn to be a professional, and that's what I did. I learned to respect my coaches at winter ball. As a catcher, I had developed quick release, so they had to retrain me to throw from the outfield. I did what I was told, paid attention to details, and I ate a lot of hot dogs during the games.

From the time I signed with the Tigers, it took me exactly 25 months to arrive in the major leagues. In my first professional season, I hit .295 at Duluth in the Northern League. In 1963, I started at Syracuse, then was sent down to Knoxville, where I began to hit with authority. But I certainly didn't think I'd be called up to the major leagues that year.

On September 10, 1963, Knoxville manager Frank Carswell told me to pack my bags and catch a flight to Washington, D.C., because the Tigers had called me up to the big leagues. But Carswell liked to horse around to keep his players loose, and I had been one of his favorite joke targets. So I was convinced that this was just another one of his pranks.

In baseball, it's commonplace to pull pranks on your teammates. And in my mind, I was too smart to fall for this one, because it just seemed impossible that I would jump from Double-A baseball to the major leagues. In my mind, I needed to go back to Triple-A Syracuse first before I was ready for the Tigers. So even though Carswell told me to get on that plane, I went to the ballpark to get ready for the Knoxville game.

When Carswell saw me, his jaw dropped. "You're supposed to be in Washington!" he said. "What are you doing here?"

It took him a minute to convince me that this was no joke—and another short while to explain how to make reservations to board the plane headed for our nation's capital. I was a 20-year-old kid from the streets of Detroit, and I didn't know much about "catching a plane."

By the time I finally made it to Washington for my first major-league game, it had started without me. I quickly changed into my uniform and hurried into the dugout. The Tigers were trailing the

Senators, 4–1. I hadn't even finished shaking everyone's hands when manager Charlie Dressen said to me, "Horton, you bat for Aguirre."

It was only the top of the fourth inning, and starting pitcher Hank Aguirre was none too pleased about this turn of events. Mind you, this was long before the designated hitter rule, so pitchers still batted for themselves in the American League. Aguirre came out of his seat in the dugout and had a few words for Dressen.

"I'm out there trying to win a ball game, and you're going to pull me for some rookie in the fourth inning?" he said. "I can still win this game."

The whole scene scared me. But Dressen just ignored Aguirre's outburst, and I was on my way up to bat. Six-foot-three right-hander Jim Hannan was on the mound. Was I nervous? Excited? Is there a difference? In those situations, you can't explain how you feel. I can't remember anything except that I lined one of Hannan's pitches up the middle for a clean base hit.

I'd finally made it to the big leagues.

A few days later, on Friday the thirteenth of September, the Tigers were back home at Tiger Stadium to face the Orioles. It looked like I would get my first major-league swings at the corner of Michigan and Trumbull when Dressen decided to insert me as a pinch-hitter for starting pitcher Phil Regan with the game on the line.

It was a 2–2 tie in the bottom of the ninth. We had runners on first and third, and one out, and Baltimore left-hander Steve Barber was on the mound. But manager Billy Hitchcock decided to call in right-hander Stu Miller from the bullpen. Dressen countered with left-handed hitting outfielder Billy Bruton to pinch-hit for me. Bruton was walked intentionally anyway, and then center fielder George Thomas hit a sacrifice fly to win the game for us, 3–2.

The next day for some reason, I wasn't thinking that I would get to play. I was in the bullpen talking to my buddies between innings—Mack, Slate, Chapman, and Terrell were all there—when word came down in the bottom of the eighth that they needed me.

We trailed, 2–0, and future Hall of Famer Robin Roberts was pitching a one-hitter for the Orioles. He'd already fanned eight batters and seemed to be cruising right along.

Catcher Gus Triandos popped out to start the eighth. Then Gates Brown pinch-hit for our second baseman, George Smith, and drew a walk. Once again, Dressen inserted me as a pinch-hitter—this time for our starting pitcher, Jim Bunning. I stepped up to the plate—my first official big-league at-bat at Tiger Stadium—and hit a Roberts fastball into the left-center field stands to tie the game. What a thrill!

The game went to extra innings, and in the bottom of the tenth, Triandos hit a home run off Roberts to give us the victory, 3–2.

My home run off Roberts remains one of my fondest baseball memories for a number of reasons. For one, my friends were all there. And of course, my father was sitting in the bleachers. He never liked sitting in the box seats, which I could get for him if he wanted. He liked the bleachers instead. Maybe he felt more comfortable there. Papa had been such an important part of my rise to the majors, and I was thrilled to know that he was there to see my first major-league home run in person. It made it even more special that it came off a pitcher who once won 20 or more games for six consecutive seasons.

Papa and I planned to meet after the game, and I was eager to hear what he had to say. You never expected praise from Papa, but I figured he would show his pride in his own way. He was late arriving, and when he finally did show up, he seemed angry, rather than happy. "Let's go," he said simply, and we hurried off.

It wasn't until later that a member of the grounds crew told me that the police had put my father in the stadium holding cell because he got into a scrap with another man in the bleachers.

Apparently when I hit the home run, Papa yelled, "That's my son! That's my son!" But the bleacher fans didn't believe him.

"If that's your son," someone supposedly said, "why are you way out here?"

And that's how my dad got into a fight on the night his son hit his first major-league home run.

# Chapter 3

**DEATH ON I-94**

WHEN TIGERS MANAGER CHARLIE DRESSEN sent me to the minors early in the 1964 season, he warned me that temporary demotions can become permanent for those who want to whine instead of work.

"You're going down on a 24-hour recall basis," he said. "I've seen guys never come back after going down on a 24-hour recall basis. You have to go down to Syracuse and work hard, Willie, because when we bring you up the next time, we plan to play you every day."

Years later, when I managed the Valencia Magallanes in the Venezuelan League, I tried to incorporate much of Dressen's managerial style into my own. He had a way of making you feel wanted, while still making you realize that if you didn't have "sweat equity" in your investment, you were bound to fail. He made me believe I could be a good major-league ballplayer, but he also told me that it was possible I wouldn't make it unless I was willing to work at every aspect of the game.

Although I was only 21 that season, there had still been speculation that I might end up as the everyday left fielder in 1964. Even during my 1963 call-up, Rocky Colavito, who had been the team's left fielder for four seasons, indirectly suggested to me that he assumed I was going to succeed him. I'll never forget the kindness he showed me while he helped me prepare to be an everyday player.

"The fans might boo you at first because they're comfortable with me out there," Colavito told me. "I'm like a pair of old shoes, and everybody loves their old shoes. But if you can just get past the boos, you'll be all right."

He reminded me that fans only boo because they care about the team and about the players. Colavito went out of his way to tell me the aspects of my game that needed improvement. Rocky sure had an arm on him. In fact, he could throw a baseball from near home plate into the outfield stands. He would talk to me about throwing and about playing the outfield. Whatever wisdom he had about the game, he shared it with me. And he taught me that helping younger players is part of being a professional. I'll never forget what Rocky Colavito taught me.

That summer, Colavito was traded to Kansas City in the deal that brought Dave Wickersham, Ed Rakow and Jerry Lumpe to Detroit. That's why there had been speculation that I was going to play left field in 1964.

But during spring training in 1964, I got off to a bad start. In February, Gates Brown and I drove to spring training together. We decided to take our time, and stop to see family and friends along the way. It seemed like a good idea until we stepped on the scales for the annual weigh-in. With the all the good food we had in Virginia and Kentucky, I was 26 pounds overweight.

Dressen was perturbed and told me that I had two weeks to lose the weight, or he was going to fine me $100 per pound.

By running, drinking nothing but water, and eating nothing but bananas, I lost it all in 10 days. The newspaper ran a photo of Dressen presenting me with a 26-pound ham as a prize for my weight loss.

But that rapid weight loss had a negative effect. I was severely weakened from shedding those pounds so fast. It felt as if I couldn't even swing the bat. It affected my hitting to the point that I didn't feel right for most of the spring.

To make matters worse, Gates Brown was sharpening his spikes with a scalpel one-day, and I inadvertently walked into the blade and severely cut my arm.

That injury also bothered me for weeks, and I really didn't feel completely healed until just before I was demoted. In fact, I remember hitting a home run the night before I was sent to the minors early in the 1964 season, so I was surprised when Dressen sent me to Syracuse.

"You remind me of a young Roy Campanella," he told me. "But you have to play every day, Willie, and you can't do that up here."

Dressen had known former All-Star catcher Campanella from their days together with the Brooklyn Dodgers. And even though I no longer played the position, I think Dressen thought I had the toughness of a catcher.

At the time, I was hitting only .163, with five extra-base hits and ten RBIs. But the timing of the demotion bothered me the most. I had just started to feel good hitting the ball. My injury was finally healed, and I was just starting to feel strong again. I wondered why they didn't just give me a few more weeks to see if I was ready to be a regular.

In light of the Colavito trade and of Dressen's faith in me, I was surprised that I only got 80 at-bats to prove myself early in the 1964 season.

What I found out later is that my father had something to do with my demotion. He didn't like me sitting on the bench, and he had gone to Mr. Jim Campbell and expressed his opinion that I'd be better off playing regularly in the minors. Mr. Campbell had become a family friend, and he respected my father's opinion. And he had also been thinking along those same lines.

Dressen's word was the law then, so I went down to Syracuse with the idea that I would be the Tigers' starting left fielder by 1965. I hit .288 at Syracuse, with 29 home runs and 99 RBIs in 1964. It seemed as if I was in a good position to win the job.

The Tigers told several of us to play winter ball for Mayaguez in the Puerto Rican League, and we did what we were told. My game was truly coming together, and by the holidays I already had 10 home runs to lead the league. I smacked a couple long home runs in Ponce that had everyone talking. One of them was estimated at more than 480 feet.

Jim Northrup was also there, and he was leading the league with a .350 batting average. Based on what I saw from Jimmy in Puerto Rico, I thought he'd be a major-league star. He was a five-sport star at Alma College, playing everything from football to golf. A gifted quarterback, Jim had offers from the New York Titans of the AFL and the Chicago Bears of the NFL, as well as from the Tigers. He accepted the Tigers' offer because their money was guaranteed, and he had to make the team in football. Jim was banging the ball that winter, and given how I was hitting and the confidence I had, it seemed as if I was about to enter a wonderful period in my life.

I could not have been more wrong.

Over the holidays, I had tried to call my parents, but across-the-ocean telephone communication in those days was dicey, even in ideal weather conditions. It took me about ten days, but I finally reached them. I distinctly remember that my mother kept asking me to come home because she missed me. Obviously she knew I couldn't do that. But she seemed sad about the distance between us.

Over the New Year's break, I drove to see my friend Alex Johnson, who was also playing in Puerto Rico. On New Year's morning, I was awakened by a group of players that included Alex, Roberto Clemente, and Jose Pagan. They somberly informed me that my parents had been in an automobile accident on I-94, just east of Battle Creek, Michigan. My father was dead, and my mother and brother Billy were in critical condition. My two nephews, Mike and Joe, were also injured, but not severely.

My parents were in my brother's car, en route to see my sister Frankie and her husband, Ken. In blizzard conditions, the car, which was being driven by one of my brother's friends, ran into the back of a salt truck.

It took me half a day to travel from San Juan to Detroit, and Gates Brown met me at the airport. The plan was to go directly to Albion Hospital to see my mom and brother, but the roads were nearly impassable. Albion was a two-hour drive away in good weather, but the conditions were so bad, we could only make it as far as the house on Edison Street.

Just as soon as I walked in the door, the phone rang. It was a doctor from the hospital. I identified myself as one of the Horton sons, and more than forty years later, I still remember what he said to me: "I have some more bad news for you. Your mom just passed."

Papa had been sitting in the front seat, in the center, and he died instantly. Billy suffered head injuries, and he was in a coma for a lengthy period; we didn't know whether he would live or die. We delayed my parents' funeral for a week as we prayed for Billy's recovery. Doctors didn't think he was going to make it.

My mom had been in the back seat with my nephews Joe and Michael. Joe was my brother Joe's child, and Michael was my sister Faye's son. They were like brothers to me, and I honestly think that my parents thought of them as their kids. They were small and I was told that my mom wrapped herself around the kids to cushion them from the impact. She took the full force. The driver escaped with just a scratch by comparison.

It was certainly the worst time of my life. I was 22, and I was still as close to my parents as I was when I was a child. It was still important to me to please my father. His presence always helped me stay on the right path, to do what was right. I wondered how my life would change without my parents.

In the midst of our grief, Tigers president and general manager Jim Campbell paid me a visit. After offering his condolences, he shook my hand and handed me a check to pay for the funerals and the hospital bills. The check was for $20,000. Remember this was 1965, and $20,000 was a tremendous amount of money. I tried to pay him back in the months that followed, but he would never accept my money.

It started to become clear to me that the Tigers had become like a second family to me, and Mr. Campbell was like my surrogate father.

Gates Brown always used to say about Campbell, "He'll take you to lunch and spend a thousand bucks, then fight you tooth and nail over fifty bucks in your paycheck." When it came to business, Mr. Campbell ruled with an iron fist. But when it came to his friends, Mr. Campbell had a heart of gold.

Through the years, I would disagree with Mr. Campbell on occasion, but we always remained close. My relationship with him was probably as complicated as my relationship with my father. In some ways, they had the same attitude. On one hand, I think Mr. Campbell was proud of what I had done for the Tigers. On the other hand, I think he believed he had to push me to be the best. Mr. Campbell knew the role Papa played in my life, and I think he felt he needed to fill that void after Papa was killed.

Throughout my career, I spent many hours talking baseball with Mr. Campbell, and I had the utmost respect for him. But as close as he felt to me, he always put his role as general manager first. Just like a father and son, we had our disagreements, particularly about money.

Almost as soon as I became the regular left fielder, I developed a kinship with the fans in the stands out there. I didn't know all their names, but I knew them. Some of them had known me since I was 12 or 13 years old.

It became my habit to take a few balls out of the bag before every game and throw them up into the stands. One day, Mr. Campbell saw me do that and said he was going to charge me five dollars for every ball I threw up there. The next day, I took the entire bag of balls out in the outfield, and threw every one into the stands.

"Charge me whatever you want," I told Mr. Campbell. My next paycheck was short, thanks to a miscellaneous deduction for those baseballs. It was worth it to me, though, because the relationship I developed with the fans in left field was as important to me as my relationship with my friends. Eventually, I started buying tickets and bringing kids to sit in left field. It wasn't hard to fulfill my promise to my dad because I truly enjoyed the fans.

When it came to contracts, Mr. Campbell always wrestled with players over every last dollar. There were some basic rules: Nobody was going to make more money than Al Kaline. If you didn't play as well as you did in the previous season, you were going to get a cut in pay. Not even Kaline was safe from the threat of a salary reduction. In 1955, at age 20, Kaline won the American League batting title with a .340 batting average. Over the next four seasons, he averaged an impressive .312. But in 1960, his average slipped to .278. In the following offseason, the Detroit Free Press ran a story about how Kaline's salary would be cut by a couple thousand dollars.

Judge Keith had one of the attorneys in his office, Nate Conyers, serve as my agent, and after we won the 1968 World Series, Conyers asked Mr. Campbell to raise my salary from $28,000 to $60,000.

Mr. Campbell didn't like that too much. "Willie isn't going to own the damn team!" he said.

Officially, I became a spring training holdout, and I was probably the most antsy holdout in the history of baseball. I didn't help my negotiating leverage because everyone knew I was anxious to get back in uniform. When my Tigers teammates were on the diamond, I didn't want to be in street clothes. Before long, I called my agent. "I'm going on the field, Nate, so you have to get this done."

Needless to say, although I received a healthy raise to more than $50,000, Mr. Campbell didn't give me exactly what I wanted.

Mr. Campbell did fight you for every nickel at contract time, but when he came back from his winter vacation, he would always have a box of candy from the Grand Canyon for his players.

Sometimes, Mr. Campbell would shock you. For instance, in 1975, I made $94,000, and after the season, I was hoping that Mr. Campbell wouldn't knock my salary below $90,000 for 1976. I'd hit 25 home runs in 1975, but my strikeouts were up, and I was nearly 33 years old. I knew that Mr. Campbell could often find reasons to drop you a few thousand dollars.

But when I got my contract in the mail, it was for $125,000! Honestly, I thought that Mr. Campbell's secretary, Alice, may have typed in the numbers incorrectly. I went down to Mr. Campbell's office to get it corrected.

"Alice," I said, "there has to be a mistake with these figures."

"No, Willie," she said. "That's the correct amount."

When I asked Mr. Campbell about it, he explained that when the Tigers acquired Rusty Staub from the Mets, he brought along a contract for $150,000. Mr. Campbell didn't think it was right that Staub, who'd batted .282 with 105 RBI in 1975, should be making that much more than I was. Although we viewed Campbell as a skinflint, he did have a code of fairness in his mind—one that probably only he understood. That raise was the biggest of my Tigers career.

Many times, I would go up to Mr. Campbell's office and talk for a couple of hours, and sometimes, we didn't discuss baseball at all. We were like family members talking—maybe even friends.

But Mr. Campbell was tough on me, just like my father was. In 1973, I was hitting over .340 in mid-June, and Mr. Campbell summoned me to his office for a chat. As I walked toward the meeting, I truly thought that Mr. Campbell was might reward me with a new contract and nice raise.

But instead of praising me, he chewed me out.

"What are you doing, slapping those dinky singles out there?" he said. "You're doing what every team wants you to do."

"What are you talking about?" I asked. "Are you looking at my average?"

He then asked whether not I was sick, or feeling ill, because he said my strength was no longer evident. It was true that my home run numbers were down at times. He then began to tell me that my game was about home runs and run production. That's what the Tigers wanted from me, and he didn't need me—or want me—to be out there trying to prove I was a .300 hitter.

"What I want you doing for this team is hitting .270 with lots of home runs," Campbell said.

I'll never forget that conversation because it made me realize that your role on a successful team is determined by how you can best serve the team—not by what you want it to be. No matter how well you think you're performing, if you aren't fulfilling your role on the team, you're letting the team down.

Conversations about baseball with Mr. Campbell always included some of his philosophy that he wanted you to think about. You could talk to him for only 15 minutes, and then spend the next couple of days chewing on the message he wanted to give you.

We didn't always agree. Much like my dad, Mr. Campbell wouldn't hesitate to tell me if he thought I was making a mistake. He and Judge Keith were both against my idea to open Club 23—my sports bar on Livernois.

They just didn't want my name associated with a bar. They thought it could be trouble, even though I explained that my concept was more of a restaurant-bar. In some respects, I was ahead of my time because I put together the kind of sports-themed bars that are commonplace today, with memorabilia on the walls and games always on TV. I think we had one of the first big-screen televisions in the city, maybe even the state.

But even though Mr. Campbell was against my decision, he would still bring his secretary, Alice, down to the club for lunch. He always supported me, even if we disagreed. To me, Mr. Campbell was family.

He and I also had different opinions on other matters, too. For instance—the Hall of Fame veteran's committee. I wouldn't allow my name to be submitted to the committee because I don't believe I belong in the Hall of Fame. To me, the Hall of Fame is for players like Willie Mays, Hank Aaron, Frank Robinson, Al Kaline and others. You say their names and you think "Hall of Fame." I put those players up on a pedestal.

Mr. Campbell would argue vehemently, comparing me to other players. "Richie Ashburn is in, and he was a good player," Campbell said. "But I would take you over him."

I would laugh, and he would continue to disagree, only conceding that it was fine if someone wanted to submit my name to the veteran's committee after I'm gone. We debated that point 10 days before he died in October of 1995. He was 71. What I've always told people about Mr. Campbell is that he was as devoted to his team as anyone I've ever met. Near the end of his life, he was a bit hurt that the Tigers organization had discarded him in 1992.

He was a smart baseball man who cared about his team and players, even though many of his players were often ticked off at him over salary issues.

A few weeks after he died in Lakeland, Florida I got a call from an attorney who wanted to talk to me about some financial matters. Much to my surprise, he told me that Mr. Campbell had named me as one of his beneficiaries in his will. He left me enough money that I was able to set up a college fund for the 11 grandchildren I had at the time.

Through the years, I've always believed that my relationship with Mr. Campbell was special. He wasn't the kind of man who laid out his feelings, but his will proved to me that he valued my friendship. And that meant more to me than the money he left in my name.

# Chapter 4

## PROFESSOR GATOR

**THE BEST HITTING ADVICE I EVER RECEIVED** sounded like gibberish the first time I heard it.

Early in my Tigers career, I would often walk back to the dugout, cursing at myself for striking out. Gates Brown would say something to me like, "Hey big man, it's the bottom of the ninth, you're on deck, and you're two runs down, with two runners on base against the Yankees. Who are the Yankees going to bring in from the 'pen to pitch to you?"

Honestly, I thought my good friend, "the Gator," was losing his mind. "What are you talking about?" I'd say, waving him off.

He never stopped jabbering at me. When I wasn't playing, the Gator would often quiz me as we sat on the bench. He'd give me various scenarios to consider—just to see how I'd answer.

"Let's say [Baltimore's Dave] McNally's on the mound," Gator would say to me. "How would he would pitch any differently than this guy?"

Or we'd be one game into a three-game series against the Yankees, and Gator would want me to name all the pitchers we'd be facing in our next series against Cleveland.

He drove me crazy for weeks with his badgering. But one day, it all started to make sense to me. Gator was trying to teach me that hitting isn't just about mechanics. It's basically a mental exercise. It's about preparation, about knowing the opposing pitchers, and about studying their tendencies.

Gates understood the science of hitting better than anyone I'd ever met. And he changed my approach to hitting. Basically, he forced me to think about hitting long before I stepped into the batter's box. He inspired me to develop my own hitting philosophy. I started to utilize some of the advice that Tigers coach Wayne Blackburn had also given me about hitting, most of which fit nicely with what Gator was preaching. It all began to come together for me.

When Mayo Smith was Detroit's manager from 1967–'70, Wally Moses was our batting coach. And he always had some funny expressions about his craft. "I can help you," he'd say, "but you have to walk to the plate yourself."

Moses would continually tell his players that if they didn't master the mental aspects of hitting, it was "a long walk from the on-deck circle to the plate."

"I'm tired of everyone always blaming the hitting coach," he told us one day. "I'm not swinging the damn bat."

Although we would laugh at Moses' approach, I understood that his message was similar to the Gator's: If you want to have a successful at-bat, your mind has to be right.

I also learned to hit by watching how the league's most skilled pitchers approached their work. Baltimore Orioles southpaw Mike Cuellar was a nightmare for me, but he made me a better hitter because he forced me to figure out why he was so successful against me.

Cuellar threw a screwball that seemed to dance away from right-handers' bats. And he changed speeds masterfully. Sometimes it seemed as if he was just lobbing the ball up there, but you still couldn't make contact.

In one game, I remember striking out two or three times against Cuellar. When I came back to the dugout I announced loudly, "He's not going to strike me out again."

Gates Brown responded quickly. "Good, big man. That's the right attitude. You'll get him next time."

"No, you don't get it," I told the Gator. "The next time, I'm going to catch one of his pitches."

Everyone laughed, but I was serious.

In my next at-bat, Cuellar threw me a change-up, and I just reached up and caught the ball. Umpire Nestor Chylak was so surprised, he didn't initially seem to know what to do with me. When he finally signaled for me to trot down to first base, Baltimore manager Earl Weaver went berserk. I'm not sure that Weaver could cite a specific rule that I'd violated, but he was fairly confident that I wasn't allowed to catch a pitch that wasn't going to otherwise hit me. It might've been a strike if I hadn't caught it. He protested the game, but it really didn't matter because we ended up losing anyhow.

If I had a chance to replay that moment, I wouldn't change a thing. I'd catch that pitch all over again. Once I'd done that, I felt as if I'd pushed Cuellar out of my head. I'd found a way to get on base against him, and I'd accomplished my mission. One of my philosophies as a hitter was not to let any pitcher ruin my tomorrow.

Through the years, I learned that doing your job wasn't just about getting base hits. When you had a runner on first base and less than two outs, you had to be more mindful of staying out of the double play. You had to hit behind the runner. You had to work the count, and take a walk if that's what the pitcher gave you.

My dad had always taught me to respect every pitcher, whether he won 20 games or lost 20. Gates helped teach me to respect the player on deck. Think about setting the table better for him. He might be swinging the bat better than you are. My hitting plan became all about winning. And as I gained more experience, the scoreboard dictated my batting stance and how I'd approach each pitcher.

I faced Hall of Fame right-hander Ferguson Jenkins many, many times in my career, and I don't think he ever threw me a strike. His best pitch was a sinker, which looked like a strike—until it suddenly seemed like it fell through a trap door. You'd swing at it, but it'd be in the dirt every time. If you really wanted to hit Jenkins' best pitch, you needed a shovel—not a bat. After a few at-bats against him, I learned to move up in the batter's box and meet his pitches before they fell through the trap door. My objective against Jenkins was just not to get cheated out of my at-bat. Unless I had two strikes on me, I wasn't about to swing at his best pitches.

It always amuses me when a player says he hit a pitcher's best fastball. "No, you didn't," I want to say. "You hit a fastball, but it wasn't his best. The pitcher clearly didn't locate that pitch where he wanted it, or you wouldn't have hit it."

Part of learning to be a good hitter is understanding that every pitcher has a knockout pitch, just like every boxer has a knockout punch. At some point, the knockout pitch is coming, and you'd better understand that.

For instance, to beat Yankees reliever Sparky Lyle, you had to have to hit his slider. You had to figure out a way to make it look like a fastball. Either you had to move your body in the batter's box or you had to foul off his best sliders. I always felt that a pitcher would almost rather walk you than have to throw you his third-best pitch.

That's why it was always tough to face Luis Tiant, Catfish Hunter, or Dave McNally in my era—because they could really paint the corners. Those guys could feed a fastball through a mail slot if you asked them to—and it would move, too.

One of the toughest pitchers I ever faced was Hoyt Wilhelm. He was the only knuckleballer I ever faced who seemed like he could put the knuckler wherever he wanted to. Wilbur Wood had a decent knuckleball, but he would throw you a fastball every now and then. Not Wilhelm. He threw a knuckle curve, a rising knuckler, and a sinking knuckler. By the time you decided you would swing, his pitch would fall right off the table. He would move that ball all around, depending upon the count. With every other pitcher in the league, I had a plan when I stepped into the batter's box. With Wilhelm, I was always just hoping for the best.

Throughout my career, I never minded facing the hardest throwers because they seemed to make more mistakes. Most of the overpowering pitchers were accustomed to getting by on their fastballs, and they made mistakes on their breaking pitches. Eventually they would hang a breaking pitch. Wayne Blackburn taught me how to push pitchers deep into the count until they made a mistake. Guys like Tiant, Hunter, McNally, and others had better breaking pitches than they had fastballs. I learned to foul off good breaking pitches and wait on a mistake. Thanks to the Gator, I began to study pitchers and learn how they pitched. Did they pitch outside or inside? I understood how they moved the ball around in different zones, and I adjusted to the way they threw. I always looked for pitches in specific highways near the plate.

I wouldn't teach my batting stance to anyone, though, because it was pretty unorthodox. I held my hands high, and I had a wiggle in my bat. The funny thing is that I didn't use that stance when I took batting practice. My regular stance didn't seem natural to me in batting practice, when there was no pressure. But when I was facing live pitching, I would allow the pitcher to set me up to hit. The stance I used evolved from watching the pitcher and allowing my eyes and my head to tell my hands and my feet where they needed to be. The idea was to relax until the instant the pitcher began his sequence.

Essentially as he went into his motion, or into his set position, I would get in sync with him. I might move closer to the plate, or up in the batter's box as the pitcher started his process. I would be set in my hitting stance at the moment he delivered. If the pitcher spotted me moving up in the box, it was too late for him to adjust. It worked for me. You have to understand the plate, and you have to make that batter's box seem as comfortable as your living room. Another good way to approach hitting is to just think of it as playing catch with the pitcher. He's throwing to you and you have to send it back to him.

At Tigertown in Lakeland, players now use the "Willie Horton Training Station." When I came to the Tigers, Blackburn helped me improve my swing by swinging at a rubber tire. When I was a minor league hitting instructor, I took that concept, and developed a method of training hitters using different tire setups. I taught players such as Jose Canseco, Terry Steinbach, and Mickey Tettleton, using this method. Every hitter is different, so every tire setup has to be different. Using tires allows you to develop a good foundation.

Being comfortable with your equipment is also important to the process. Early in my career, I'd check my swing and the bat would snap in two pieces. My teammates seemed shocked, and people began talking about my strength. Shortly thereafter, Tigers manager Charlie Dressen convinced me to start using a heavier bat.

Before that, I was using bats that weighed 32 to 34 ounces, and 34-and-a-half inches long. On Dressen's advice, I started using bats that weighed 38 to 40 ounces, and 35-and-a-half inches long. I saw the difference in my hitting immediately. I started to use more of the field, and I wasn't pulling every pitch.

During my career, I didn't see too many players using bats as heavy as mine. I always noticed that players who came over from the National League seemed to favor heavier bats because the N.L. was a fastball league. Orlando McFarlane wasn't considered a power hitter, but when he came to the Tigers from the Pittsburgh Pirates in 1966, I noticed that he swung a heavy bat. Tony Taylor also came from the N.L., and he used a heavy bat, too. In the American League, only Frank Howard seemed to use a bat like mine.

Bat manufacturers customize bats for each major-leaguer, but when I first came into the league, I used the K75 Rocky Colavito model because I liked the barrel of that bat. But when I finally got the opportunity to customize my own bats, I combined three different styles. I took my handle from the Al Kaline S2, the barrel from the K75, and the meat of the bat from Gates Brown's M110 model. It was probably no coincidence that I chose the bat styles of three players who I admired immensely.

To be comfortable at the plate, everything had to be perfect for me, including my helmet. That's why the two helmets I got from the Tigers early in my career were *the same two helmets* I was using when I retired after the 1980 season. Everywhere I went, I just repainted them to match the colors of my new team. When I was beaned in 1971, I was urged to switch to a helmet with an ear flap. But I simply couldn't get comfortable at the plate in a helmet like that. Believe it or not, there were plenty of players who weren't picky about their helmets. In fact, Norm Cash couldn't even get comfortable wearing one. He stuck with the protective liner that went inside his cap.

To me, one other piece of clothing was important on the field. To this day, when I see people selling Willie Horton "game-used jerseys," I can tell you if it's really mine by looking at the bottom. I had a 54-inch chest and I'm only 5-11, so my shirts came long. I would cut all of my shirts the same way because I didn't like that extra material hanging down.

As a rule, ballplayers don't like new equipment. On the Tigers, Mickey Stanley was the best at re-lacing a glove, so we went to him to fix our old gloves rather than get a new one.

People marveled at my strength in the 1960s, but I never did a lick of weight training. My strength developed naturally, although my training as a boxer with the medicine ball and heavy bag probably helped.

I boxed out of the local recreation center, and I usually fought older competitors. When I was 17, I won a Golden Gloves championship. It was held in Windsor, Ontario, Canada, right across the river from Detroit, and it was televised.

Unfortunately, my dad saw me on TV and he told me I was never going to box again.

In those days, you were expected to work during the offseason. When I came home from winter ball in 1961, my dad got me a construction job laying bricks and building walls. A summer of that kind of work will probably help you more than weightlifting. It seemed to me that you wanted to stay away from weightlifting because you didn't want to become muscle-bound to the extent that it would slow down your bat speed. Flexibility was always my objective. And for a great, inexpensive training session, I'd slice a tire inner-tube and just stretch it between my arms.

It's hard to say exactly when I started to understand how to be a major-league hitter. But there was a hot stretch near the start of the 1965 season when I began to realize the vulnerability of most pitchers. That May, I batted .389 with 17 extra-base hits and 25 RBIs in 26 games. In one three-game series at Washington from May 11–

13, I went 8-for-13 with 10 RBIs. At one point, I reached base 10 consecutive times. And I set a new record of five RBIs in one game at D.C. Stadium.

"It took them two years and $22 million to build D.C. Stadium," wrote the late Detroit Free Press sportswriter Joe Falls. "Willie Horton all but demolished it in three days."

Falls kept track of my first seven home runs that 1965 season, and according to one of his stories, they traveled 440, 420, 400, 390, 420, 400, and 425 feet.

Right after the trip to Washington, we went to Boston, where I had another two-home-run game. One of my home runs cleared the Fenway's Green Monster in left field, and the screen, and landed in downtown Boston.

"If I had his power," Gates Brown told Falls, "I'd be hitting 50 home runs and making 70 grand."

At that time, Bob Swift was the Tigers' acting manager because Charlie Dressen was recovering from a heart attack. "(Willie) is my left fielder now, no matter who pitches," Swift told Falls. "I hope he stays out there till 1985."

Today, baseball managers rely heavily on statistics to make in-game decisions. I always told former Tigers hitting coach Bruce Fields—a man I admire greatly—that there's both good and bad that comes with that. When you look at a player's statistics against a certain pitcher, you don't know whether all of his hits came at a time when he was in the best streak of his career, or whether they came when the pitcher was in the worst slump of his career. Maybe the hitter had 10 bad days all season, and three of them came against one particular pitcher.

All I know is that when I was hitting well, I didn't much care *who* was on the mound. I just wanted to know how he'd been throwing the ball lately—how's his control? The history is important, but it shouldn't be an overriding factor.

As a hitter, I always respected my scouting reports. They were more useful to me than raw numbers alone. You see, all good pitchers pitch different ways to different batters. They're either going to pitch you inside or outside—whatever's successful for them. I kept a book on every pitcher I faced. They're not going to change what they do. They're just going to keep pitching you in the same area, so it's up to you to make the right adjustments. You have to learn to foul-off good pitches, while still staying aggressive and looking for your pitch.

When I first came to the majors, I played full-time. And I'm thankful for that because I'm not sure I would have had such a long career if I was platooned. If I would've been used strictly against left-handers, I might've washed out. Even though conventional wisdom says I should've been able to hit lefties better because I batted right-handed, it simply wasn't true in my case. Initially, I couldn't get comfortable with them. The motion and the look of a southpaw would often confuse me at the plate.

Some left-handed pitchers would add to my confusion by wearing their baseball cap tilted to one side, or their uniform bunched to one side. It always seemed to me that their motion purposely included some little tick, stutter, or pause designed to break a hitter's concentration at the plate. To me, they always looked like they were going to throw to first base.

One reason that young hitters struggle against left-handed pitchers is that they're more of a mystery to them. You just don't see too many premium left-handers in the minor leagues. And organizations tend to rush left-handed prospects to the majors quicker because they're often in short supply.

I had brief stints in the majors in 1963 and 1964, and I finally started playing full-time in 1965. But I really didn't hit left-handers as well as I should have until about 1968. In 1966, for example, I batted .246 against lefties, and .271 against right-handers. In 1967, I batted just .236 against lefties and .300 against right-handers. But in 1968, I hit .301 against left-handers. After that, I consistently hit for a higher average against left-handers than against right-handers. I just needed experience to find my comfort level.

My dad always insisted that the route to success involved "keeping your eyes and ears open—and your mouth shut." Early in my career, I especially heeded that advice. I would talk to Rocky Colavito, watch Al Kaline, and listen to Gates Brown.

One thing I learned specifically from Kaline was how compose myself after a knockdown pitch. When Al got knocked down, he'd pick himself up, flick the dirt off his uniform, and set himself as if he was just striding up from the on-deck circle. Usually the next pitch was an off-speed pitch, and Al would hit it right up the middle. His approach began to be my approach.

But clearly, Gates had a big influence on my career because he helped me keep my mind on my hitting. He made me think about the game in ways that no one else had. If a manager or a coach had told me that, maybe it wouldn't have sunk in. But Gator was one of my closet friends on the team. We even roomed together early in my career. And one time, I brought him to my old neighborhood and introduced him to my neighbor in the projects, Norma Jean Sterling. They ended up getting married.

In my mind, when the Gator instructed me about hitting, it was like getting singing lessons from Aretha Franklin or acting lessons from Sidney Poitier. Gates might have been the purest hitter on the Tigers in those days. Kaline and I still talk about that all the time.

What impressed me is that Gates adjusted to whatever role he was given. He batted over .300 in his three minor league seasons, and in 1964, he played regularly for the only time in his career. He hit .272 with 15 home runs and 11 stolen bases. Gates was a stocky man, but he could run.

During spring training in 1965, some members of the media wrote that I was going to take Gates Brown's job because he had played left field the year before. That bothered me immensely because as a player, you aren't trying to take anyone's job—you're just trying to get in the lineup. It's not accurate to suggest that anyone takes anyone's job in spring training because it's always an open tryout. If it were up to me, Gates and I both would've played. I believed he was good enough to play regularly. In fact, at one point, Charlie Dressen considered moving Kaline to center field, and using Gates in left and me in right.

Sometimes general manager Jim Campbell would say that he didn't have any trade offers for Gates, but others in the organization would tell Gates that he had five or six offers. Presumably, Campbell wanted to keep Gates because he understood how vital he was to our team, whether he was playing 50 games or 100 games.

Gates was also a great clubhouse guy, always making jokes but also always offering words of encouragement. It was no surprise that he became the Tigers' hitting coach after he retired as a player. I wasn't the only one who Gates helped on our team. It was like he had a master's degree in hitting science.

The funny thing is that Gates Brown hated batting practice. In spring training, I always wanted to be in his group because I knew he'd give me his swings in the batting cage.

While we were hitting, Gates would go the water fountain and spray water all over the front of his shirt so the coaches would think he'd worked up a healthy sweat. When the rest of us were finished hitting, Gates would go to trainer Bill Behm for his rubdown. "Boy, I'm tired," Gates would tell Behm. "I've had a rough day."

# Chapter 5

## EXTRA CASH, NIGHTLY POKER, LIGHT ON THE MAYO

MICKEY LOLICH RODE A MOTORCYCLE. Denny McLain had a lounge act. Pat Dobson and John Hiller were real pranksters. Glib Norm Cash was the center of attention at every party. Gates Brown was a nightly card player—and he wasn't playing solitaire.

When Mayo Smith gave up his job as a New York Yankees scout to become manager of the Detroit Tigers on October 3, 1966, he must've felt as if he was taking over a fraternity house as well as a baseball team.

Between the lines in that era, no major-league team was more devoted to winning than the Tigers were. And outside the lines, no major-league team was more devoted to howling at the moon. In 1968, we came from behind after the seventh inning to win 40 different games. We also pushed a plane into a pool at an Anaheim hotel because it seemed like a fun idea at the time. We once produced 97 extra-base hits, including 42 home runs, in a single month. We also were involved in four bench-clearing brawls in a single season. We had rifle arms in our outfield, and we had a *real* gun in our clubhouse because McLain had a permit to carry a concealed weapon.

We were a crazy mix of competitiveness and juvenile behavior. On one hand, we couldn't wait to start the late night, post-game poker game. On the other hand, we were known to stay in the clubhouse 90 minutes after a game to analyze why we had lost. On more than one occasion, a Detroit ballplayer would spend the night at the stadium because he was so angered by his personal performance.

One night in Boston, right fielder Jim Northrup, miffed by a bad day at the plate, called Tigers general manager Jim Campbell at one o'clock in the morning to see if Campbell could get the lights turned on at Fenway Park for some extra batting practice.

Northrup's attitude that night reflected a team-wide commitment toward winning a pennant. It was a team that wanted success very badly. Most of us had grown up together in the Tigers' farm system, and we were like a family. We were a tight-knit, loyal group of guys. When you found one Tigers player in those days, you probably found most of us.

In 1966, we lost our lovable 67-year-old manager Charlie Dressen—and soon after, we lost his replacement, Bob Swift. Dressen suffered his second heart attack on May 16 and died August 10. I wept the night he died. Charlie was my first big-league manager, but he was more like a grandfather to me. He liked to tell me stories about other successful players, particularly black players, with the hope that I'd be inspired to realize my potential. As a manager, he could be tough, but kind at the same time.

Swift was one of our assistant coaches, and he took over as manager after Charlie's heart attack. But on July 14, *he* was hospitalized with cancer. Bob died right after the season. He was only 51. Our third base coach, Frank Skaff, became manager midway through 1966, but how can you succeed under those circumstances? The emotion of that season was simply overwhelming. We were 13 games over .500 with Dressen and Swift in charge through the first 83 games, but only one game over .500 the rest of the way. As soon as Swift was hospitalized in July, we lost 12 of the next 15 games. But despite the difficulty of the season, we still managed to win 88 games and finished just 10 games behind the A.L. pennant-winning Baltimore Orioles.

Mayo Smith's personality was probably the right fit for the Tigers going into the 1967 season. Some guys like to manage like they're playing a board game, moving guys all around as if they're trying to prove they're worth their pay. Mayo wasn't like that. Although he had managed in the 1950s with the Cincinnati Reds and Philadelphia Phillies, he really wasn't as well-known in the baseball world. He'd been a minor-league outfielder for almost two decades and spent half a season with the 1945 Philadelphia Athletics. Mayo was a player's manager. He found a lineup he liked, and he stuck with it. He liked veterans. If you were a veteran, he figured you knew what you were doing and he left you alone. He was a decade younger than I am now, but Mayo always seemed like he was 70 years old to us.

He didn't like confrontations. Actually, I'm not sure he even liked talking to his players very much. If you asked Mayo a question, he would ask you to elaborate a little bit more. When you were done explaining, Mayo would say, "You answered your own question" and then move along.

Mayo essentially inherited players who were accustomed to policing themselves. The players ran the clubhouse at Tiger Stadium, and we held each other accountable. The manager and coaches laid down some guidelines, and we enforced them. We were comfortable with each other. When a player wasn't performing the way he should, one of us would say something to him. We respected seniority, and we all understood that younger players were supposed to follow the lead of the older players. There was a clear chain of command in the locker room and on the field.

Our catcher, Bill Freehan, was the quarterback. Billy would talk to everyone and we followed him. If Bill told us to move around in the outfield, we moved.

We were all about respect and teamwork. That's what made us so successful. We knew that outfielders needed to listen to the second baseman or shortstop when the throws came in from the outfield. And it didn't matter whether Al Kaline was a better hitter or that I hit more home runs, we knew that center fielder Mickey Stanley was the boss

47

in the outfield. On a base hit up the gap, Stanley would always call us off or let us know if he couldn't get to it.

There wasn't one guy on our roster who wouldn't accept help from his teammates. Some guys were more stubborn than others, but when we walked out the clubhouse door, we were a unified team. That's how you win.

We felt comfortable getting on each other because we were so close. Northrup could kick my butt if he didn't think I was working hard enough, and I could get on him if I didn't like his attitude in a game. Northrup, Stanley, and Freehan had all played together, dating back to their first pro season with Duluth in 1961. I had played with Denny McLain, Northrup, and Stanley in Knoxville in 1963. I played with Don Wert and Ray Oyler in Syracuse. Norm Cash, Dick McAuliffe, and Kaline had played together on the Tigers since 1961. Gates Brown and I had both made our major-league debuts in 1963. Even Bill Behm had been our trainer in the minors and then was promoted to the Tigers with us. Even our team physician, Dr. Clarence Livingood, was also the family physician for most of us. That's the kind of bond that team had.

But sometimes when you entered our clubhouse, it was like a trip to Neverland. The Tigers were a team of colorful characters, and that may have been one of the keys to our success. We were always having fun. You could never be sure what sort of shenanigans would take place behind those doors. Mickey Stanley and I were the best of friends, and when we were in the same room, we were like a couple of puppies—we were always wrestling. Jim Price would come after me all the time looking for a playful wrestling match.

Cash was one of the most fascinating characters. He was also the most superstitious player on our team. If he was in the middle of a batting streak, he wouldn't wash his uniform. He wouldn't even want anyone to touch it. He'd go so far as to call the clubhouse attendants on the road and tell them how to deal with his uniform. It had to go directly from the bag to a hanger. When Cash was going well, his uniform was dirty enough to stand on its own.

The other crazy thing about Cash is that I don't know that I ever saw him use his own bat. That's crazy when you consider he won a batting title with a .361 average in 1961.

He would wander around the clubhouse, pulling bats out of his teammates' lockers. "Hey this bat really feels good," he'd say. "Are you gonna use this one today? Let me try it out. I think there's a couple of hits in this one."

Cash would cork a few of his bats and use them in batting practice to see how far he could drive a ball. Clearly he wasn't going to use those bats in a game because you could see the cork on the end of the bat.

Gates Brown was another player who would occasionally grab another player's bat to pinch-hit. One day, he grabbed one of Cash's practice bats and got busted by umpire Nestor Chylak, who could see the cork sticking out. Cash liked to have those bats to see how far he could drive a ball in batting practice. You could tell they were for practice because he made no effort to hide the cork. Gates had no idea he had an illegal bat in his hands.

Cash could drive Mayo crazy. One day the Yankees brought in Steve Hamilton from the bullpen with Cash due up next. Hamilton was 6-foot-7 and he'd played in the NBA with the Minneapolis Lakers. More importantly, he had a three-quarter throwing motion and a wicked slider. He was murderous against left-handed hitters. In 1967, left-handers batted only .171 against him. In 1968, they batted just .184.

Standing in the on-deck circle, the left-handed hitting Cash saw Hamilton coming into the game and walked right back to the dugout. He put his bat in the rack and sat down.

Mayo rushed over and said, "Norm, I didn't put in a pinch-hitter. You're still in the game!"

"Mayo," Cash responded. "I couldn't hit Hamilton when we were in the minors, I've never hit him in the majors, and I probably won't hit him today. Any good manager would put in a pinch-hitter for me right now. If you don't, we're just giving them an out. Why do that when we can still win this game?"

Stormin' Norman liked to win, but he also liked to joke around. In the summer of 1973, Nolan Ryan was throwing his second no-hitter of the season—unfortunately, it was against us. In the bottom of the ninth at Tiger Stadium, Norm came to the plate with a piano leg instead of a bat. He'd already fanned three times using a bat against Ryan, and he thought he couldn't do any worse with a piano leg. Umpire Ron Luciano, of course, wouldn't let him use it, and Cash eventually popped out using a regulation wooden bat. But everyone had a good laugh when Cash entered the batter's box with that piano leg on his shoulder.

Mayo would grin and bear most of our antics, but there were some lines he wouldn't let us cross. Once, when we were in the midst of a losing streak, we were headed out west. Mayo never liked those trips because he thought we got into too much mischief in California. He told us we were going to have a bed-check out there, and Tigers coach Wally Moses reminded us when we all gathered to play poker that night.

Gator and I roomed together, and nearly everyone was gathered in our room, either playing cards or watching. Right before midnight, everybody returned to their rooms to await Mayo's call. After each player got the call, he would just come back down to our poker game.

Awhile later, everyone was back in our room, including right-handed reliever Fred Lasher. He kept asking everyone who came in if Mayo had checked on them. It turned out that everyone had been called but Lasher. That made him furious. He stormed to Mayo's room and busted down the door.

"Aren't I a member of this team, too?" he screamed at Mayo. "I'm as important as anybody else is! You should've checked on me."

Mayo always worried about us when we played in California—and for good reason. Everyone seemed to have too much fun in the sun, including me. And there was one particular party that got me into trouble. I knew some of the Four Tops from Detroit, and one night in California, they threw a party in my honor. I remember telling Gates about it, but he refused to go. He figured that nobody at the party was going to care that the Tigers had a game the next afternoon.

Willie's parents, Clinton and Lillian ("Sis") Horton.

Family: Ruth, James, Helen, Frank, Frankie, Robert, Dad, Joe, Virginia / Henry, Mom, Faye, Ray, Mabel, Billy, Willie.

Willie's elementary school in Stonega, Virginia.

Willie's mother's church.

Railroad tracks where young Willie met his friend Larry Munsey.

Arno, Virginia—Willie's birthplace.

Willie, Larry Munsey, and their Little League team.

Willie's childhood home in Virginia.

Michigan Sportsman of the Year award. (Painting by Walt Terrell)

Gloria Horton and her father, Sam Reid.

Willie pauses for an interview in the 1970s. *(Photo courtesy of Bill Eisner)*

...e of Willie the Wonders's favorite pictures.

From left to right, Mickey Stanley, Gates Brown, Mickey Lolich, Willie, and Bill Freehan. *(Photo courtesy of the Detroit Tigers.)*

An old-timers game at Tiger Stadium in the early '90s. *(Photo courtesy of Bill Eisner)*

Gloria's parents, Sam and
Thelma Reid.

Gates Brown, Tigers manager Billy Martin,
and Willie relax after a big game in 1972.

Women's social at Club 23.          Men's social at Club 23.

Willie the Wonder played in 2,028 major league games!

Willie drove in 1,163 career RBIs.

Willie racked up 1,993 career hits.
*(Photo courtesy of Mark Dehem)*

Willie (a.k.a. "Mull Digger") slugged 325 career home runs.

In 7,298 major-league at-bats, Willie stole just 20 bases.

Willie swings for the fences in spring training, circa
1970. *(Photo courtesy of the Detroit Tigers)*

Willie is considered one of baseball's all-time
strongest players.

Willie was all smiles on this day in 1964.

Willie tunes up during spring training in the early '60s.

Thousands of youngsters imitated their idol's famous batting stance.
*(Photo courtesy of the Detroit Tigers)*

Many baseball experts say that Willie belongs in baseball's Hall of Fame in Cooperstown, N.Y.

# DETROIT SCORER'S ASSOCIATION
## NEWSPAPER BOX SCORE

Played at **BRIGGS STADIUM**

League **METROPOLITAN** ............ Class **CHAMPIONSHIP** ............ Date **6/9/59**

| Team NORTHWESTERN | | AB | R | H | RBI |
|---|---|---|---|---|---|
| CHARLES BOYD | 2B | 4 | 2 | 1 | |
| BOB MARSHALL | SS | 2 | | | |
| WILLIE HORTON | C | 4 | 3 | 2 | |
| JOHN HOLMES | CF | 5 | 1 | 2 | |
| MATTHEW SNORTON | 1B | 4 | 1 | 2 | |
| ALEX JOHNSON | RF | 3 | 1 | 1 | |
| CLARK NEYLAND | 3B | 3 | 1 | 1 | |
| TYRONE PETERSON | LF | 3 | 2 | 2 | |
| BILL STREET (RH) | P | 0 | | | |
| JERRY MIXON (RH) | P | 3 | 2 | 1 | |

(NW 7) NEYLAND WALKED - 2ND ON PB + PETERSON BEAT OUT HIT TO 3B - NEYLAND OUT AT PLATE ON MIXON GROUNDER TO SS - BOYD SAFE ON ERROR - MARSHALL WALKED (RBI) - HORTON FORCED MARSHALL AT 2B - MIXON SCORING

Total ............ **31 13 12**

| Team CASS TECH | | AB | R | H |
|---|---|---|---|---|
| ROY KRUPA | 3B-LF | 5 | 2 | 2 |
| JACK TRELOAR | 2B | 4 | 1 | 2 |
| CARMEN FANZONE | SS | 3 | 2 | 1 |
| RON POSOCH | 1B | 3 | 2 | 2 |
| DOUG VILNIUS | CF | 3 | | |
| FRANK PALAZZOLA | LF-RF | 4 | 1 | 2 |
| TOM MULLINS | RF | 2 | | |
| LARRY HARRISON | C | 3 | 1 | 1 |
| GEORGE COJOCARI (RH) | P | 2 | | |
| AL STUBBE (RH) | P | 0 | 1 | |
| RON ORLOWSKI | | 1 | | |
| RAY KRUPA | 3B | 1 | | |

(CT 6) FANZONE WALKED AND SCORED ON POSOCH' LO DOUBLE TO LC + TO 3RD ON INFIELD OUT AND SCO PASS BALL

Total ............ **31 10 10**

*Batted for **MULLINS AND FLIED TO LF** in the **6TH**
**Batted for ............ in the ............
***Batted for ............ in the ............
****Batted for ............ in the ............

| TEAM | 1 | 2 | 3 | 4 | 5 | 6 | 7 | 8 | 9 | 10 | 11 | 12 | Tota |
|---|---|---|---|---|---|---|---|---|---|---|---|---|---|
| NORTHWESTERN | 1 | 0 | 3 | 0 | 6 | 1 | 2 | | | | | | 13-1 |
| CASS TECH | 0 | 6 | 0 | 0 | 0 | 2 | 2 | | | | | | 10-10 |

Errors **PETERSON — JOHNSON — NEYLAND — TRELOAR 2 — FANZONE**

LEFT ON BASE CASS **12** NW **5** | (RBI HARRISON - KRUPA - POSOCH 4 - PALAZZOLA 2 - HORT

2 Base Hits **FANZONE - POSOCH 2 HORTON** | MIXON — PETERSON — HOLMES — MARSHALL 2 SNORTO

3 Base Hits ............ | **TRELOAR**

Home Runs **HORTON    SNORTON** | (21-11)

Hits Off **STREET    5** in **1²** Inn. Off **MIXON    5** in **5's** Inn. Off ............ in ............ | PO-A CASS TECH 2B, NW 21-9

Off **COJOCARI 7** in **4¹³** Inn. Off **STUBBE** in **2²³** Inn. Off ............ in ............

Struck out by **STREET    0** By **MIXON    6** By ............

By **COJOCARI 4** By **STUBBE 2** By ............

Stolen Bases **SNORTON**

SAC **MULLINS - MARSHALL**

SAC FLY - MARSHALL - HORTON

Base on Balls Off **STREET    3** Off **MIXON 5** Off ............

Off **COJOCARI 4** Off **STUBBE 2** Off ............

Double Plays **TRELOAR TO FANZONE :**

WP **STREET — COJOCARI**

Winning Pitcher **MIXON**    BK- COJOCARI    Losing Pitcher **COJOCARI**

HIT BY PITCH- STUBBE (8

PB HORTON — HARRISO

Umpire **KUNKA (PLATE) HOOPER (1ST)** Scorer **MORRIS MOORAWNICK**    Remarks **(NW3) HORTON HOMERED ABOVE 3**

DECKER (3RD)    MARK IN UPPER DECK RC FIELD (CT 2) PALAZZOLA SINGLED TO RF- MULLINS SACRIFICE

HARRISON SINGLED TO LF SCORING PALAZZOLA AND TOOK 2ND WHEN LF OVERTHREW CATCH - COJOCARI LINED

KRUPA SINGLED TO RF SCORING HARRISON - TRELOAR AND FANZONE WALKED - POSOCH CLEANED BASES WITH GO

DOUBLE OFF RC FIELD BARRIER AT 370 MARK- VILNIUS WALKED BY NEW PITCHER MIXON - PALAZZOLA SINGLED

SCORING POSOCH - (NW 3) PETERSON, MIXON AND BOYD WALKED - MARSHALL SAC FLY TO LF EVERYONE ADV

MIXON SCORED ON BALK AND BOYD SCORED ON HORTON'S SAC FLY TO RF (NW 5) BOYD' SINGLED TO RF - M

SACRIFICED - HORTON SAFE WHEN 2B MAN THREW PULL 1B OFF BAG ON GROUNDER- HOLMES SINGLED TO RE SCORING

HORTON HOMERED OVER 400-FT MARK IN LC FIELD (RBI 3) - JOHNSON WALKED - (STUBBE PITCHING) NEYLAND HIT TO

...HNSON TO 3B WHEN 2B MAN MUFFED THROW FOR FORCE AND SCORED ON PETERSON SINGLE TO CF - NEYLAND

...ND SCORED ON MIXON'S SINGLE TO LF (NW 6) HORTON    89    DOUBLED OFF LC FIELD BARRIER AND ... PRINTING C

...SCORED ON SNORTON'S SINGLE TO RF

Willie's high school city championship scorecard from 1959. Willie and the Northwestern Colts defeated Cass Tech, 13–10.

Act No. 53
Public Acts of 2004
Approved by the Governor
April 7, 2004
Filed with the Secretary of State
April 8, 2004
EFFECTIVE DATE: April 8, 2004

## STATE OF MICHIGAN
## 92ND LEGISLATURE
## REGULAR SESSION OF 2004

Introduced by Reps. Richardville, Waters, Hardman, McConico, Reeves, Woronchak, Plakas, Anderson, Stewart, O'Neil, Rocca, Gieleghem, Drolet, Woodward, Pappageorge, Phillips, Rick Johnson, Minore, Zelenko, Kolb, Jamnick, DeRossett, Spade, Lipsey, Bisbee, Murphy, Tabor, Koetje, Kooiman, Voorhees, Hager, Ehardt, Meyer, Julian, Hummel, Newell, Vander Veen, Dennis, Howell, Williams, Ruth Johnson, Sheltrown, Bradstreet, Shackleton, Adamini, Brown, Gaffney, Cheeks, Smith, Stallworth, Hunter, Hood, Tobocman, Farrah, Paletko, Pastor, LaJoy, Law, Brandenburg, Bieda, Meisner, Wojno, Acciavatti, Clack, Condino, Vagnozzi, DeRoche, Taub, Accavitti, Amos, Stakoe, Garfield, Gleason, Robertson, Milosch, Shaffer, Hoogendyk, Nofs, Wenke, Ward, Byrum, Emmons, Steil, Sak, Nitz, Stahl, Sheen, Huizenga, Farhat, Elkins, Moolenaar, Palsrok, Walker, Gillard, Casperson and Mortimer

# ENROLLED HOUSE BILL No. 5200

AN ACT to designate October 18 of each year as Willie Horton Day in the state of Michigan.

*The People of the State of Michigan enact:*

Sec. 1. The legislature recognizes the fundamental contribution that Willie Horton has made to the city of Detroit and the state of Michigan through his humanitarian works. Raised in a Detroit housing project, Willie fulfilled a boyhood dream by playing for his hometown team, the Detroit Tigers. Throughout his career, Willie has been involved with such organizations as the United Way, the Boys and Girls Club of America, Meals on Wheels, and the Foundation Fighting Blindness. His dedication to helping the youth of his city and beyond has been a hallmark of his playing career and in the years since he left the game. In 1967, Willie used his ambassadorship and goodwill to help crush the violence that erupted during the riots in Detroit. In 2000, the Detroit Tigers further honored this man by retiring his number and erecting a statue in his image at Comerica Park. In recognition of this great man, the legislature declares October 18 of each year to be known as "Willie Horton Day".

This act is ordered to take immediate effect.

_____
Clerk of the House of Representatives

_____
Secretary of the Senate

Approved    4/7/04     3:25 p.m.

_____
Governor

On April 7, 2004, Michigan governor Jennifer Granholm signed House Bill No. 5200 into law, proclaiming October 18 as "Willie Horton Day" annually throughout the state.

Michigan state representative and majority floor leader Randy Richardville presents Willie with a copy of House Bill 5200.

Freman Hendrix helps celebrate the first annual Willie Horton Day.

Northwestern High teammates Walt, Willie, Richard and Marshall.

Willie with niece Pat and nephew Johnny.

Willie and family at Northwestern field dedication ceremony.

Willie with the Tigers scout who signed him, Lou
D'Annunzio. *(Photo courtesy of Mark Dehem)*

Willie's statue at Comerica Park in downtown Detroit. *(Photo courtesy of Bright Imaging Group)*

WILLIE HORTON
"WILLIE THE WONDER"
BORN OCTOBER 18, 1942 ARNO, VIRGINIA

DETROIT TIGERS OF, DH 1963-77 TEXAS RANGERS, CLEVELAND INDIANS, &
TORONTO BLUE JAYS DH, OF 1978    SEATTLE MARINERS DH 1979-80
A HOMETOWN HERO WHOSE ACCOMPLISHMENTS ON AND
OFF THE FIELD ARE A CREDIT TO THE CITY OF DETROIT

ACHIEVEMENTS AND HONORS
RAISED IN A DETROIT HOUSING PROJECT AND OVERCAME ADVERSITY
    TO BECOME A TIGER HOMETOWN HERO
WAS A BASEBALL STAR FOR DETROIT'S NORTHWESTERN HIGH SCHOOL
    AND PLAYED DETROIT SANDLOT BASEBALL
WAS INSTRUMENTAL IN HELPING CRUSH THE VIOLENCE THAT ERUPTED
    DURING THE 1967 RIOTS IN DETROIT
BATTED .326 HIS FIRST SEASON WITH THE TIGERS
HAD 100 OR MORE RBI IN 1965 104 AND 1966 100
THREW OUT LOU BROCK AT HOME PLATE IN THE PIVOTAL GAME FIVE
    OF THE 1968 WORLD SERIES
LED THE TEAM IN HOME RUNS 1968 36, 1969 28 AND 1975 25
HIT 325 CAREER HOME RUNS, 1163 RBI, AND HAD A .273 LIFETIME BATTING AVERAGE
WAS ELECTED TO FOUR ALL STAR TEAMS AS A TIGER
HAD HIS UNIFORM NUMBER 23 RETIRED JULY 15, 2000
SCULPTORS: JULIE & OMRI R. AMRANY          CO-SCULPTOR: GARY TILLERY
DEDICATED  JULY 15, 2000

The plaque on Willie's statue. *(Photo courtesy of Bright Imaging Group)*

Friends, family, and fans gather to see Willie's statue
unveiled and his jersey retired on July 15, 2000.

Willie and Clarence
"Pee Wee" Thomas.

Lenny Green, Bobby Miles and
his wife, Zelma, and Gloria.

Tigers front office representatives at the North-
western High ceremony. From left to right, Bob
Raymond, Steve Quinn, Duane McLean, Charlie
Jones, John Westhoff, and Al Avila.

Willie, with his children and grandchildren, pose before the
closing of historic Tiger Stadium, September 27, 1999.

A longtime love affair: Willie
Horton and Tiger Stadium.

Willie the Wonder has signed thousands of autographs over the years for his many fans.

The Tiger Stadium grounds crew
in the mid-1990s—one of the
best in the country.

At his jersey retirement ceremony, Willie shows his thanks to Tigers owner Mike Ilitch.

No other Ti
will ever w
Willie's nur
ber 23 agai

Willie gives an emotional speech to a packed Comerica Park, as his wife, Gloria, and broadcaster Ernie Harwell look on.

I don't recall too much about the party except that somehow we ended up at a house owned by singer Glen Campbell. The sun came up and we were still there, and I had to have someone drive me straight to the ballpark.

When I arrived, the Gator was there, shaking his head, letting me know that he'd made the right choice not to attend that Hollywood bash.

To be honest, I tried to tell Mayo that I couldn't play that day because I felt lousy. But Mayo, to his credit, said, "You're going to play."

As it turned out, I hit a home run in that game and drove in three runs and probably never felt worse in my life. But that's the way we all were back then. No matter what happened the night before, once the game started, we were all about winning. I remember my relatives would come and visit me from down south. We'd stay up all night talking, but I'd play the next afternoon without thinking twice about it.

The only time I can remember Mayo being truly angry with us came on a road trip to Anaheim to play the Angels. We stayed at a hotel that proudly displayed an old fighter plane out in front. Late one night, after too many drinks, some of us "relocated" that plane to the middle of the hotel pool.

At four o'clock in the morning, Mayo caught wind of it and promptly hauled us all out of bed. It was the first time any of us had ever seen him mad. I could barely stop from laughing, though, because he came downstairs wearing a nightshirt with the slits down the side, and I'd never seen anyone wear one of those except on TV. It looked like an old lady's nightgown from the turn of the century.

"I don't care who did it!" Mayo said, fuming. "Everyone is going to help get it out of the pool." We tried, but we weren't able to get that plane out of the pool, and a wrecker had to be called in to do the job.

We usually didn't get into too much trouble on the road, though, because we were too busy playing cards. On the road, Gates Brown and I held a regular poker game in our room. He was the head organizer, and when we checked in to a hotel, Gates would always buy 100 one-dollar bills from the front desk to make sure we'd be ready for the game. Gates, John Hiller, Jon Warden, Pat Dobson, and Tommy Matchick always played. Sometimes Cash or Northrup, McLain, or others would join us.

The regulars always liked McLain to play in those games because he wasn't nearly as good a card player as he was a pitcher. They nicknamed McLain "the Dolphin" because he was a "fish" at the poker table. He would be playing five-card stud and have a two, three, nine, seven, all different suits showing, and he'd stay in. Everyone would be looking at each other, like what is he *doing*? But Denny was Denny.

Because we were as close as brothers, we sometimes acted like it—meaning we didn't always play nice. I've never been a successful gambler, so I didn't play much. But I would go to the games anyhow—I saw them as social events. Cash was the same way. He wasn't much of a gambler, but he always wanted to be where the party was. Sometimes, I would simply be the Gator's bank. "Let me hold a twenty," Gator would say to me, and the next thing I knew, we were partners in some poker pot.

McLain always played the role of big shooter in these games. He always wanted to be the big king. When he played cards, he liked to wear a Japanese smoking jacket. He was always talking on the phone during the games. And even though he always had a pocket stuffed with money, Denny was always short when it came time to ante up.

Like I said, we were as close as brothers, and sometimes brothers fight each others. One night, we were in the middle of a game, and Denny was on the phone ordering some food, and his antics started to irritate Northrup.

The game was high-low, split the pot, meaning the best hand and worst hand shared the pot. As usual, Denny was light, so he was pulling chips out of the pot to show how much he owed.

With bets at one or two dollars apiece—and three raises allowed, the pots would sometimes grow to a couple hundred dollars, this one included. The games could get serious because none of us had the contracts that today's athletes do. A couple of hundred dollars was still a nice sum for us.

On this particular hand, McLain ended up winning half the pot, and when that happens, the other winner gets your "lights" because you actually owe the pot.

But Denny swept his "lights" into his own pile, and Northrup spotted the move. His temper boiled over. He grabbed McLain's arm, and said "those are mine." McLain claimed he wasn't light on the pot. "You lyin' son of a gun," Northrup said, as he reached across the table and ripped McLain's black-and-white smoking jacket right in half.

I really don't remember for sure, but I'm guessing Jimmy must've had a bad day on the field because he was angrier than he should've been.

"I'm tired of Jim Campbell protecting you," Jimmy said.

The next thing I know, money was flying everywhere and my teammates were yelling and pushing. Gator and I broke up the fight before it really got out of hand.

Shortstop Ray Oyler probably had had too much to drink because I think he thought he was still in the military. When the scuffle started, he grabbed Gates Brown. I still remember Oyler trying to get in the middle of the scrap and big Gator just holding him by his head.

Meanwhile, some guys—myself included—were picking up the money that was scattered on the floor. It was probably the only time I ever won at poker.

Today, Warden always jokes that when the fight broke out, he got up, stretched, said, "Where has the time gone? I'd better get to bed" and then scrambled out of the room. His theory was that if management came down to break up a fight, they weren't going to punish Northrup, McLain, Cash, or me, but Mayo might have wondered what a rookie was doing up there with a bunch of veterans.

"It would have been, 'Hey, rookie, I'll see you in Toledo,'" Warden says, laughing. "So I got my rear end out of there."

I should take a moment here to talk about Oyler because he was probably one of the forgotten heroes of 1968. The 165-pound Oyler was probably one of the slickest fielding shortstops I ever saw in the major leagues, but he had trouble hitting his weight when he was with the Tigers.

I never quite understood that because I played with him at Syracuse in Triple-A ball, and he hit 19 home runs one season. The season before that, he hit 23 doubles and nine home runs. But at the big-league level, he just couldn't find any confidence at the plate. You could've rolled the ball up to him, and I'm not sure he could've hit it.

For a joke, the guys gave Ray a "Popeye bat" with a big barrel on it. He handled the ribbing pretty well.

Supposedly Oyler, who had spent time in the Marines, was 22 when the Tigers drafted him in 1960. And he was supposedly 28 when Mayo Smith joined the team in 1967, but Oyler looked as if he was in his late 30s. When we acquired pitchers John Wyatt and Earl Wilson, both of them told us that Oyler had been their sergeant in the service. Wyatt and Wilson were both listed as three and four years older than Oyler, and they didn't see how that was possible.

"He must have joined the service when he was 14 years old," Wyatt used to say.

But I respected Oyler because he was willing to bunt, or hit behind the runner, to help the team. He also won games for us with his defense. Often Oyler, batting eighth, would lay down a sacrifice bunt to move a runner into scoring position to allow our pitchers to drive him in. Our pitchers could all swing the bat, and most of them might have been better major-league hitters than Ray. Heck, Earl Wilson probably hit more home runs in one season than Oyler hit in his whole career.

In addition to their contributions on the field, Warden, Dodson, Hiller, and Price kept us all loose with their antics. And I was frequently the target of their pranks. My concerns about flying were well-known, and the guys liked to mess with me on that. One time, they locked me in the bathroom on the team flight. It was like I was stuck in an elevator, going up and down, up and down. It seemed as if I was in that bathroom forever.

Another time, one of those three guys posted a note on my locker, saying I had to call some doctor because tests I had taken for hemorrhoids showed internal bleeding. I was nervous and worried, but then I caught them snickering and I figured out what was going on.

What I liked about our team is that we always seemed to understand when it was appropriate to pull pranks. When we needed to relax or to get our minds off a losing streak, you could count on funny comments and jokes. And everybody had a nickname, too. Don Wert was "Coyote" because he didn't say much. I became "Roids" because I suffered from hemorrhoids. Freehan and Joe Sparma were dubbed "Big Ten" because Freehan had played tight end at Michigan, and Sparma had played quarterback at Ohio State. Jim Northrup was "the Gray Fox" because he was prematurely gray. And I always called Jim Price the "Big Man" because he always seemed like he was destined to wear a suit some day in the business world.

Price and I actually played against each other in 1964 when I was playing Triple-A ball in Syracuse, and he was in the Pirates' organization playing for Columbus.

In one game, Bob Priddy, who eventually made it to the majors, was pitching for Columbus. He hit my Syracuse teammate Oyler "right in the coconut," as Price likes to say. I was up next, and I didn't even look at Price as I stepped in the batter's box. But as I was taking my practice swings, I told Price that if Priddy's pitches even got close to my head, I was coming after Price. Price nodded and then went out to the mound for a chat.

Years later, Price told me what he said. "What I told Priddy was that if he threw high and inside to you, you were going to come after him with a baseball bat."

Outfielder Wayne Comer, from Shenandoah, Virginia, was one of my good friends on the team, and we spent a lot of time together. Even today we keep in touch. I recently visited him at home in Virginia to celebrate an anniversary of baseball in that area. When Comer played for the Tigers, we called him Shank. Shank was actually a fine outfielder and a dependable role player in 1968. He also liked to run with the big dogs, and occasionally he'd get himself into sticky situations at various watering holes.

One time, some of us were having a drink and a burger at the Brass Rail in Minnesota, and Wayne spotted a group of soldiers at the bar. Wayne's impishness got the best of him. He went up, and one-by-one, he asked each soldier where he was from. He would then make an insulting remark about his state. The joke seemed to play pretty well until he got to the last soldier and he suggested, in his own colorful way, that Oklahoma was the worst state of them all. We ended up fighting our way out of the place. I tell this story simply to show that we had a one-for-all and all-for-one attitude. We looked after each other.

Most successful teams have a player who keeps everyone loose and on their toes at the same time. Gates Brown could help a player out of a batting slump, and he could have the entire team doubled over in laughter because of something he said.

Gates always drew a crowd around him because you never knew what might come out of his mouth. Once, we were playing one of those rare 11 a.m. games in Minnesota, and Al Kaline had the day off. That shifted me from left field to right field, and Gates started in left.

At that early in the morning, the glare of the sun was directly in your face in left field and I was mighty thankful I was in right. Bob Allison hit one ball that bounced off Gator's chest, and then Harmon Killebrew drove a ball that bounced off Gator's head.

When Gator came back to the dugout, he was mad about the errors, and he blamed it all on Mayo Smith. Believe it or not, he started cussing out Mayo for giving him the start.

"You know full well that I shouldn't be out playing in left field this early," Gator screamed. "You know that I like to play poker late at night."

Mayo was dumbfounded. He didn't know what to say, so he turned to batting coach Wally Moses and asked, "What's he talking about?"

Moses shrugged, and everyone else was laughing because Moses was keenly aware that Gator liked to stay up late playing poker.

Then McLain came into the dugout and decided to needle Gates. That was only fair because Gator liked to needle everyone else.
"It's bad enough that I have to face Minnesota with eight good hitters in their lineup," McLain said. "But now I find out that my biggest enemy is sitting on the bench with me."

We all laughed because with the way McLain was pitching then, he could overcome just about any mistake we made. McLain also knew that the Gator could take a ribbing.

The Gator knew he wouldn't usually be called upon until late in a game, so he liked to hang out down in the bullpen, especially at Tiger Stadium, because the relievers always had plenty of food spread out like a smorgasbord. Hot dogs, pretzels, and peanuts were always on the menu. One night in the fifth inning, Mayo called down to the bullpen for Gates to come pinch-hit.

The guys in the bullpen told me that Gates had just dressed up a couple of hot dogs, and had eaten only one of them when he got the call from Mayo.

"You guys will eat this if I leave it here," Gates said as he wrapped up his ketchup-slathered dog and stuck it in his jersey.

This was 1968, and Gates was stroking the ball like Ted Williams. Not surprisingly, he ripped a line drive down the right-field line and slid head-first into second base with a double. Gator rolled over to get up, and the umpire looked at him with panic in his eyes. "Don't move, Gator!" he yelled. "You're hurt."

There were ketchup stains streaking down Gates' jersey, and it looked as if he was bleeding profusely. Gator told the umpire it was an exploded hot dog and to keep quiet because he didn't want Mayo knowing he was eating every night at the all-you-can-eat bullpen buffet.

As he often did, Mayo inserted a pinch runner for Gator, who came out holding his side because he didn't want Mayo to spot the ketchup stain.

Another time, Gates hit a home run off Boston pitcher Lee Stange and a hot dog fell out of his uniform as he was rounding the bases.

We had many great characters on the Tigers to keep us all loose and enjoying ourselves. But there was no question who the team leader was. Al Kaline was easily the most respected man in the clubhouse. He never played a day in the minor leagues. He was 18 when the Tigers signed him in 1953, and he won an American League batting title when he was just 20. He wore the English D continuously from 1953 until 1974. Then he went into the broadcast booth. He has essentially been a Tiger for more than half of a century.

Players called him the "The Line" because Mr. Campbell wouldn't pay anyone more than he paid Al. I preferred the nickname "The Lion" because he was the king of our jungle. When he walked in our clubhouse, he was so light on his feet you couldn't even hear his cleats click.

To me, Al was the Abraham Lincoln of our team He was humble and quiet, but when he spoke his words were powerful.

Some guys wondered why Al never said much. But former trainer Jack Homel explained to me that Al's reserved demeanor probably reflected how he arrived in the major leagues. When Al came to the Tigers in 1953, he was an 18-year-old high school player joining a team that had a lineup heavy with veteran players. Johnny Pesky was 33 and just a year from retirement. Outfielder Pat Mullin was 35. Catcher Matt Batts was 31, and there were a couple of other starters 30 or over.

"He was a kid in a man's world," Homel said. "When you come to a team in that situation, you're just expected to keep your mouth shut and play. That's what Al did and that just became his personality. He just stayed in that world."

To this day, Al and I are the best of friends. I learned a lot from hitting behind him, especially the professional manner in which he approached hitting. Early in my career, I kept my distance, mostly out of respect for who he was.

But as I grew into a man myself, I began to realize that if you had a question for Al, he had an answer. He was a private man. He wasn't like Cash, or Gates, or Rocky Colavito, who all loved to talk. He wasn't going to come up to you and start telling you how to become a better hitter. That wasn't Al's style. But if you went to him, he'd give you everything you needed. He was one of the classiest ballplayers I ever came across in my career.

Perhaps my bond with Al was cemented forever on May 30, 1970, when I performed an emergency medical procedure on him that I'm told saved his life.

We were playing a game at County Stadium in Milwaukee when Brewers second baseman Roberto Pena sliced a 380-foot line drive into the right-center field gap. Center fielder Jim Northrup and right fielder Kaline both tried to make the catch, but they collided violently. The ball deflected off Northrup's glove, and he immediately started chasing down the ball. The bases had been loaded with Brewers, and Jim wanted to keep some of those runners from scoring.

I immediately noticed that Kaline wasn't moving. I was in a full gallop from left field to right. Milwaukee bullpen coach Jackie Moore was the first to get there and he could see Kaline gasping for air, but he couldn't get Kaline's mouth open.

By the time I got there, Al had turned blue. I kneeled over his chest and performed an emergency first-aid procedure that I had learned from my boxing days. Always concerned about a boxer swallowing his mouthpiece, we were taught to push on the chest to help force open the jaw. I did that and forced my three fingers down Al's mouth and pulled out his tongue. Milwaukee's trainer Curt Rayer was also there helping me. Al had swallowed his tongue after the collision, and the blockage in his throat prevented him from getting air.

Unfortunately for me, when I got Al's jaw open, he bit down on my hand—hard! I screamed loud enough that some people thought I was severely injured. I still have the mark on my hand where Al got me. I often tell people that the bite mark is the best autograph you can get because no one can take that one from me.

I'm thankful that my boxing training came back to me when it did. In an emergency, it's easy to forget your training.

Pena ended up with an inside-the-park home run, and we eventually lost that game 9–7. But I don't think anyone on the Tigers felt bad about the loss after Al survived that scary moment in the outfield. He didn't play the next game, but he was in uniform and didn't have any lasting effects.

Every player on our roster appreciated Al for who he was and what he meant to the organization. He was also one of the classiest players in the game, and on the Tigers, he was the standard by which all others were judged.

Every successful team has players whose competitiveness fuels success. Tigers second baseman Dick McAuliffe and pitcher Earl Wilson were just that type.

Once the game started, we were all business. But McAuliffe was all business two hours before the first pitch. We called him Mad Dog. Before the game, he didn't want people talking to him. It was almost like he was in a trance, and he'd be perturbed if you disturbed him. He also played with an edge to his game. He respected players who tried to take him out at second base on a double-play ball because that's the way he played.

And no one competed with more ferocity than Wilson. I remember a game against Baltimore at Tiger Stadium when Wilson was pitching masterfully, going into the ninth inning with a 4–1 lead. He'd given up only three hits, and the Orioles weren't making good contact. Wilson had them off balance.

Then in the ninth inning, Frank Robinson homered on the first pitch, and Boog Powell and Brooks Robinson followed with solo shots in rapid-fire succession to tie the game. Boom. Boom. Boom. To this day, I've never seen a team lose a three-run lead as quickly as we did. Mayo pulled Wilson out of the game, and reliever Tom Timmerman then gave up the winning run on a double by Davey Johnson.

After the game, Earl was furious that Mayo didn't have a reliever up throwing in the bullpen to replace him after he gave up the first home run.

Mayo was flabbergasted. "Earl, you were pitching a three-hitter," he said. "You looked like you were coasting, and if I had someone up throwing, you would've been mad at me for that." Earl was just steamed that we lost the game, and Mayo was a convenient target. Earl hated losing.

Another time in Baltimore, Earl was saying before the game that Frank Robinson had his number, and he was darn tired of giving up big hits to him. Robinson was perhaps the most competitive player I ever played against. When Robinson slid into second base to break up a double-play, he sometimes would knock the pivot man onto the outfield grass. Robinson never received enough credit for his hitting ability. I remember one time early in my career when we had a pre-game meeting about the Orioles. We started talking about how to pitch to Robinson, but Charlie Dressen cut off the discussion because he said Robinson could hit a pitch in any location. "You just have to go right at him and hope for the best," Dressen said.

On this day in 1966, Earl had a different plan. "I'm going to drill his ass," he said, defiantly. "I'm going to bust him between the neck and the collarbone."

In the first inning, Earl gave up a couple of singles to Luis Aparicio and Russ Snyder, and then Robinson strode to the plate. Earl threw high—inside smoke up above the neckline. Robinson just raised his hands and blasted the pitch clear out of Memorial Stadium to give the Orioles a 3–0 lead.

Earl just raised his hands over his head and walked right off the mound. He took *himself* out of the game!

Clearly Mayo Smith inherited a team primed to win a pennant. We had the talent, and we were gaining the experience. In 1966—a year before Mayo got there—everyone in our starting lineup hit 10 or more home runs, except Jerry Lumpe. At 31, Kaline had finished third in the batting race and had hit 29 home runs; he still seemed in the prime of his career. I was only 23 and had just completed my second 100-RBI season. Norm Cash hit 32 home runs, and Dick McAuliffe hit 23. Jim Northrup had smacked 16 home runs in just 123 games, and he looked very much like a consistent 20–25 home run guy.

Freehan was only 24, and he was already a two-time All-Star and one of the top defensive catchers in the game. From 1965–'66, Bill posted a .996 fielding average and threw out about 36 percent of runners trying to steal on him.

Team president Jim Campbell could see even in 1965 that we had the makings of a championship-caliber team. That's why on June 14, 1966, the Tigers traded Don Demeter and a player to be named later (Julio Navarro) to the Boston Red Sox for Earl Wilson and Joe Christopher. Earl solidified our pitching staff. He boasted a 2.59 ERA in 1966, and when he pitched, it was like having an extra big bat in the lineup. He might've been the best-hitting pitcher in the American League. Also that season, Denny McLain won 20 games for the first time. Mickey Lolich won 14 games, and it was clear he was going to be a dominant pitcher. We also had high hopes for right-handed pitcher Joe Sparma, the former Ohio State quarterback. Personally, I thought he threw as hard as any pitcher in the American League. When we first started, I thought he was going to be another Sandy Koufax. I would say Sparma threw his fastball in the high 90s.

In 1967, McAuliffe moved full-time to second base, and Ray Oyler became our starting shortstop. Mayo's theory was that we had plenty of offense, and that Ray would make our defense stronger.

Even dealing with the tragic deaths of Charlie Dressen and Bob Swift in 1966, we had still contended. Now with a fresh start and a new manager, the Tigers wouldn't be content just to contend. We were thinking about winning. When I looked at our lineup and compared it to the rest of the American League, I saw no reason why we couldn't win multiple championships.

# Chapter 6

**1967**

**DURING SPRING TRAINING OF 1967,** I tore my Achilles so badly that a leading orthopedic surgeon recommended that I have surgery that would sideline me for the entire season.

Amazingly, that wasn't the worst news of the summer.

Playing through that injury wasn't nearly as excruciating as seeing the city of Detroit engulfed in flames, with people dying and tanks rolling through the neighborhoods where I played sandlot baseball as a child. The aching in my ankle wasn't nearly as painful as seeing National Guard troops marching up 12th Street with their eyes panning the houses for snipers.

By July of 1967, I expected to be in the midst of the American League pennant race. Instead, I found myself standing in the midst of an urban riot. There I was, standing in full Detroit Tigers uniform, on the hood of my car pleading with the rioters and looters not to destroy more homes and lives.

This was supposed to be a summer of fun in the Motor City. All winter, fans had been talking about our chances to win Detroit's first pennant since 1945. We were hungry for success. New manager Mayo Smith had been on all of the sports shows, saying we were going to compete for the American League title. We figured our pitching staff was as talented as any in the league. The Red Sox had Jim Lonborg, Gary Bell, and Jose Santiago. Minnesota had Dean Chance, Jim Merritt, Jim Kaat, and Dave Boswell. We could match with Mickey Lolich, Denny McLain, Earl Wilson, and Joe Sparma. All four of those Detroit pitchers could easily win 20 games.

After my injury, the Tigers flew me to California to meet with a leading sports medicine expert, and he told me flat-out that my season was over before it began. That answer was unacceptable to me because I had trained aggressively all winter to be ready for our pennant drive. With my German shepherd, Champ, at my side, I'd run up and down the Lodge Freeway service drive all winter long to reach a high level of conditioning. I was not going to let that go to waste.

Ultimately, it was my decision whether to have surgery. I informed our team physician, Clarence Livingood, that I would try to play through the injury and have my surgery after the season. He consulted with Dr. Russell Wright, who worked with both the Detroit Lions and Tigers, and they came up with the idea of me playing the entire 1967 season in a soft cast. The cast was protected with a high-top boot, similar to the ones that Johnny Unitas wore in the NFL.

The hope was that if I sat out the first three weeks of the season, my Achilles would heal enough to let me play most of our games. We also consulted with Mayo, and we all agreed that if the Tigers had a significant lead, I'd come out of the game. The idea was to minimize as much strain on the ankle as possible. It was not an ideal situation, but I was able to play 122 games that season. My injury wasn't the Tigers' only medical woe that season: Al Kaline also missed five weeks midseason with a broken hand.

Injuries or not, the Tigers started the 1967 campaign with a 25–15 record. But we had a rough June, finishing below .500 for the month. Still, as July rolled around, we were still close enough to make a run at the pennant. We were a confident team, and we mistakenly believed that our pennant chase would be the big story in Detroit as the summer heated up. But we had no idea that baseball would seem like a trivial pursuit near the end of July.

On July 23, we split a doubleheader against the New York Yankees. But we didn't realize that while we were competing against Mickey Mantle, Elston Howard and the Yankees, a riot had started in the area around Tiger Stadium. We could see smoke billowing above the stadium roof, but we just assumed there was a major fire nearby.

Even when we were told to exit Tiger Stadium immediately because there was rioting, none of us could really comprehend what was happening on the streets. How do you explain that people—many of whom had never even had a parking ticket in their lives—would suddenly become part of an unruly mob?

People have often asked me why I drove to the epicenter of the riot, and I really can't explain my actions. Thoughts were just whirling around my mind, and I just wanted to be able to do something to help. This was my community. These were my people. Members of my family were living in the eye of this riot. Honestly, I didn't understand why this was happening. Team officials were really pressing us to leave the area quickly. Most of the players didn't even shower. I didn't even change out of my uniform. I jumped into my car and drove over by 12th Street, near the area where I had delivered Michigan Chronicle newspapers as a child. I had walked these streets a thousand times without a fear in the world. But what I saw on those streets that night scared me. Houses had flames dancing across their roofs. Cars were overturned. Small groups of youngsters were roaming the streets, looting and vandalizing the local businesses. It looked like a war zone. To me, it looked like the world was coming to an end.

I got out of my car, climbed on the roof, and started shouting at people until I got their attention.

"Go home, Willie!" somebody said. "Don't stay down here. We don't want you to get hurt."

Supposedly, the 1967 riots began when Detroit vice squad officers raided an after-hours drinking club on 12th Street and Clairmount. There was a large party going on inside in celebration of two returning Vietnam veterans. Apparently, a large group of people gathered outside to protest the arrests. Black people being arrested by white police officers. Racial tension had already been at a boiling point, and this blew the lid off.

There have been studies about why the rioting began, and they pointed to many different factors, including the community's mistrust of the police and economic hardship. It certainly was a changing political climate because of the war in Vietnam and the civil rights movement. But I certainly wasn't thinking about any of that as I stood on my car and asked members of my community to go home and be with their families.

They were burning up and tearing up the neighborhood. "Why are you doing this?" I kept asking. "Why?" But no one had an answer. "Whatever message you're trying to make will surely be lost in the violence," I said.

People did listen, but not many stopped their assault on the city. More people expressed concern for my safety. Eventually, I climbed down and got back into my car.

The rioting went on for five days. Forty-three people died from the violence, and 1,189 were injured. More than 7,200 were arrested—one of them an 82-year-old man. More than 400 homes were burned and more than 2,500 businesses were either looted or destroyed.

That night, I drove in and out of the riots without incident. People recognized me that night, and later, some would thank me for at least making an effort to quell the violence, even if it was a failed one. No one tried to harm me that night, and my car never got a scratch. Maybe that was the night that I embraced my community for the first time as an adult.

I went back down there over the next few days—once because I heard that Mickey Lolich was on one of the tanks. He was in the National Guard, and I was told he had been called to active duty. Other times because I felt I had to do something to help my community. The riot had a profound impact on my life, and certainly it affected our ballclub.

Because of the riots, we didn't play for four days. When we resumed play in Baltimore, we were six games over .500 and starting to make a serious run at winning a very tight A.L. pennant race. We won four of our last six in July, and then posted a 21–14 mark in August to strengthen our position. Going into the final two weeks of the regular season, the Boston Red Sox, Minnesota Twins, Chicago White Sox, and Detroit Tigers all had a chance to win the pennant. The Tigers were trying to win their first since 1945, and we felt confident, although we suspected that the race would come down to the final day. We were right.

In the final two days, Carl Yastrzemski and the Red Sox beat the Twins twice to eliminate them. We controlled our own destiny. All we had to do was sweep a doubleheader on the last day of the season against the California Angels, a team that was in the middle of the pack.

In the first game, I smacked a two-run home run off left-hander Clyde Wright in the first inning, and I doubled later. I ended up scoring three runs, and we won the game 6–4. Joe Sparma pitched seven strong innings, and Bill Freehan went 3-for-3. We thought we were on our way to a pennant.

But in the nightcap, the Angels played us hard. Jimmy Northrup hit a two-run homer in the second inning to help us build a 3–1 lead. But we couldn't hold it, even with Denny McLain on the mound. In the third, Jim Fregosi hit a run-scoring double, and Don Mincher hit a two-run homer to give the Angels the lead. By the bottom of the fifth, the Angels were up 8–3. But we wouldn't go down without a fight. With two out in the seventh, Dick McAuliffe hit a two-run single to make it 8–5.

Even trailing by three runs going into the bottom of the ninth, we had some confidence, and it grew when Freehan doubled and Wert walked to start the inning off Minnie Rojas. Then the managing began in earnest. Mayo Smith pinch-hit Lenny Green for Mickey Lolich, who had come out of the bullpen to help keep us in the game. Angels manager Bill Rigney then brought in left-hander George Brunet to pitch to the left-handed-hitting Green. Then Mayo brought in Jimmy Price to bat for Green. Even after Price flew out to left, I think we believed we'd rally to tie or win because Dick McAuliffe was up. Mac was an All-Star second baseman that year, and in 1966 and 1967, he had a combined total of 45 home runs. He also had some clutch hits, including one earlier in the game.

"Mac" hit the ball on the nose, but right at Angels second baseman Bobby Knoop, who turned it into a quick double-play. It was the only double-play McAuliffe hit into the whole season. The team was devastated, but nobody blamed Mac.

Even though it looks like we lost on the final day, pennants are never won or lost on the final day. They're lost months, weeks and days before. We lost it in the final week when we only won three of seven games. We lost the night before when we gave up six runs to California in the eighth inning and lost, 8–6. We lost it in mid-September when we didn't sweep the seventh-place Washington Senators. We lost it in early July when we lost seven in a row, including four to the Senators.

Injuries did undermine us in 1967: I like to think that Al and I would've been worth a few wins each had we been healthy. Also, Denny McLain suffered a mysterious foot injury late in the season and missed a few starts. No one knew exactly how he hurt his foot. It wasn't the first time he was involved in controversy, and it wouldn't be the last. With the riot as a backdrop to our pennant chase, fans really didn't embrace the battle for first place as they normally would.

But we learned about ourselves in 1967. We came to understand that there's a fine line between winning and losing. We realized that those games in July were as important as the games in September. And the riots reminded us that, given the unhappiness in the world, it truly was a privilege that we were getting paid to play a game we loved.

When we lost to the Angels on October 1, 1967, we couldn't view the loss as having any grand purpose. But early in the 1968 season, it became clear to me that our team had an assignment even more important than winning a pennant. It seemed to me that there was some divine inspiration at work here. It seemed to me that the Tigers' real undertaking in 1968 was to help unify the city of Detroit—to bring black and white together. To restore harmony to an area that had been a battleground for four days the summer before. And to heal the city. Maybe we needed to lose that final game of 1967 to fully appreciate our role.

# Chapter 7

## THE PEOPLE'S CHAMPIONSHIP

THE ECHO OF GUNFIRE THAT HAD DEFINED the summer of 1967 on the streets of Detroit was replaced by the sweet tones of Ernie Harwell, whose voice owned the night in the Motor City in the summer of 1968. People still tell me that if you drove down any block in the city that summer it was like hearing Harwell in stereo. His lyrical delivery seemed to be coming from all directions. It was a hot summer, doors and windows remained open, and Harwell seemed to be a guest on every porch—a visitor in every home. People would be walking down the street with a transistor swinging from a wristband, not wanting to miss a game, an inning, or even a single pitch of the 1968 season. Everyone in the city—black or white, rich or poor—was listening to Harwell during what can only be described as a magical season.

In 1967, the city was on fire. In 1968, the Tigers were on fire.

It was the year of the tiger in China that year, and fans began to embrace the idea that the Chinese calendar had forecast our success on the ballfield. We really didn't need an omen. No clubhouse speeches were necessary to remind us that we were expected to win the pennant in 1968. We all believed we should have won in 1967, and we were determined to make sure we made no mistake in 1968.

Curiously, we lost on Opening Day, but then we won nine in a row and kept on rolling. Rookie left-hander Jon Warden, who remains a dear friend to this day, won three of those games. He'd made the jump from Class A baseball directly to the majors, and now he was the first three-game winner in the major leagues. When a Sports Illustrated reporter asked Jon how many more games he could win as a rookie, Jon said, "I should win 45 or 50."

Jon made the team because we needed an improved bullpen, and with that sense of humor, he fit right into our clubhouse. We were a confident bunch. The Tigers moved into first place on May 10 and we never looked back. Nobody was going to catch us. We won 103 games and finished 12 games ahead of Baltimore.

What I remember most about 1968 is that we never believed we were out of any game. In 40 of our victories, we were tied or trailing in the seventh inning. Fans began to expect our comebacks, and because of that, there was always energy and emotion spilling out of the ballpark. If we were trailing going into the seventh inning, people would start to clap and to bang those old, green, wooden seats. As you stepped into the batter's box, you could feed off the rhythm of the cheering. It was intimidating to play against us in Tiger Stadium.

People viewed us as a three-run homer club, but we could beat you in many different ways with many different players.

For example, utility infielder Tom Matchick had just three home runs for the season, but one of those was a two-run shot in the bottom of the ninth on July 19 against Baltimore. We trailed 4–2 going into the ninth, but Tommy's homer gave us the win, 5–4. A week later, reliever Daryl Patterson entered a game against the Orioles at Memorial Stadium with the bases loaded and nobody out in the bottom of the sixth. He struck out Fred Valentine, Brooks Robinson, and Davey Johnson to get us out of a jam. Patterson went the rest of the way, and we won that one, 4–1.

During the 1968 season, Jim Northrup smacked four grand slams and broke up three no-hitters. On June 24, Northrup hit grand slams in two consecutive at-bats in a 14–3 win at Cleveland. He was the first major-leaguer since Baltimore's Jim Gentile in 1961 to hit grand slams in consecutive at-bats. Then five days later, Northrup hit another grand slam to beat Chicago, 5–2, which set a new record of three grand slams in a week.

My roomie Gates Brown also had what is arguably the best pinch-hitting season in baseball history. In 1968, he batted .455 as a pinch-hitter, with 18 hits in 40 at-bats. He also drew eight pinch-hit walks.

On August 11, he walloped a home run in the 14th inning to help us beat the Red Sox, 5–4, in the first game of a doubleheader at Tiger Stadium. In the nightcap, we scored four in the ninth—capped by Gator's game-winning single—to beat Boston, 6–5.

Gator always liked to remind us how often he had to be the hero. "You guys go out there and screw it up for eight or nine innings," he'd say, "and then I have to come in and bail you out."

Our pitching staff also saved us on more than one occasion. Denny McLain had one of the most remarkable seasons ever by a major-league pitcher—and I wasn't at all surprised. The first day I met him, I knew he was destined for major-league success.

On April 8, 1963, the Chicago White Sox had to choose between protecting McLain or a right-handed pitcher named Bruce Howard on their roster. When the Sox kept Howard, the Tigers claimed McLain. He started with Duluth that season in the Northern League, but after going 13–2 with 157 strikeouts in 141 innings, the Tigers promoted him to Knoxville, where I was playing.

"I'm not here to stay," McLain told us. "I'm going to the majors."

McLain was an amazing pitcher. With a rising fastball and overflowing confidence, he moved up just as quickly as he predicted. By the end of the 1963 season, he was playing with the Tigers. In his first 21 innings in the major leagues, he fanned 22 batters.

It took him two seasons to gain enough experience in the majors to be dominant. And from 1965 through 1969, I don't think there was a better pitcher in baseball. In that time period, I wouldn't have taken Bob Gibson over McLain. For those five seasons, McLain was 108–45 with 1,006 strikeouts. For five years, he put up Hall of Fame numbers.

In 1968, Denny was almost untouchable. He was 14–2 by the end of June, and on July 27, he won his 20th game of the season. He was just blowing batters away with his fastball. On September 14, with two runs in the bottom of the ninth, we beat the Oakland A's, 5–4. I had the game-winning hit—a single over the left fielder (Port Huron, Michigan, native Jim Gosger) and Denny got his 30th victory.

He would finish the season 31–6 to become the first major-league 30-game winner since Dizzy Dean in 1934. Denny was the first American Leaguer to win 30 since Lefty Grove in 1931.

When it came to competition, Denny was a fire-breather at all times. Although I wasn't on the mound when Mayo Smith came to visit, we all heard the stories about what they said to each other. It was never a pleasant experience for Mayo.

"What the heck do you want, Mayo?" Denny would say.

"Well, I just want to see how you're feeling," Mayo would say.

"Do you have anyone in the bullpen better than me?"

"Well, no. But I just want to make sure you're OK."

"Mayo, get the heck off the mound."

"OK, Denny, go get 'em."

If Denny would've trained more, he could've been one of the greatest players in the game. I don't think he ever ran 100 wind sprints in his life. He also drank a case of Pepsi almost every day. He had cases of it stacked around his dressing stall.

Even if he would've done 20 percent of the training that the rest of us were doing, he might have won 20 games a season for a decade. He had strong legs and a flame-thrower arm. He was overflowing with talent, and he wanted greatness. We all loved playing behind Denny because he was a quick worker. He wanted the ball now, and he was usually ready to throw before the batter was set. Two hours and 30 minutes was a long game when Denny was on the hill. He could pitch a complete game in less than two hours. He challenged hitters, and with his stuff, he could be effective with that strategy. With the trust he had in his defense, he didn't fear letting the other team hit the ball.

"The business of pitching up or down or in and out is all bunk," McLain told reporters before the '68 World Series. "You just go out and pitch your game."

True to form, Denny joked about how he'd handle Lou Brock's speed. Denny said he wasn't good at holding runners on base, so he had a unique plan. "I'm either going to get Brock out or let him hit a home run. That'll keep him off the bases."

That was Denny McLain. He pitched the way Frank Sinatra sang: He did it his way.

With McLain in our clubhouse, every day was an adventure. He didn't sing when he played the organ professionally, but he would always be humming around the clubhouse. "Fly Me to the Moon" was one of his favorite tunes, which always seemed appropriate. The first time I ever saw a portable phone was in the visitor's clubhouse in Cleveland, when McLain called his wife, Sharyn, who was in a hospital back in Detroit.

He told her he had a plane waiting for him at the Cleveland airport to fly him back to Detroit.

"The game will take two hours, and with the ride to and from the airports, and with the plane ride I will be at your bedside in five hours," McLain told his wife.

He was always confident about his ability to get outs quickly. And that game played out just as he told his wife it would. I bet he was by her side right when he said he'd be.

McLain, whose father-in-law was Hall of Famer Lou Boudreau, was involved in plenty of crazy stuff—and most of it we didn't know anything about. But when he started carrying a gun, I moved my locker across the room from him. That just scared me. McLain could be mysterious—and a bit of a loner—but between the lines, he was about winning. There was never any question about his will to win.

His pitching brilliance was a staple of our success in 1968, but our hero changed every day. Almost everybody seemed to have his moment in the spotlight. We really did seem like a team of destiny. In terms of consistency, Dick McAuliffe was unquestionably our spark plug. He scored 95 runs, and produced 50 extra-base hits. His batting average was only .249, but he batted 35 points higher with runners in scoring position. He batted .364 with the bases loaded. His aggressiveness at the top of the order always gave the team a lift, and maybe we realized that even more after he was suspended for five games for charging the mound and injuring Chicago's Tommy John on August 22 at Tiger Stadium.

On ball four, John's left-handed fastball sailed over Mac's head. Both of them were jawing at each other as Mac trotted to first base. John had good control, and probably that's why McAuliffe believed John was throwing at him. Suddenly, Mac charged the mound and the benches emptied. John went low, and turned his shoulder toward McAuliffe, presumably to protect himself. But that backfired when McAuliffe's left knee rammed into his shoulder. John was lost for the season with a separated shoulder. The league suspended Mac for five games. Then we went into New York and promptly lost four out of five to the Yankees. We all realized in that series how important McAuliffe was to the team.

Other than that series against New York, it really did seem as if everything went right for the Tigers in 1968. People talk about our pitching and hitting that season, but they forget that we led the majors in fielding that season. Bill Freehan and Mickey Stanley were both Gold Glovers that season, and McAuliffe made only nine errors. Ray Oyler had only eight errors at shortstop, and I don't think any other shortstop in the American League fielded his position any better than Ray did in '68.

In terms of hitting, we led the American League in home runs and runs scored. We scored 671 runs that season. The Red Sox had the second-best offense, and they finished 57 runs behind us. We clobbered 185 home runs, and no team was within 50 of that.

And we didn't even need that much hitting because our pitching was exceptional. Mickey Lolich won 17 games that season, and Earl Wilson posted a 2.85 ERA and Joe Sparma won 10 games. Among our relievers, Don McMahon (2.02), Patterson (2.12), John Wyatt

(2.37), John Hiller (2.39), and Pat Dobson (2.66) all had ERAs under 3.00.

The night we clinched the pennant—when we beat the Yankees on September 17, 1968—was symbolic of how we played all season. We won the game in our last at-bat. We received a terrific pitching performance. We were flawless in the field, and Bill Freehan threw out a couple of guys trying to steal second base. It was a team victory, and some of the unsung heroes were at the forefront. Joe Sparma pitched a five-hit complete game, and he walked just one batter.

With two out in the ninth inning of a 1–1 game, Kaline, batting for Norm Cash, drew a walk off Steve Hamilton. We knew Mayo wouldn't let Cash bat against Hamilton after the grief he took the last time he considered letting Cash face the tall lefty. Next, Freehan singled to left. Then Mayo put in Jim Price to bat for Oyler. The Yankees brought in righty Lindy McDaniel to pitch, and so Mayo countered with the Gator, who hits from the left side. Gates drew a walk to load the bases.

Up stepped Don Wert. "Coyote" had struggled through a tough season—he only batted .200 for the season. But this was his moment in the sun. Two outs. Bases loaded. Bottom of the ninth. The pennant on the line. McDaniel wound and delivered, and Coyote singled sharply to right field. Bedlam reigned in Detroit.

1968 was an amazing summer. Everywhere, there were bumper stickers and billboards that read "Sock it to 'em, Tigers," which was a takeoff on a phrase from Laugh-In, which debuted that year on NBC. The newspapers were on strike for several weeks that summer, and maybe that relieved some of the tension as well. There were no stories about what had happened the previous season. Everyone was just talking about the Tigers. When we were on television on Saturday afternoons with George Kell doing the play-by-play, everyone in the state seemed to be watching.

Someone even wrote the team a silly song that was played continually on the radio.

*We're all behind our baseball team*
*Go get 'em, Tigers!*
*World Series bound and pickin' up steam*

*Go get 'em, Tigers!*

❖❖❖

As we prepared to meet the Cardinals in the Fall Classic, we felt as if we had only one issue to resolve. Where was Kaline going to play?

On May 25 of '68, Al suffered a broken arm when he was hit by a pitch from Oakland A's pitcher Lew Krausse. Al missed a month, and during that time, it seemed as if our outfield—Mickey Stanley, Jim Northrup, and me—simply took charge.

There was some crazy talk about trading Kaline for a shortstop, but no one in our dugout would have wanted that, even though our starting shortstop Oyler was only hitting around .135.

Our team was all about Al Kaline. He made us tick—whether he played or not, and we all knew he had to play in the World Series.

In recent years, ESPN has called the decision to move Stanley from center to shortstop—to open up a spot for Kaline in the World Series—the fourth greatest coaching decision of all-time. But it was actually the players who developed the plan. We talked about it frequently, and we even joked about it as we got into September.

I remember Northrup teasing Stanley as the three of us were standing in the outfield before a game late in the season.

"What are you going to do, Mickey?" the Gray Fox asked. "You know Willie's going to play everyday, and we know the Cardinals have nothing but right-handers in their rotation. So you know I'm going to play everyday."

The logical decision was to move Stanley to shortstop. He was the team's best all-around athlete, and we all believed Mickey could play anywhere on the diamond, including pitcher. What's sometimes forgotten is that Stanley would often take ground balls with the infielders before games. He just liked taking ground balls.

Northrup would always joke with Stanley. "You could make more money if you switched to shortstop." Northrup's theory was that there weren't many good-hitting shortstops in the game then, and Stanley's .259 average with 11 home runs would look great to any general manager looking for a shortstop.

There wasn't anyone else on the Tigers who could've made that move as smoothly as Stanley. Neither Northrup nor I could've played there. And people say that Dick McAuliffe could've moved back there because he'd started out as a shortstop. But then Stanley would've had to move to second base—and then we would have had two players out of position in the World Series. The obvious choice was Stanley. The only question was who would tell Mayo that's what the players wanted.

Eddie Mathews finally said he'd do it, and we knew he was the man for the mission. Eddie had 500 career home runs, and given how much reverence Mayo always had for the veteran players, we knew he'd buy into the plan, so long as Mathews presented it to him.

Mayo went along with the plan and issued the order as if it had been all his idea. Maybe he'd been thinking about it. Who really knows? Mayo certainly wanted to find a way for Kaline to play, and this wasn't a charity move by any stretch of the imagination. Even though Kaline got off to a slow start in 1968 and had only played 102 games because of injuries, he still batted over .300 after July 1. He batted .327 in September, and for the season, he hit .386 with runners in scoring position.

Stanley played the final nine games of the regular season at shortstop, and looked very comfortable there, committing only two errors. But the media, especially the national media, thought Mayo's decision was foolish. The Series was too big a stage, they insisted, to launch such an experiment.

But then again, not many members of the media believed we had much of a chance against the Cardinals. Before the World Series, the Tigers were listed as 8–1 underdogs on the betting line. We were a bit miffed to read, as well, that some of the Cardinals—Bob Gibson in particular—believed that the opponents they'd faced in the National League had more talent than we did.

Eddie Mathews didn't play much for us in 1968, getting most of his at-bats as a pinch hitter. He had already said it would be his last season. But Eddie was an important clubhouse guy, and his leadership was important heading into the World Series. He had played for the

Milwaukee Braves in the 1957 and 1958 World Series.

Right before the series started with Game 1 in St. Louis I recall that Stanley, Northrup and I were all sitting in the clubhouse, acting more nervous than we should have been. Eddie came in and shooed us out on the field. "Go out and have some fun," he said. "Enjoy being in the World Series."

That was an important reminder because we played better when we were having fun. We didn't have any fun in Game 1, though. Bob Gibson's 1.12 ERA in 1968 was the best baseball had known since 1914, when Red Sox hurler Dutch Leonard established the record of 0.96. Gibson was almost invincible in Game 1, with one of the greatest pitching performances in World Series history. He set a record with 17 strikeouts, and we managed just five hits off him. He struck out Kaline and Cash three times each, while Northrup, Freehan, and I were victimized twice.

We were beaten soundly, but even though the Cards chased McLain after five innings, I don't think we were overly concerned by the one loss. Lou Brock hit a home run and swiped a base, which was a sign of things to come.

I remember Northrup breaking the tension in the clubhouse about Gibson's performance, saying, "I didn't know God was black."

In Game 2, Mickey Lolich was the hero, going the distance and striking out nine. Lolich also hit the first and only home run of his 16-year career. He'd borrowed one of Al Kaline's bats, and Al joked afterward that he wouldn't let Lolich use his bats again "because he's taking all the hits out of 'em."

Cash and I also smacked home runs in Game 2, and maybe that was important simply because there had been much written before the World Series about how our power wouldn't be as effective in spacious Busch Stadium. The Cardinals only hit 30 home runs at home all season. Busch reminded us of the coliseum in Oakland, except the ball carried better at Busch. In one of our first batting practices, Bill Freehan hit the glass windows of the Stadium Club in deep left-center field, and the local reporters seemed impressed. We never doubted our power, but the fact that one of our pitchers cleared the fence there—and that we hit three home runs total—should have sent a message to the Cardinals.

My home run came in the second inning, and it carried 10 rows beyond the 335 marker. The late right-hander Nelson Briles served me up a slider down and away, and I knew I hit it well. It was our first home run of the Series, and it felt as if the Tigers were off and running. But it was actually Lou Brock who was off and running.

Brock's speed and his bat had become significant factors in the Series. As the Series moved back to Detroit for Game 3, he had three hits and stole three bases, and we lost, 7–3. We dug ourselves an even bigger hole in Game 4. Baseball is a team game, and a player only gets up four or five times in a regulation game. But Brock and Gibson seemed to be carrying the Cardinals all by themselves. Gibson struck out 10 more batters, and Brock smacked another home run and stole his seventh base of the Series. We lost, 10–1, and many people— maybe even some of our own fans—thought all the fun of the summer of 1968 was coming to an end.

But we didn't feel that way. After that game, Northrup said, "We're giving Gibson too much respect. We're giving the Cardinals too much respect. We have to go out there and play the way we know how to play."

We talked about how we had to minimize the damage Brock was doing on the basepaths. Somebody had to step up and harness him. But nobody suspected it would be me.

# Chapter 8

## WE KNEW LOU WOULDN'T SLIDE

EVERYONE IN THE BASEBALL WORLD SEEMED shocked that Lou Brock didn't slide in Game 5 of the World Series. But everyone on the Detroit Tigers would've been surprised if he had slid.

When the ball left my hand in the fifth inning, I believed the throw was going to nail Brock at the plate because our scouting reports indicated that he'd developed some bad habits.

Brock was probably too dominant for his own good in 1968. He stole 62 bases in 74 attempts during the regular season, and he'd swiped an unprecedented 294 bases over a five-season span. During that era, Brock and all of his teammates—and maybe even the entire National League—began to believe that he owned the basepaths. He always raced from first to third on a base hit. And he always scored on a single from second base. Our scouting reports indicated that no one was challenging him. Teams were just conceding runs to his world-class speed.

Given that kind of treatment, it was easy to understand why

Brock began to take his dominance for granted. According to scouting reports, he usually drifted around third base, and Cardinals third base coach Joe Schultz usually didn't offer him much guidance because Brock didn't need it. Lou always had the green light on the basepaths. Likewise, the on-deck batter usually didn't move up to the plate to signal Brock when to slide on close plays because Lou never *had* close plays.

Before the Series started, the Tigers outfielders vowed we would challenge Brock if the situation presented itself.

Unquestionably, the throw I made to nip Brock at the plate was the most important moment in my professional career. The general consensus seems to be that the throw was the turning point of the 1968 World Series. But plenty of people deserve credit for making that play possible.

Going into Game 5 at Tiger Stadium, we were already trailing the Cardinals 3–1 in the best-of-seven series. And in that contest, we were already down 3–0 after the Cardinals' first at-bats. In the fourth inning, we chipped away at their lead with a pair of runs. Mickey Stanley tripled to start the inning, and Norm Cash drove him home with a sacrifice fly. Then I launched a triple out near the 440-foot marker in center field, and Jim Northrup chased me home with a single to right, cutting the Cardinals' lead to 3–2.

As I said before, we were confident in our ability to come from behind. But we also knew that we couldn't afford to surrender any more runs. When Lou Brock doubled with one out in the fifth, we all understood that the World Series might hinge on our ability to prevent Brock from scoring.

Cardinals second baseman Julian Javier stepped to the plate. Since he batted right-handed, I was fully expecting him to hit the ball in my direction. Many years of training would all come together at this exact moment of my career. It had started with my father, who taught me to listen to my coaches and respect my opponents. My old teammate Rocky Colavito played a role in that throw because he had helped me with my outfield play when I first joined the Tigers. So, too, did Charlie Dressen, who was the law to me in my first couple of seasons in the major leagues. And although Gates Brown had primarily talked about hitting, he also made me realize that I had to start mentally preparing for a game the minute I got out of bed in the morning.

Being in the outfield with Kaline and Northrup also helped me with my positioning. In my early years, I would chase balls into the corner a lot. But by watching those guys, I learned to play the caroms the right way. Playing a ball off the walls is just like billiards; you simply have to understand your angles. There were others, too, but the biggest influence on that throw was probably Mickey Stanley because he had spent hours with me, talking to me about patrolling the outfield. He'd helped me tremendously with my throwing motion.

Remember, I had been a catcher in high school, and I had a quick release—a short-arm motion designed to throw a ball from home to second. Stanley had worked with me about positioning my body to get more on my throws. He was an incredible outfielder. In fact, he didn't have a single error in the outfield in 1968. When I watched him make plays in center field, I often felt as if I should take off my glove and applaud. Nobody in the league could climb a wall like Stanley. When he went up a wall, it was like steps had suddenly appeared to get him above the fence line.

In terms of the throwing motion, Stanley always told me, "It's like being on a bus and reaching up to pull the cord to let the bus driver know you need to stop—reach up, extend the arm, and pull down."

Likewise, I had studied how our pitchers worked against hitters. That's why I knew Javier would probably hit the ball in my direction because Lolich was going to work him down and in. Based on all of my knowledge, I moved out of my normal position. And when Javier lined that single, I was right there to cut the ball off and fire it in—in one fluid motion.

My objective on that throw was to hit our third baseman, Don Wert, right on the nose. He was my cutoff man in that situation. People tend to forget that catcher Bill Freehan also made that play happen. I've always said that Freehan was as important to our team as Johnny Bench was to the Cincinnati Reds in their heyday.

After I uncorked the throw, it was Freehan's call to either let it come through to home plate, or to instruct Wert to cut it off and fire to second and prevent Javier from taking an extra base. This was the kind of fundamental baseball that made the Detroit Tigers successful in 1968.

Freehan read the play perfectly. He realized the throw was on line with good velocity, and he could see that Brock had broken stride around third base. Brock thought he was home-free. But Freehan let the throw come through and blocked the plate beautifully. And just as our scouting reports indicated, Brock didn't slide. Frankly, I think Brock was shocked that I even tried to throw him out at the plate.

The next batter, center fielder Curt Flood, then hit a routine fly ball to me in left, and we were out of the inning. As we came to the infield, I hugged and thanked Stanley.

"Squirrely," I said. "You were right there with me on that throw. All that time you helped me with my defense paid off."

Although I had plenty of important hits in my career, I never felt prouder than I did at that moment because I had worked harder at my defense than anything. Hitting came easier to me, but I had to work at defense. And at that moment, I felt as if I didn't take a back seat to any left fielder in the American League.

People also forget that in Game 2, manager Mayo Smith removed me from the lineup in the seventh inning of an 8–1 victory. Ray Oyler went to shortstop, while Stanley went to center, and Northrup went to left. Sportswriters portrayed that situation as me being lifted for defensive purposes, and I was insulted and angry.

Much later, Smith would tell me that he was simply giving me some rest, thinking that he didn't want to risk me re-injuring my Achilles, which had given me trouble off and on during 1968. But my removal from Game 2 may have motivated me even more in Game 5. I had thrown out six guys that season trying to get an extra base off me, and there were only two or three other left fielders in the A.L.— Carl Yastrzemski among them—who threw out more.

After the fifth inning, we still needed runs to win the game and force a Game 6 back in St. Louis. We got them in the seventh, with Mickey Lolich starting our rally. With one out, he singled to right, ending the day for Cardinals starter Nelson Briles. St. Louis manager

Red Schoendienst then brought in left-hander Joe Hoerner to pitch to Dick McAuliffe. Mac responded with a big hit, pulling one of Hoerner's offerings between first, where first baseman Orlando Cepeda was holding Lolich on the bag, and second baseman Javier.

Mac understood how pitchers worked. He noticed that Hoerner liked to pitch inside, so he decided that the hole on the right side of the infield looked rather inviting.

Stanley then walked to load the bases, and Al Kaline drilled a two-run single to give us a lead we wouldn't lose. Norm Cash also singled off Hoerner to drive in Stanley and give us a two-run cushion.

The funny thing is that Mayo would've been second-guessed for not lifting Lolich for a pinch-hitter if Lolich hadn't delivered. But Lolich had hit a home run in Game 2 of the series. In fact, he had two hits and two RBIs in that game, and he was pumped up. More importantly, we wanted Lolich to stay on the mound because we all knew that if you were going to get to Lolich, you had to get to him early. He got tougher as a game wore on. And in Game 5, Lolich was getting sharper with each passing inning.

After the game, Brock complained that he'd gotten his foot in safely under Freehan's tag. But according to the *Detroit Free Press,* Cardinals play-by-play broadcaster Harry Caray said replays showed that Brock was indeed out. And still photos provided even more evidence.

But even with the victory, the Tigers were still down three games to two in the Series—with a long way to go. But Game 5 had to be demoralizing to the Cardinals, and it was a huge morale boost in our clubhouse. The tide had started to turn. Even before my throw nailed Brock, Freehan had thrown him out trying to steal in the third inning. Brock led the inning off with a single, but Freehan called for a pitchout and cut him down. Before then, Brock had stolen seven bases against us, and he was hitting over .500 in the Series.

There wasn't anyone like Brock in the American League, so we had to learn how to deal with him. Before the Series, we talked about Brock more than any other Cardinal, including Gibson. The year before, Brock batted .414 with seven stolen bases, two doubles, a triple, and a home run to lead the Cardinals over the Boston Red Sox in the World Series. But after Game 5 in 1968, he didn't seem so invincible anymore.

Although it's easy for me to say now, I believed going into the World Series that it would be either Mickey Lolich or Earl Wilson who would be our pitching hero—and not Dennis Dale McLain.

I felt that McLain had probably pitched too many innings during the regular season, and I suspected he was getting tired.

While winning his 31 games, McLain pitched 336 innings. That was 116 more than Lolich and 112 more than Wilson. If everything else were equal, I would've taken McLain against anyone. But McLain had 28 complete games that season, and no one in baseball had thrown that many. Bob Gibson had the same number of complete games, but he threw 34 fewer innings. And remember, Denny wasn't a highly conditioned athlete.

Although Lolich would win the MVP of the 1968 World Series, we still needed Denny to win one game for us. That was Game 6.

Stakes were higher at the World Series. The spotlight was brighter. The pressure was more intense. But Denny was still Denny.

Before the Series started, reporters asked McLain if he was going to be nervous in Game 1. "No, I'll probably be more nervous when I play Vegas," said McLain, referring to his two-week organ-playing gig after the season.

The night before the Bob Gibson–Denny McLain showdown in Game 1, Denny played the organ at the Sheraton Jefferson's Gashouse Parlour. He even played there after the game. The players and their wives were all there the first night. As I've said before, when you found one of us in 1968, you found most of us. Jim Northrup served as emcee, and we all had a good time.

At one point, Denny joked, "I may not be a better pitcher than Bob Gibson, but I'm sure I'm a better organist."

We weren't the kind of team where everyone was tucked in bed by 9 o'clock. Everyone started to head to their rooms after 11, and supposedly Denny played encores until just after midnight.

When Al Kaline was asked about it, he told the *Detroit Free Press*, "That's just the way Denny relaxes."

Denny was also ticked off that he'd been removed from Game 1 after only five innings. The *Free Press* reported that Denny and Mayo had to have a morning meeting early in the Series to clear the air.

But we all knew that none of that mattered because when the game started, Denny was always a bulldog on the mound.

Heading into Game 6 back in St. Louis, a local writer asked Mayo if losing to Gibson in Game 1 destroyed any of McLain's confidence.

All of the Detroit writers laughed, and Mayo said, "Obviously you don't know Denny McLain."

Weary or not from a long season, McLain was dominant in Game 6. With a 13–1 thumping of the Cards, we tied the Series at three games apiece. Denny scattered nine nits, fanned seven, and didn't walk one batter. Meanwhile, we pounded starter Ray Washburn and the next two Cardinals pitchers, Larry Jaster and Ron Willis. Kaline was 3-for-4 with a home run and four RBI. Believe it or not, Northrup had another grand slam. I had a couple of hits, too, including a double and two RBIs.

This forced a deciding Game 7—still in St. Louis, against the legendary Bob Gibson. But clearly we were a more confident team. Gibson had dominated us with 17 strikeouts and a shutout in Game 1, and then gave up just one run in Game 4. He'd actually won three games against the Red Sox in the 1967 World Series, and he now owned a new major-league record of seven consecutive World Series wins. But somehow, we believed we could beat him in a deciding game. When Mayo asked Lolich to pitch on two days' rest, Lolich thought that Mayo was talking about a relief role. But when Mayo told him he'd be starting, Lolich said he was ready.

And he was.

I thought Mayo made the right call to pitch Lolich in Game 7 because Mickey had an amazingly strong arm. He always seemed to be as strong at the end of the season as he was at the beginning. Even in a game, he always seemed to start strong, go into a relaxed mode, and then finish a game like a bulldog. I don't recall ever seeing him tire out. And even though he was a lefty, he seemed to be able to get right-handers out with regularity. He fanned about 23 percent of the right-handers he faced that season and over 30 percent of the left-handers. His ball moved sharply, and I did not like taking batting practice against him.

I truly think that McLain made Lolich a better pitcher, too. He woke Mickey up to the truth of how talented he really was. McLain wasn't shy about saying what he thought about how his teammates played. He would tell Lolich, "If I had your arm, I'd just go out there and blow 'em away." He was always needling Lolich.

Lolich was masterful in Game 7. It was a scoreless duel between Gibson and him until the seventh inning, when Cash and I delivered back-to-back two-out singles. Then Northrup hit a long fly to center field. People say that Curt Flood misplayed the ball, but when Jimmy made contact, I knew the ball was going over Flood's head. Flood did lose his footing for a moment, but it didn't matter because he wasn't going to flag that ball down. It was well beyond his reach.

Cash and I scored, and Jimmy legged out a triple. Then Bill Freehan doubled him home for a 3–0 lead. That's all the support Mickey needed. We added another run in the ninth when I got us going with a single. Mayo put in Dick Tracewski to run for me, and he eventually scored to make it 4–0.

With two out in the bottom of the ninth, Lolich surrendered a home run to Mike Shannon. But then he got Tim McCarver to pop to Freehan to wrap up the Series.

We had beaten Gibson in the clinching game.

"We're champions of the world!" Earl Wilson kept saying over and over in the clubhouse. "We are champions of the world!"

It's difficult to describe the feelings you have after winning a championship. We were like a family and we celebrated like a family. We were all thrilled for Kaline, who had played for the Tigers since 1953, and had finally won it all. Despite the criticism Mayo took for reconfiguring our regular lineup for Al, he hit .379 in the Series, with 11 hits in 29 at-bats, including two doubles and two home runs. He also had eight RBIs. Only Northrup matched Al's RBIs.

Meanwhile, Stanley performed extremely well at shortstop—so well that people were saying he should be moved there permanently. He committed a couple of errors, but there wasn't a moment when anyone on the team believed the move was risky. I was very proud that I batted .304 in the Series, with a double, triple and home run, plus five walks. Through the years, I'd learned to take what the pitcher gave me. And Gator had taught me to respect those hitting behind me. Those walks seemed like base hits to me in the World Series.

And with an ERA of 1.67 and three victories against the Cardinals, Mickey Lolich deserved the MVP—and he got it.

Brock ended up batting .464 against us, but he wasn't a significant factor in Games 6 and 7. He didn't steal a base in either of those games.

The clubhouse was raucous as we celebrated the championship. Tigers owner John Fetzer, a buttoned-down executive, was in the room taking swigs out of Stanley's bottle of champagne like he was one of the players. McLain had stolen the microphone from NBC analyst Joe Garagiola and was trying to interview *him*. Broadcaster George Kell, an ex-Tiger himself, was celebrating so much, you would've thought he was still on the team. Sportswriters say they don't care which team wins, but we were with those guys every day, and we could see on their faces that they cared. The late *Detroit Free Press* and *Detroit News* columnist Joe Falls certainly cared. He was Mickey Stanley's neighbor, and he congratulated everyone after the game. He told it "like it was" in his column every day, but he was a caring man. He interviewed me 30 to 40 minutes after the game and, my feet *still* weren't back on the ground.

"I looked over at the top of the left field wall in the seventh inning, and I saw Rudolph the Red-Nosed Reindeer," I said to Falls. "Christmas came early! Man, oh, man. I've never been this happy in my life. Never. Never. Never."

That night, Tigers fans flocked to Detroit Metro Airport to greet us when we got home from St. Louis. But the authorities were so concerned about the security risk that we were re-routed to Willow Run Airport near Ypsilanti. Over the next few weeks, the city just overflowed with love for the Tigers. Instead of killing each other like they'd done the previous summer in the riots, people were hugging each other. Black and white, blue-collar workers and white-collar workers—they all came together in one citywide celebration. The newspapers reported that downtown Detroit had the feel of Mardi Gras when we won the championship.

In the Tiger Club at Comerica Park today, there's a quote of mine on the wall. It says, "I believe the '68 Tigers were put here by God to heal this city."

Though I said that 37 years ago, I still believe that as passionately today. My spirituality just tells me that there was a connection. God knew the city of Detroit needed something to restore some harmony to our neighborhoods, and the 1968 Tigers did the work for Him.

Years later, 1968 Tigers relief pitcher Jon Warden was eating in a Cincinnati restaurant wearing a Detroit Tigers cap. He was approached by an elderly man who asked Jon if he was from Detroit. Jon's wife coaxed him into telling the guy that he had actually pitched for the 1968 championship team.

The guy's eyes lit up and he shook Jon's hand. "Thanks for saving our city," he told Jon. "Thanks for saving our city."

# Chapter 9

## BEANBALLS AND BILLY

FOR YEARS, LEFT-HANDED PITCHER RICH HINTON assumed that I was angry with him for drilling me in the eye socket with a fastball. But despite the beaning, I believed that Hinton actually saved my life.

Hinton was a rookie making his first major-league start for the Chicago White Sox at Tiger Stadium on Friday, August 27, 1971, when a heater sailed on him in the bottom of the third inning. He clearly knew he'd uncorked a wild one because he sounded an alarm the instant he released the pitch.

"It got away from me!" he screamed.

It was a night game, but as I stepped into the batter's box to face Hinton, a bit of twilight still peeked into the ballpark. I never saw the ball clearly. But I recall hearing Hinton's warning yelp, and I reacted by dipping and turning my head to the left. Had I not reacted to Hinton's warning, the 85 to 88 mph pitch could've struck me right on the temple. When you don't pick up the ball right away, you're in serious danger. Usually I would've turned away to the right and fallen back at the same time. That movement also might've put the ball on a direct path to my temple. For some reason, I turned left and it struck me in the right eye.

Eight years later, when I joined the Seattle Mariners, Hinton and I actually became teammates. When we were introduced, he seemed to be concerned about how I was going to react to him. I told him that my attempts to contact him after the incident were simply to thank him for warning me. In my stance, I crowded the plate, and pitchers habitually put me on the ground. I knew who was throwing at me and who wasn't. I was confident that Hinton's pitch got away from him.

Dr. Clarence Livingood, our team physician, theorized in the local newspapers that the pitch might've also just nicked the visor of my helmet, which had slowed the ball's velocity enough to prevent permanent eye damage. My eye was grotesquely swollen shut, and my face looked as if I had resumed my boxing career and gone 10 rounds with Muhammad Ali. Although there were no broken bones, there was nerve damage that required surgery. Livingood wouldn't even offer an opinion about how long I'd be out of action, and manager Billy Martin only told the press that it would be longer than 10 days.

It was close to a month before I returned to the lineup, and even then, I had some fear. I had reasons to be scared about my career. Seven weeks before, Tony Conigliaro, then playing for the California Angels, had called an early morning press conference to announce his retirement because of deteriorating eyesight—the result of a 1967 beaning.

In 1982, Conigliaro, 37, suffered a massive heart attack. And at age 45, he died of pneumonia in 1990. But at age 19 in 1964, he hit 24 home runs as a rookie outfielder for the Boston Red Sox. The following year, he jacked out 32 round-trippers to capture the A.L. home run crown at age 20. At 22, he became the youngest player ever to hit 100 career home runs. But on August 18, 1967, Tony C. was struck in the face by a fastball from California Angels pitcher Jack Hamilton at Fenway Park. There's a famous *Sports Illustrated* issue with Conigliaro's disfigured face on the cover. His cheekbone was fractured and his eyesight was damaged so badly, he missed the entire

1968 season. He was able to come back and play a couple of seasons, but his injury had long-term consequences. His improvement turned out to be only temporary.

The season before Hinton beaned me, on May 31, 1970, Baltimore Orioles center fielder Paul Blair was carried off the field in Anaheim after suffering a broken nose and multiple facial fractures when he was hit by a pitch from Angels reliever Ken Tatum.

Blair was an improving player who had batted .285 with 26 home runs in 1969. But after his beaning, Blair just wasn't the same hitter. That was clear to everyone in baseball. As I started my recovery, I couldn't help but think of Blair and Conigliaro. It was worrisome. That's why I'm thankful, even today, that Billy Martin was my manager that season. But at the time, I was angry with his approach to my injury.

Injuries are just part of baseball. Right before Hinton's pitch found my face, I had just returned to the lineup after missing a week with an injured wrist. And in 1970, my season ended in late July because of torn ankle ligaments. Those injuries were easily resolved. When the injury healed, I played again. But this injury involved psychological bruising, as well as nerve damage. Shortly after the beaning, I worried that I might not see pitches clearly ever again.

Martin, to his credit, pushed me to return to the lineup quickly. Twenty-nine days after the beaning, I went 3-for-3 in my return against the Yankees on September 25 at Tiger Stadium. I ended up playing the last four games of that season. Truthfully, I was furious with Martin at the time because I felt that he was forcing me into the lineup before I was ready. I resented his actions.

At the time of the beaning, I was actually flirting with .300 for the season. But when I ended the season with an 0-for-11 slump to drop my average under .290, I wondered if Billy knew what he was doing.

Not until Martin insisted that I play winter ball in Florida did it occur to me that my skipper was actually trying to speed up my recovery. Veterans just didn't go to winter ball. But Martin realized that if I didn't regain my comfort level in the batter's box, I was going to think about the beaning all winter. No one talked about sports psychologists in those days, but Martin clearly was trying to get my mind ready for the 1972 season. Everyone knows the old adage that if you're thrown from a horse, you have to climb back on it as soon as possible. But that idea really didn't mean much to me until Martin insisted that I face as much live pitching as possible before the 1972 season.

What I know today is that 0-for-11 slump at the end of the 1971 season—and my winter ball at-bats—might've been some of the most important at-bats of my career. Even if I'd had an 0-for-50 slump to end the season, I'd feel the same way today.

Martin understood that he had to be tough on me to help me feel normal again. Not only did Martin insist that I play winter ball, he came to Florida with me. His favorite coach and good friend, Art Fowler, was also down there working to reconstruct my swing. The two of them forced me to take batting practice with a barrel around my chest because they wanted me to stand straighter in my stance to give me a better look at the pitch. At first, they wanted me to wear a helmet with an earflap, but I couldn't get comfortable with that. By standing straighter, they convinced me that I would never again lose sight of a pitch.

When I look back on my major-league career, I think that Billy Martin was the smartest manager I knew. No manager was willing to sacrifice more to make his players better. I don't mean to suggest that I agreed with every move he made. Billy was a tyrannical manager, and he didn't send candy and flowers to his players. He was direct and confrontational. Some managers leave veteran players alone, feeling that they've proved themselves capable of being professionals. But that wasn't Billy's approach. He didn't care who you were; he would be in your face if he didn't think you were pushing yourself to achieve the standards he established for his players.

Back on August 6, 1969, Billy was managing the Minnesota Twins. And during a trip to Detroit to play us, he got into an argument with his pitcher Dave Boswell behind the Lindell A.C. on Michigan Avenue. Billy punched his lights out, and two months later, he was fired. The following October, the Tigers hired him to replace Mayo Smith. Billy visited every Detroit player to discuss his expectations.

Honestly, I was impressed that he came to my house and sat in my living room, rather than just sending me a letter.

Martin laid it on the line for me. He said he believed I could be a better ballplayer than I had shown in the two previous seasons. "If you play at times the way I saw you play when I managed in Minnesota, you're going to get a lot of splinters sitting on the bench," he told me.

I was already a three-time All-Star by then, and I had been a .300 hitter in 1970. I can't say I was ready to hug Martin when he laid those words on me. But over the years, I realized that Martin was always motivated by winning. He wanted his players to succeed, and if he had to offend some people along the way, or hurt his own reputation to accomplish that, he was willing to pay that price.

That night, he assessed my strengths and weaknesses for me. It was such a serious conversation that I started to laugh when Martin abruptly said, "OK, grab your coat. We're going to Gates Brown's house."

At the Gator's bar, we held some serious baseball discussions about where our team was at, and then we shot pool most of the night. That was Billy Martin. When he was serious, he was like an army general addressing his troops. But when the work was done, he wanted to be one of the guys and have a good time.

Jim Northrup would probably still say today that he disliked Martin because Martin pushed him probably harder than anyone on the team. But I would argue that Martin made Northrup a better player because he played him against some tougher left-handers. Not wanting to be embarrassed, Northrup learned to handle those pitchers.

"You can score a run without getting a hit," Martin liked to say.

And that's the way he managed. He didn't believe that you needed three-run homers to win games. He liked the leadoff walk, a swipe of second, a ground ball to the right side of the infield, and a sacrifice fly. He liked bunts, hit-and-run baseball, and manufactured runs. It was aggressive baseball. And in subsequent years, it came to be known as "Billy Ball." He was very tough on his pitching staff, too. He liked his pitchers to protect his hitters, and he rode all of his pitchers mercilessly about surrendering too many walks. "Walks set up big innings," Martin would say.

Billy liked to manage his team, and he never wanted anyone—even a veteran—to become comfortable with his place in the lineup. He wanted his players to believe they had to re-earn their starting positions every day.

Martin didn't hesitate to shake up his team. He proved that on August 13, 1972 when he put together the strangest possible lineup to shake us out of a slump. Norm Cash batted leadoff, and shortstop Eddie Brinkman, a .224 career hitter, batted cleanup. Batting third, I hit a home run and a triple. Cash had a couple of hits, too. We won, 3–2, over the Cleveland Indians.

In his three seasons as Tigers manager, Martin was able to get under everyone's skin at one time or another. Billy and I had our issues, particularly in our first spring training in Lakeland, when we had a disagreement over what I considered an unreasonable pinch-hitting appearance he wanted me to make.

Specifically, I remember Martin telling me that if I wasn't in a game by the sixth inning, I wasn't going to play that day, and I was free to finish my running ritual. My training habits were well established. Gates would drive my car to the park with my bicycle in the back. I would don army clothes and run from the Holiday Inn to the ballpark on the path around the lake. When the exhibition games moved past the sixth inning, I would do my sprints, put on a sweat suit, and ride my bike back around the lake to the hotel.

In my mind, my schedule was cleared with Martin. But one day, we were playing the Los Angeles Dodgers, and after I returned to my room, coach Frank Skaff knocked on my door. "Did we win?" I asked, not thinking this was anything but a social call.

"No," said Skaff, "the game is still going on, and Billy wants you to pinch-hit."

"Pinch-hit?" I said. "By the time you drive me back over there, the game will be over. What are you going to do? Hold the game up till we get there?"

"No, I'm not driving you," Skaff said. "Billy wants you to ride your bike back around the lake and then pinch-hit."

"Ride my bike?!" I said. "People will be home by the time I get

As Willie wraps up his speech, he gets a
standing ovation.

Willie and granddaughter Alisia.

Willie, Ernie Harwell, Judge Keith, and Mr. Ilitch.

Willie and officer Janet
Butler from the Detroit
Police Athletic League.

Willie and his cousin Ernest Horton Jr.

Willie's daughters and granddaughters celebrate in 2000.

Willie with former Tigers trainer Bill Behm and his wife, Donna.

Willie and the one and only
Gator—Gates Brown.

From left, Willie, Arsene Bondy,
Gloria, and Bonnie Bondy.

Willie, Gloria (second from right), and their immediate family.

Dominique, Willie, Sam, and Al.

Willie with Judge Damon
Keith and Mother Keith.

Willie and Gloria, a partnership based
on love and deep religous beliefs.

Gates Brown, Bob Milano and
his father, Angelo, and Willie.

Willie and Northwestern principal
Larry Lattimore.

Willie poses with Mr. and
Mrs. Nate Conyers.

James Slate revels at Willie's Wall
of Fame.

Deryl, Reverend and Mrs.
Baker, and Willie.

Dr. Tom Dickerson and his wife celebrate
Willie Horton Day in 2004.

Three Detroit Tigers leg-
ends: Al Kaline, Willie, and
Mark "The Bird" Fidrych.

Willie loved hearing from
fans in the bleachers.

Timeout for a fan photo.

30th anniversary of the 1968
world champion Detroit Tigers.

Immediate Horton Family reunion picnic in 2000.

A Horton Family banquet.

Celebrating with children and grandchildren in 2000.

Horton Family at the Northwestern field dedication in 2004.

Willie and Tigers general
manager Dave Dombrowski.

Willie and Hall of Famer Eddie
Mathews sign autographs at a
reunion of the 1968 Tigers.

Willie and close friend and agent Mark Dehem pose
in front of Willie's statue at Comerica Park.

An up-close look at Willie's 13-foot-tall,
stainless steel statue.

Immortal Investments publisher Michael Reddy and author Kevin Allen pose with "The People's Champion."

The Old English D at Comerica Park.

James and Joe Lewis, close frends in Flor

Willie is introduced at his 2000 jersey retirement ceremony, surrounded by young local ballplayers.

Willie's family awaits the on-field ceremony at Comerica Park.

1968 teammates. From left,
Mickey Lolich, Lenny Green,
Gates Brown, Willie, Al Kaline,
Earl Wilson, and Mickey Stanley.

sportswriter Joe Falls offers his congratulations.

Mr. Whiting, center, and his guest.

Willie and Mr. & Mrs Shears.

2000 reception with family and friends.

Talking baseball with Hector Cruz.

Seattle friends Jim and Sharon Brown.

Publisher Michael Reddy, Willie, and Al Kaline. *(Courtesy of Brooks Photo)*

Willie with daughter Pam and Tigers owner Mike Ilitch in 2000.

Longtime Tigers broadcaster Ray Lane.

Judge Damon Keith has been a tremendous influence for most of Willie's life.

With sons Al, Darryl Williams, and Deryl.

Gloria's sister, Melba Barnett, enjoys the
Northwestern Field dedication in 2004.

illie and the "other" number 23,
rk Gibson.

Willie has always been very accommodating to the media and to the fans.

Gloria and Willie with Dr. Robert Raubaurt and his family.

Willie with Mark and Karen Dehem.

Willie poses with nephew Johnny, left, and Johnny's son David.

Judge Damon Keith, a Detroit legend.

Willie's terrific friends—Mr. and Mrs. Mickey Stanley.

Willie reminisces with Coach Walter Owens.

Willie with former Lions great Billy Sims; Mr. Hockey®,
Gordie Howe®; and Howe's agent Del Reddy. *(Photo
courtesy of Lynn Gregg)*

Bob Resch, left, and Jim King of Music
Town Productions, writers and producers
of the song "Willie the Wonder."

Wayne County Executive Robert Ficano
helps celebrate Willie Horton Day.

NBA Hall of Famer Dave Bing and
Willie at Unsung Hero Award dinner
*(Photo by Darryl W. Horton)*

Marguerite Bodiford is always smiling.

Bob Reynolds, Morris Hood Jr., Bill Maxey, and Quinton "Rocky" Watkins.

Willie with talented pro and good friend George Brooks, of Brooks Photo Specialists.

Gloria Horton and Immortal Investments publisher Michael Reddy.

Dr. Kenneth Burnley and Detroit Tigers designated hitter
Dmitri Young (wearing a 1970s Willie Horton road jersey)
congratulate Willie at Northwestern High.

Tigers outfielder Rondell White
and Gloria Horton at Northwestern field dedication.

Willie's sister Virginia, nieces, and a friend.

there. I'm not going."

Billy was clearly just trying to provoke me. Forty-five minutes later, the phone rang and team president Jim Campbell was on the phone, saying he wanted to see me in his office the next morning.

Early the next day, I was in the clubhouse ready for the meeting, and Billy acted as if nothing had happened. He was talking about how we had lost a tough game. He didn't say a word about my refusal to ride five miles for a pinch-hitting assignment.

When we entered his executive office, Mr. Campbell started the meeting by saying that it's important to always have good communication between the manager and the players. Clearly, Mr. Campbell could see that Martin and I somehow had our wires crossed on what was expected of me. But before Mr. Campbell could finish his statement, Martin leaped up out of the chair and threw a pipe at Mr. Campbell.

Apparently, it was a pipe that Mr. Campbell had given Martin as a gift. Billy screamed, "You can keep your pipe! No one will *ever* tell me how to run my team!"

Obviously, I didn't have anything to say, and Mr. Campbell just told me to go back to work. Martin left the team for a couple of days, and Tony Taylor was put in charge. I saw Billy in front of the hotel and tried to talk things over. He just grumbled at me and walked off. The next day, there was a knock on my door. When I opened it, Martin walked in and started talking.

"First, let me tell you that I was I wrong to ask you to pinch-hit the way I did," Martin said. "But you were wrong for challenging me. When it comes to this team, you have to remember that I'm the captain of this ship and what I say goes. I'm the one who gets fired if we don't win. I have the responsibility."

When he was done, he shook my hand, and I told him that I appreciated his effort to make peace. After that, I had a better understanding of Martin. I vowed that if I ever got the chance to manage, I'd embrace some of Martin's philosophy. Say what you will about Billy Martin, but you always knew where you stood with him.

Martin could be extremely funny, and his humor played well with the media. He was making $35,000 when he was fired by the Twins, and the Tigers gave him a raise. After the Tigers fired Martin, the Rangers gave him a hefty raise to lure him to Texas. They fired him, too, but supposedly the Oakland A's broke the bank to hire him. The New York Yankees gave him even more money when they hired him. In fact, when I was coaching for Martin in New York, he'd essentially joke that if he got fired a couple more times, he was going to be the richest man in baseball.

My biggest issue with Martin came in the 1972 playoffs, when he started me in only three of the five games against the Oakland A's. I had battled injuries throughout the season, and it hadn't been my best one by any means. But Martin knew that I would've played through those injuries if given the chance.

We lost that best-of-five series in the last game. In Game 5, Martin left me on the bench and started Duke Sims in left field, even though Sims hadn't played left field for us and had limited major-league experience there. We'd claimed Sims off waivers in early August, and he played 25 games as Bill Freehan's backup catcher, plus four games spelling Kaline in right.

Gates Brown still believes the Series might've turned in the ninth inning of Game 1, when Martin pulled me out of the game. The score was tied, 2–2, and we had runners on first and third with nobody out. I was due up against right-handed Rollie Fingers, but Martin decided to play the percentages and use Gator as a pinch-hitter because he hit left-handed. But Gator popped out, and then Jim Northrup hit into a double play to end the inning. We ended up losing that game in the 11th.

No one can say what would've happened if I'd been allowed to bat for myself in that situation, but I like to think that I could've driven in that runner from third. Four years before, in the 1968 World Series, I'd proved my ability to produce in big games. If the Tigers had taken Game 1 in 1972, maybe we would've won that series.

As angered as I was by what happened in 1972, it might surprise you to know what I've said for years—that if Martin would've been our manager in the late 1960s, we might've won three or four World Series instead of just one. We weren't a broken team—or over the hill—when Martin took over in 1971. But we were banged up from injuries, and I think Martin got all that he could out of us, especially in '72.

In 1969, there were probably a series of factors that hurt our chances to repeat as champions. Dick McAuliffe was injured in July and was lost for the season. Our chemistry also wasn't the same. Eddie Mathews had retired, and he was missed around the clubhouse. It was also an expansion year, and the Tigers lost Jon Warden, Ray Oyler, Wayne Comer, and young pitchers Mike Marshall and Dick Drago, who could've helped us. The Tigers brass thought the expansion draft went better than expected because the team didn't lose Gates Brown or Tom Matchick, but our chemistry was certainly altered. John Wyatt was also released before the 1969 season.

Interestingly, we actually scored more runs in 1969 than we did in 1968, but we also gave up 109 more runs. Our pitching probably wasn't as sharp, and we definitely didn't play as well defensively as we did in '68. We also didn't have the same knack for coming from behind to win games. In my opinion, we weren't hungry enough. We were still celebrating our championship. We really didn't get going until August, when we were 21–9, but then we suffered through a sub-.500 September. We ended up with 90 wins that season and finished 19 games behind the Baltimore Orioles.

One of the few regrets I have about my career is that we didn't seize our opportunities for championships the way we should have. People talk about the Oakland A's dynasty, but I thought our team was as strong, if not stronger than the A's.

Mayo Smith might've been the right manager for us in 1968 because we were a self-starting team. We were driven to success. We didn't need a manager harping at us. But I think we would've won again in 1969 if Martin had been our manager. He wouldn't have allowed us to keep celebrating our 1968 championship. He wouldn't have let us get complacent. We needed our tails kicked in 1969, and that just wasn't Mayo's style.

Some of my teammates felt that Martin took the fun out of the game because he was such a dictator in the dugout. But I remember having plenty of good times under Martin, especially after the team acquired Frank Howard in 1972. He's the man I called Big Daddy.

As the Tigers chased the A.L. East title in late August, management bought Frank from the Texas Rangers. He was 6-foot-7, 255 pounds, and he certainly was as powerful as anyone who ever played the game. He had been the National League rookie of the year for the Los Angeles Dodgers in 1960, and his career was filled with incredible feats of power. He was one of the few men to hit a ball over Tiger Stadium's left-field roof. In 1968, while we were winning a pennant in Detroit, big Frank went on a tremendous home run tear for the Washington Senators. In one span of 20 at-bats, he hit 10 home runs. He finished with 44 that season.

From almost the minute he got to Detroit, Frank and I became friends. Soon, we decided to become roommates. The first day I woke up with Frank on the road, I heard him on the phone ordering room service.

"I'll need eight scrambled eggs with cheese, six pieces of toast, four milks, half an apple pie, and a couple of steaks," Frank said.

In my sleepy haze, I thought, "Man, I got myself a good roommate. He's ordering breakfast for me." Just then he turned to me and said, "And what do you want, Willie?"

Big Daddy and I still keep in touch, and as this book was being written, he was hoping to get involved with the new major-league team in Washington, D.C.

But when I think of Frank, I think of him coming down to my Club 23. He loved playing Gladys Knight and the Pips' "Midnight Train to Georgia" on the jukebox. He'd be dancing around the club, snapping his fingers to the music, and when he snapped his fingers, it was like someone firing a 45-caliber pistol. "We're all on that last train to Georgia!" he'd say with a laugh.

When my training camp barbecue for players and fans grew too big for me to take care of it all by myself, it was Big Daddy who stepped in to help. He helped pay for some of the supplies, and he worked the grill with me in Lakeland. Frank was the strongest man I'd ever met, and he had one of the biggest hearts of anybody I'd met in baseball. He truly is a beautiful man.

Eddie Brinkman was our shortstop on that 1972 team, and he and I were tight. Remember, I had played against him as a teenager in

Altoona. We had a lot of history, and we had a lot of fun together as major-leaguers. People sometimes forget how well Eddie played for us during that period. In 1972, he set a league record of 72 consecutive games without an error, and that wasn't broken until Cal Ripken played 95 consecutive games without an error in 1990. Uncle Ed, as we called him, had only seven errors that season, in 156 games. And he won the Gold Glove. He was a lifetime .224 hitter, but I thought he was actually a better hittter than even he knew. In my mind, he was a decent hitter when the game was on the line, or when there were runners in scoring position. He also had a terrific sense of humor. He hit .327 in April with a handful of extra base hits. One day, he came into the dugout after scoring a run and tried to look exhausted. "I'm just tired from carrying you guys," he said with a grin on his face.

The Tigers could've saved some money if they'd just gotten one room for the three of us, because Eddie was always down in our room lying on the floor. We would talk baseball till all hours of the night.

Eddie Brinkman will be most remembered for the night we captured the A.L. East. During a live television interview, he said we were all "a great bleeping bunch of guys."

But Eddie didn't actually say "bleeping." He uttered The Word you cannot say on television. We always kid Eddie because if anyone else made that comment, he would've been heavily criticized. But Eddie was such a lovable guy that he actually picked up some promotional appearances out of it. From what I heard, he was quite a hit on the ladies shows.

It's funny how some players can get away with non-conforming behavior because it's part of their personality and charm, while others can't. I still laugh when I remember how Gates Brown would sometimes show up at formal team gatherings with an open shirt and a big gold chain, while the rest of us were all dressed in suits. If I did that, someone from the team would've been on me. But nobody would say anything to the Gator because that was just part of his personality. He was a leader on our team, and he was a colorful character. The Tigers needed Gator to be Gator.

The Tigers finished third in 1973. Billy Martin was fired in late

September because of his continuing differences with the front office. He was a non-conformist, but he wasn't a lovable character. Management had been clear to him all along that if they could find a reason to fire him, they would. But Martin accepted that. In fact, he told me later that if his reputation had to suffer to make his teams better, he was willing to accept that.

What I know is that he did what he thought was right to make me a better player. In fact, I believe that Martin extended my career by six or seven years. I played until 1980—much longer than others in my age group. I think I lasted as long as I did because I heeded some of the advice that Martin gave me about my conditioning and my approach to the game.

When Ralph Houk took over as manager in 1974, I thought the change might not be in my best interests. I was right. As it turned out, Ralph Houk was the reason I didn't play my entire career in a Detroit Tigers uniform.

# Chapter 10

## REMOVING THE OLD ENGLISH 'D'

WHEN THE DETROIT TIGERS TRADED ME TO the Texas Rangers on April 12, 1977, I told the media that "it was probably best thing for me," even though in my heart, I knew it was a lie.

The Old English D was a part of my life. It wasn't tattooed on my body. It was tattooed on my heart—and in my mind. When Mr. Campbell traded me, it was a shock to my system. It was like my father was disowning me.

Even though Mr. Campbell completed the deal to bring left-handed reliever Steve Foucault and $25,000 cash to the team, I knew that the trade wasn't his idea. It was obvious to me that Ralph Houk was behind it.

What bothered me the most about leaving the Tigers was that Houk told the media he had spoken to me about embracing a new role on the team but that I "wouldn't accept that role." He told the media that he wanted me to become more of a role player, and that I had resisted. But there was no such discussion. I had no idea what Houk was thinking because he didn't communicate with me whatsoever.

I certainly understood my situation on Opening Day of 1977. Remember, I was going to be 35 at the end of that season and one-by-one, my 1968 teammates had begun to leave, either through retirement or in trades. Al Kaline had retired after the 1974 season. Norm Cash was released on August 7, 1974, and Jim Northrup was unceremoniously sold to the Montreal Expos the same day. Before the 1976 season, Mickey Lolich had been dealt to the New York Mets in the deal that brought Rusty Staub to Detroit. By the start of the 1977 season, John Hiller, Mickey Stanley, and I were the only holdovers from that World Series squad. I knew I wasn't going to play 162 games in 1977. I was hoping I might play 100 games and get close to 400 at-bats.

Houk was trying to rebuild the team, and we had a surplus of outfielders. Ben Oglivie was on that squad, along with Ron LeFlore and Rusty Staub. Houk also wanted to give young Steve Kemp a chance to play out there. He saw Kemp as a key building block for the future, and I could see that, too. The Tigers also had some quality infield prospects emerging, including Alan Trammell and Lou Whitaker.

But just two seasons before, I had been named the American League's Outstanding Designated Hitter, after hitting .275, with 25 home runs and 92 RBIs. I thought that I'd play 100 to 105 games at DH and in the outfield in 1977, and that I'd serve as a mentor to Kemp. To be honest, I looked forward to that because I remembered how much Rocky Colavito had helped me early in my career. As a player, I felt it was important to give back to the game. And I felt it was important that I pass along the knowledge I'd learned. A baseball team is like a family, and you should do what you can to guide and tutor the younger members of the family.

It's funny that on the day Houk was quoted as saying that I wouldn't accept my new role, Kemp was quoted as saying that I'd done all I could to help him become comfortable in the organization.

It was a tough situation for Kemp because he felt like he was trying to take my job. But I told him not to worry about that. He was

22. I was 34. I told him not to let the boos bother him. I told him what Colavito had told me: Fans get used to a ballplayer and appreciate him like they appreciate a comfortable pair of shoes. At first, they don't think the new shoes will be as comfortable as the old ones. But sooner or later, they get used to the new shoes, and they make for a comfortable walk.

I told him that when fans boo him, it just means they care about what goes on with the team. And those who boo will cheer even louder once they get comfortable with you.

"I really like Willie," Kemp told the Detroit Free Press the day I was dealt. "I respect him as a person and as a player. He was a good fellow. He tried to help me. He gave me advice, and he tried to give me some extra confidence. I felt he was behind me all the time."

Do Kemp's remarks give the impression that I was a man who didn't understand his role?

Any suggestion that I didn't want to stay in Detroit is simply untrue. Detroit was my city. It was my home. I had grown up in the Jeffries projects, and I had learned to play ball on the inner-city fields. I had stood on the hood of my car and spoke to a mob during the 1967 riots. I owned and operated Club 23 on Livernois, just a few miles from Tiger Stadium. Why would I want to leave the Tigers?

My relationship with Mr. Campbell might've allowed me to block that trade. But knowing Mr. Campbell the way I did, I knew that when Houk asked him to trade me, Campbell felt obligated to do so because he strongly believed that a GM must support his manager. Mr. Campbell always put the team first—even above his personal feelings. He was a man of principle.

When it came to my career, Mr. Campbell often acted as if he were my father—or at least my guardian. Maybe if I would've gone to him at the start of the 1977 season and told him how badly I wanted to stay in Detroit, he might've tried to persuade Houk that it was best to keep me around. But because I saw Mr. Campbell as a father figure, I think I wanted to prove something to him. In the back of my mind, I think I believed that if I went to Texas and had a great season, then Mr. Campbell would bring me back home.

I probably also wanted to prove to Houk that I was still a productive major-leaguer. I remember thinking that I was going to go to Texas to do for the Rangers what I wanted to do for the Tigers in 1977. I wanted to contribute on the field as a player, and as a mentor to the younger players.

To be honest, I was a bit insulted by the trade. I had played in four All-Star games, while Foucault, 27, had been a .500 pitcher in just four major-league seasons. He'd signed as a third baseman, switched to catcher, and only tried pitching after suffering a serious knee injury.

Was that the best deal the Tigers could work out? When I got to Texas, I was determined to have a strong season.

. I shed some tears on my last day with the team, but I kept my composure the best I could for my final interviews as a Tiger. The media reported that I showed no anger or bitterness. And they accurately portrayed me as being more hurt than mad.

On the day the trade was announced, we were on the road in Toronto. After I was told of Campbell's decision, I returned to the field and finished batting practice. I wanted to say goodbye to my teammates, particularly Mickey Stanley, who was a very close friend.

This was what I told the media that day: "As long as I live, I will be part of the Tigers, part of Detroit. I've been a member of this organization since I was 17 years old. I'm never going to outgrow that. The Tigers and the city of Detroit are two of the most important things in my life.

"I'd be lying if I said I'm not going to miss the organization. It's been a part of me for too long. The ballpark [and] the people who work there will be a part of me until the day I die. I'll remember them wherever I go."

The late Joe Falls, then a Detroit Free Press columnist who would become a good friend through the years, wrote that the trade seemed "pretty callused on the part of the Tigers.

"Let's come right out and say it," Falls wrote. "Willie was always more than just a ballplayer to the city of Detroit. He was the first black star the Tigers ever had—the only one who gave the black community a sense of pride. He was one of their own—a kid off their streets who came up the hard way and made it. Who wouldn't be proud of someone like that?"

Joe wrote that I appreciated everyone in the game, including the grounds crew. It was true that I considered most of the groundskeepers my friends. I would occasionally take them to dinner and invite them down to my club for a drink. Falls said that he admired that I left with class and didn't criticize the team. There was no temper tantrum. In the Detroit newspapers the next day, I even thanked Houk for playing me in left field in spring training so the Rangers would know that I could still play in the outfield.

"I liked [Willie] because he had all the basic instincts of honesty, integrity, and decency," Falls wrote. "These traits were ingrained in him, and I always liked to think his parents had something to do with that. In his own way, Willie Horton was a regal man."

His words meant a lot to me. While I was proud of how I played the game, I've always known that it was more important to be judged as a man than as a player.

That's why it bothered me so much that Houk said I wouldn't accept a lesser role. The truth is, he never once discussed it with me. Not once. I used to call him "Major Smile" because people warned me that there wasn't always truth behind his smile. But I never really believed Houk was like that until the moment I was traded.

Before I left the Tigers clubhouse in Toronto that afternoon, I shook hands with everyone, and reserved my firmest grip for Steve Kemp. "Remember what I told you," I said. "Just relax."

In the sports world, trades often are boiled down to one line in the transactions column of the newspaper. But they are truly traumatic events to the players involved. Your family, your business relationships, and essentially your life is thrown into chaos.

Club 23 had become a fixture in the community. After I opened it, I wanted someone to help manage the business, so I turned to a former classmate at Northwestern High School. Her name was Gloria Reid. In high school, I had run around with her brother Sam, and she didn't like me initially because she thought I was keeping Sam out too late and getting him into trouble. But I had always been impressed with the way Gloria carried herself. She had gotten herself a good job at Ford, and I remember when I asked her to work for me, she said, "I don't know anything about running a club."

But she took the job, and she worked with my friends Donald Wayne Neeley and Bob Reynolds to turn Club 23 into a successful operation. I was very proud of my club. Many of the players from other teams would visit when they were in Detroit, and it became a regular hangout for airline pilots. People from Wayne State University would come over. We served good food. One of our specialties was the Boomer Burger, named in honor of one of my many nicknames. My sister Virginia worked at the club and made many of those Boomer Burgers. When Magic Johnson was in high school playing summer basketball at St. Cecelia, he would come into Club 23 for a Boomer Burger. And on the night of the 1971 All-Star Game in Detroit, there was a long, long, long line to get into my place.

People knew me because I was a ballplayer, but Club 23 also reminded people that I was a Detroiter. We worked with other businesses in the area to help kids find jobs because unemployment was high in those years. We also bought tickets to take local kids down to Tiger Stadium.

One day in 1975, Mayor Coleman Young came into Club 23 looking for me. He said he needed my help to calm down a mob that had formed in protest of the shooting of a black youth by a white bar owner on Livernois. The bar owner had come across some kids breaking into a car. As it turned out, the youngster who was killed had actually stolen my wife's car—twice. But when a mob of 700 people formed on Livernois around that bar, Mayor Young was concerned that another riot would break out. When he asked me to come out and address the crowd, I did it because this was my home. There was some looting in the area and some property damage. And one man was badly beaten. But Mayor Young's approach seemed to work, because the few hours of violence didn't evolve into a full-scale riot.

We made money on Club 23, and I probably would've made more if I'd listened to Gloria. I always put money back into the business when I should've been putting more money in the bank. Gloria started out as the manager, but over time, she became a companion—and then my wife. And that was the best decision I've ever made.

When I was traded, I knew that Club 23 wasn't going to be able to survive. Gloria was crucial to the business—but she was coming with me to Texas. There are so many details to deal with when you're traded. For instance, my sister Ruth and her husband—I called him Mr. Robey—used to attend every Tigers game. I'd leave them tickets at the box office, and they'd just walk on over from the Jeffries projects. Suddenly, I was worried about how they were going to attend the games. But my teammate Ben Oglivie immediately said he'd take care of them.

Oglivie and I only played together for three full seasons, but we became the best of friends. The Tigers had a habit of having new players room with me, and when "Benji" came over from the Boston Red Sox for Dick McAuliffe, we hit it off right away. We had very different approaches to physical fitness, though, which was quite interesting at first. Remember, this was 1974. And when I woke up one morning to see Benji on the floor with his legs crossed doing meditation and yoga, it scared me.

"He was exercising by lifting himself up on two fingers!" I remember telling Bill Behm.

Actually, it was Benji who got me thinking about the role proper nutrition plays in an athlete's conditioning. Benji was 6-foot-2 and weighed 160 pounds. My diet wasn't as strict as his, but I began to think about eating less fried food and more vegetables. By the end of my career, I was probably in better shape than I was at the beginning. In fact, during my final two seasons in the major leagues, my playing weight was 210 pounds.

It was hard saying goodbye to Ben Oglivie. But considering his approach, I certainly wasn't surprised that he played until he was 37 years old—or that he had some great seasons late in his career, hitting 41 home runs one year for the Brewers.

You'd think it would've been hardest to say goodbye to my teammates. But it was also hard saying goodbye to the support personnel—like the members of the grounds crew, and certainly Bill Behm.

Bill had been taking care of me since I signed my first professional contract, and we had some funny moments together over the years—like the first time I chewed tobacco in the outfield. I ended up vomiting in left field. Behm had a birth defect that caused him to limp, but no one hustled out on the field to tend to his players with more urgency than Bill. When he saw me get sick, he raced out there like an Olympic sprinter. He might've given my old Northwestern classmate Henry Carr a run for his money that day.

"Willie, what's the matter?" Behm asked.

"I swallowed my chewing tobacco and threw up," I said.

"You have to be careful that you don't accidentally swallow it," Behm said.

"You mean I'm not supposed to swallow it?" I asked, incredulously. "Nobody told me that."

Behm laughed so hard that the game was held up a couple of minutes longer than it should've been.

Another funny moment with Behm came in 1968 when I re-injured my Achilles tendon chasing a fly ball. When I went down in a heap and didn't get up, Mayo Smith and Behm both sprinted out of the dugout toward the outfield.

Along the way, Mayo pulled his hamstring and went down like he'd been shot. Behm had to stop and treat Mayo, and he eventually ended up helping carry Mayo off the field. Meanwhile I was left lying in the outfield. My teammates all had a good laugh about that one.

When you're saying goodbye to your friends, you remember all the laughs you shared with them. And saying goodbye to the people at Tiger Stadium was like saying goodbye to my family. Remember, I had worked at the stadium when I was a kid and essentially had been around the corner of Michigan and Trumbull for two decades.

As sad as I was, I took some comfort in the knowledge that I was going to a team that wanted me. Some members of the media wondered where I was going to play for the West Division contending Rangers because they had recently acquired Claudell Washington from the Oakland A's, presumably to play left field. They had two right-handed designated hitters in John Ellis and Tom Grieve.

But I knew they didn't trade for me so I could sit on the bench. Having gone through a trying experience with the non-communicative Ralph Houk, I went to manager Frank Lucchesi when I got to Texas and told him I was ready for whatever role he had for me, and that I wanted to help the young players as much as I could.

This was a young, hungry ballclub, and I was excited about playing for a team that believed it could win. Somehow that season, the Rangers found 519 at-bats for me, including more than 400 as the cleanup hitter. I batted .348 in May, hitting safely in 15 of 20 games that month. In one game against Kansas City, I walloped three home runs and had five RBIs in a 7–3 win at Royals Stadium.

After some games, I'd call Mr. Campbell and tell him to "check the box score" the next day in the paper. I called Mr. Campbell often that season, and not because I wanted to razz him. In my heart I knew he was following my performances as if I were still playing for him. I knew that he cared what happened to me. I think he was as proud as I was that I helped the Rangers win 94 games that season. That was 20 more wins than the Tigers had under Houk. I finished the season batting .289 for Texas, including .313 on the road.

In retrospect, it was one of the best seasons of my career. I really enjoyed playing with the Rangers. And I think we might've won the Western Division if management hadn't fired Lucchesi on June 22. In spring training, Texas infielder Lenny Randle had attacked Lucchesi after Lucchesi benched him. Lucchesi suffered a fractured cheekbone, and ended up suing Randle. I can't help but think that this had something to do with the firing because we'd just won 10 of 13 games when Lucchesi was canned.

Eddie Stanky, 60, replaced Lucchesi. Stanky promptly quit a day later either because he was homesick or because he didn't like the "modern player." Both were given as his reasons for leaving. Connie Ryan filled in as interim manager, and then six days later, we got Billy Hunter, the former St. Louis Browns and New York Yankees infielder. He decided to conduct spring-training-style practices right then during the hot Texas summer. We finished eight games behind the Royals in the West, and to be honest, we were a tired team by the end of the season.

I really didn't think much about Houk after that until the moment in 1979 that I became the 43rd major-league player to hit 300 career home runs. The two-run shot came in Seattle off Tigers ace right-hander Jack Morris. The blow was a big deal in Seattle because they hadn't had much history yet. Just before my next at-bat, they stopped the game and brought out a fourth-grader who had caught the ball—and he gave it to me.

I remember when I was rounding the bases after hitting number 300, I thought about my major-league career. And after the game, I told the media that I dedicated that home run to Mr. Campbell and to Ralph Houk.

Years later, I ran into Houk at an Upper Deck Legends game, and I politely told him I had something I wanted to get off my chest. I told him there were no hard feelings, but I was curious to know why he had told the media that I wouldn't accept my role, when in fact, he had never even said a word to me about what he expected from me.

He stuttered, stammered, and eventually said that he'd been misquoted. It was hard for me to believe. I didn't think he was being straight with me—just like he hadn't been straight with me in 1977.

After my last full season with Houk in 1976, I began to think about how I'd approach managing if I was ever given the opportunity. I was sure I'd communicate better with my players than Houk ever did. I figured I'd manage like a combination of Charlie Dressen, Casey Stengel, and Billy Martin.

If given the chance, I would demand as much from players as Martin did. I would push them to be the best players they could be. But I wanted to be more of a teacher. I wanted to motivate, inspire, and encourage younger players as Dressen had done for me. And I wanted to have good rapport with my players the way Stengel did all those years. I never played for him, but it was clear that Casey Stengel got along with his players. I believed I could be a good manager if given the chance. What I didn't know at the time was that I would be managing in just two years.

# Chapter 11

## MY OTHER WORLD SERIES

WHEN A RINGING TELEPHONE WAKES you up at three o'clock in the morning, it's usually not good news. But the pre-dawn call I got on November 4, 1978, was a mixed blessing. My friend Cookie Rojas had been forced to resign as manager of the Valencia Magallanes in the Venezuelan League, and team owners wanted to talk to me immediately.

The fact that I was playing in the Venezuelan winter league at age 36 just goes to show what a strange journey the 1978 season had been for me. Cookie's mandate with the Magallanes had been to assemble a roster capable of winning the Caribbean World Series. But that was no easy task because everybody plays quality baseball in that part of the world. They just love their baseball down there, and Valencia's park was always packed when we played. The winter-league rosters are always full of promising major-leaguers. The pitching is good, and the hitting is better. There are no easy games in the Venezuelan League.

At the start of the winter season, it looked as if Rojas had picked the right players to do the job. Major-leaguers Jerry White, Tim Blackwell, Mitchell Page, and Rodney Scott were on our team, along with a solid-hitting minor leaguer named Dave Coleman. Mike Norris was also on the pitching staff. We looked impressive early on, launching the season with a lengthy winning streak. I was hitting over .300, and I enjoyed mentoring the younger players.

But then the Magallanes suffered one of those inexplicable losing streaks. One loss became two; two became three; and when a slump hits four and five, everyone starts to tighten up. Before we knew it, the Magallanes had lost 10 games in a row. Given the expectations that management had placed on Rojas, it seemed likely there'd be a shake-up. We figured the lineup would be juggled, and maybe we'd sign a new player or two.

But when the team's directors rousted me from a sound sleep in the middle of the night, I didn't know what to expect. They summoned me to the office immediately, and before the sun came up, they'd offered me the manager's job. This came as quite a surprise. Pablo Penton, one of the owners of the team, would tell me later that the board of directors had debated whether to "go back to the States" to hire an experienced manager or to hire me. They decided on me because they believed I had good rapport with the players. Apparently, Rojas had also recommended me as he was headed out the door, and they respected him, even though our talented team was now at .500 for the season after 20 games.

Initially, I had reservations about taking the job because I felt indebted to Cookie. He'd given me the opportunity to play in Venezuela at a time when I really needed it—for a variety of reasons.

It wasn't an easy decision to replace him because I honestly felt that he was saving my life in Venezuela. I still tell him that today. Cookie brought me down there and took care of me when I was going through the strangest time of my career. And as it turned out, my Venezuelan managerial experience was one of the highlights of my career.

The 1978 major-league season had been rough on me. First, the Rangers shocked me with a trade to the Cleveland Indians during spring training. Then the Indians released me over the Fourth of July weekend. I was out of work 10 days when the Oakland A's signed me. I thought I'd found a new home. When I got there, the A's were a few games over .500. And analyzing the division race, it seemed that a team could win the A.L. West with fewer than 90 wins.

I distinctly remember telling A's owner Charlie Finley that if we could deal for another big bat—like Toronto's Rico Carty, who was rumored to be available—I felt we could contend. I got off to a good start in Oakland, hitting over .300. We also had Mitchell Page (who would later join me in Venezuela), and a 24-year-old kid with a lot of potential named Tony Armas. With some good breaks, I felt like we could really make some noise. I was sure of it.

Then a few weeks later—just as I'd suggested—the A's actually did trade for Carty. But who did we send to last-place Toronto in return? A minor-league pitcher named Phil Huffman—and me. After hitting .314 with Oakland, I went to Toronto and hit only about .200 there. But that wasn't the worst of my troubles.

Before a Blue Jays game against the Tigers in Toronto, my three sons were involved in a frightening altercation outside Exhibition Stadium. An overflowing crowd was jamming into the game, and there was congestion near the players parking lot. To this day, I'm not sure exactly how events unfolded, but my wife, Gloria, remembers that some bystanders made unseemly remarks to my sons, and words were exchanged. A fight ensued. Gloria had my daughters with her, and she was trying to protect them. She was screaming. Someone tried to lead her inside to safety, but she wouldn't leave us. "Those are my boys and my husband," she said, and handed off the girls to a woman, who took them inside.

As I was making my way over to help my boys, a member of the Royal Canadian Mounted Police—on horseback—saw me running toward the melee and thought I was planning to join the fight. Presumably, he didn't know I played for the Blue Jays, but either way, he struck me upside the head with a billy club. Then his horse raised up and came down on my son Deryl Lamar's foot—and broke it.

Not knowing who'd hit me, I turned around and slugged the horse. For the next month, people all around baseball were talking about how Willie Horton knocked out a horse. I don't know if I knocked him out, but the horse did go down. Blood was running down my head. Two of my sons, Darryl William and Al, were standing back-to-back, fighting against the crowd. I had bats in the trunk of my car, and the danger level was high enough that I thought about getting them.

"Don't let Willie get those bats!" Gloria said. It was certainly one of the scariest moments I've ever experienced—maybe scarier than the night I addressed the mob during the 1967 riots.

Finally, a Blue Jays executive arrived and informed the police that I was a ballplayer, and we were escorted into the building. But the ordeal wasn't over. As the doctor began to examine my injuries, we realized that the police had handcuffed my sons and were trying to cart them off to jail. It took some time to untangle the mess.

Apparently, I kept telling Gloria I was fine, but I really wasn't. At the hospital, doctors told me that I'd suffered a concussion, but it was far more severe than anyone realized. Over the next few weeks, my vision was hazy, and people were telling me that my mind wasn't right. Sometimes I was disoriented—and depressed. Other times I would be angry. I would be in the outfield, but I couldn't maintain my focus. When the season was over, I was trying to drive from Toronto to Detroit and I ended in Cleveland in front of the ballpark. That's when I knew that my brain wasn't functioning properly. Today, I'd probably be diagnosed with post-concussion syndrome. No one called it that then, and the treatments that were prescribed didn't seem to work.

What seemed to bring me back to reality was my decision to play winter ball.

When the season was over, I didn't know what my baseball future would be. When Pablo Penton and his manager Cookie Rojas suggested that I travel to Venezuela to play a 60-game winter ball season for the Valencia Magallanes, it seemed like a good idea. Penton was also a scout for the Oakland A's and knew my reputation. They were willing to pay me $5,000 per month, plus bonuses, and living accommodations in a nice condominium. Retirement was a possibility for me at that point, but I thought that if I played well enough down there, some major-league team would sign me before spring training.

Usually players with more than three years of major-league experience aren't allowed to play in winter ball unless they're natives to that country. But Penton, a part-owner and vice president of the team, petitioned Major League Baseball commissioner Bowie Kuhn to let me play, on the basis that I was trying to recover from my concussion. Kuhn gave his blessing, and soon, Gloria and I were on our way to Venezuela, along with our daughters Pam and Gail.

My friend Louis Burrell had to stay with me all the time because I would want to go running in the middle of the night. Cookie helped me re-train my mind. In fact, he trained me like a racehorse. He just worked with me all the time. And even after he was fired as our manager, he told me that he wanted me to have the job.

To be honest, I don't think the Magallanes realized that I had some very strong ideas about managing, even though I'd never managed a ballclub before. Their board of directors was surprised at some of my moves and shocked by my opinions on personnel moves, too, especially when I told them I didn't want to add a major-league All-Star shortstop to the team as we headed into the Caribbean World Series.

Management also looked at me a little funny when I went in and asked them to give my native Venezuelan players more money because I felt they were underpaid.

"You're like a labor union leader," Pablo said to me.

"You have to give these boys what they deserve, and you have to keep them happy," I said. "You can't just take care of the star players. You have to spend time with each of them."

According to league rules, you had to play three native players at all times, and I always felt it was important to make sure the native players realized how much I valued their contributions. I also wanted to make sure the role players felt needed.

Pablo's a dear friend of mine today, and we still laugh about the time I decided to insert a pinch-hitter—a guy named Rafael Carel—

for myself, with the winning run on second base in an important game. Carel was a backup catcher, and hadn't yet distinguished himself as a player when I made the move.

In my mind, it was the right moment to motivate Carel. I figured if we were going to win the Caribbean World Series, he might need to be a key player. And I also felt that some of the native players needed a morale boost. I also wanted to see what Carel was made of.

After making that move, I had to pass the owners' box seats as I walked back to the dugout.

"Are you crazy, Willie?" Pablo asked. "What are you doing?"

"I know what I'm doing," I told him.

Fortunately for me, Carel smashed a triple and we won the game. And as the season progressed, he became a more confident player and an important player for our team.

What's interesting about my player/manager job is that once I accepted it, my mind began to become sharp again, and I started to emerge from the fog of my concussion. It was almost as if the added responsibility forced my mind to heal itself and deal with the extra workload.

The Magallanes went on a roll after I took over and we made up ground quickly. We won the regular season and playoff crown. And after we won our league title, there was plenty of excitement about our possibility of winning the Caribbean World Series, which was held that year in Puerto Rico. In that part of the world, the Caribbean World Series is as important as our World Series. Even today, Caribbean World Series games are broadcast on Spanish-speaking stations in Miami and other parts of the United States with a large Hispanic population.

The Caribbean World Series dates back to 1949, and Venezuela was one of the original competitors. Many top major-leaguers have played in the tournament. Through the years, the Caribbean World Series has included major-leaguers Don Zimmer (1955), Earl Battey (1958), Tommy Davis (1960), Manny Mota (1971), Carlos May (1972), Bobby Valentine (1973), and even my old Tigers teammate Norm Cash. Cash played for the Venezuela team that finished second in 1959, and he's best remembered for hitting two home runs and driving in eight during the tournament.

Rules allow teams to pick up three native players for the tournament, and the Magallanes management wanted me to add Cincinnati Reds shortstop Davey Concepcion. By then, Concepcion had already been a regular National League All-Star. He'd won four Gold Gloves and had hit .300 that season. Many people thought that he was the best shortstop in the game during the 1970s.

But I told the owners I didn't want Concepcion because we had a young native shortstop named Alexis Rodriguez, who had blossomed into one of our top players. I couldn't look him in the eyes and tell him I was benching him because we could sign Concepcion. It wouldn't have been fair to Rodriguez.

Owners were upset by my decision. We had an intense argument over the Concepcion issue. Likewise, I disagreed with management about how we should've handled the situation when a couple of our star players, Mitchell Page and Rodney Scott, wanted to go home for Christmas. To me, it didn't seem fair that some players could go home and others could not. My position was that if Page and Scott left, I didn't want them coming back.

"We're all on this ship together," I told Mitchell and Rodney, "and nobody jumps ship when we're still sailing."

Pablo begged me to take them back, and eventually I relented, but I made no promises about how I would play them. I didn't start either one of them in the first two games of the playoffs—not bringing them in until the fifth or sixth inning. I think the other players respected me for that decision. Mitchell and Rodney were young men then, and they still had some growing up to do. Later, they would tell me they appreciated my approach with them. Imported players wanted more relaxed rules in winter ball, but I had a stringent set of rules for our team, and no one was exempt from them.

Essentially, I made good on my promise to myself that my managerial style would be a blend of Billy Martin, Charlie Dressen, and Casey Stengel. I thought I was tough when I had to be, much like Billy. But I came to be park early every day to work with the young players. I talked to them and tried to give them confidence. I told them stories like Dressen did. And I tried to keep the clubhouse loose like Casey did.

We didn't have Tim Blackwell to catch for us in the Caribbean World Series because he had only signed a contract until December. Apparently, Rojas had been anticipating signing another catcher late in the season, but that catcher backed out. Blackwell agreed to extend his stay until after the playoffs, but he wouldn't go to the Caribbean World Series. We ended up using major-leaguer Bo Diaz at catcher.

The Caribbean World Series includes the top teams from the Dominican Republic, Puerto Rico, Venezuela, and Mexico. You play each team twice, and the team with the best record is declared the champion.

In the opener, New York Mets pitcher Nino Espinosa of the Dominican Republic beat us, 1–0, on a two-hitter, and the board of directors was nervous. "Don't worry," I said. "We're going to win this thing." And we did.

We didn't lose another game. Page wrapped it up for us when he hit a three-run homer in the ninth inning to beat Mexico's Enrique Romo, 9–6, to win the final game. Romo pitched for the Pittsburgh Pirates. We had to win that game, too, because if we lost, we would've been tied with the Dominican Republic. If there had been a tie, we would've had a playoff game—and we were out of pitchers.

Much to my delight, Alexis Rodriguez hit over .300 for me and played flawless shortstop. He was the runner-up in voting for the top shortstop in the tournament. That was important for me, because I'm not sure they would've let me back into Venezuela if we would've lost that series. Everyone had questioned my decision not to take Concepcion. But White batted .522 in the series, and Page drove in 11 runs. He was simply amazing.

Obviously winning the 1968 World Series was a more important moment in my baseball career, but when we won that Caribbean World Series Championship game in Puerto Rico, we celebrated as if we were champions of the world. We weren't any less excited than we were in 1968. It was a proud moment, particularly for me, because when I came down to Venezuela, it was possible my career was over. I proved down there that my bat still had pop, and maybe more importantly, I proved that I could contribute beyond my playing ability.

My time in Venezuela really helped me considerably because I hit .313 and finished among the top 10 hitters in the league. The Seattle Mariners liked what they saw from me and gave me a tryout contract in late January. The only negative of my Venezuela experience was that my daughters Pam and Gail contracted an eye disease, and we were worried for a couple of days that they might lose some of their eyesight. You can imagine how hard it is to concentrate on baseball with that on your mind.

Pablo Penton told me a couple of times that he thought I could manage in the big leagues because I seemed to be getting the most out of my players. Frank Robinson had become the first black manager in the major leagues with Cleveland in 1975, and it appeared that the league was opening up more to racial equality.

Mostly, I was thinking about getting my chance to play again with the Mariners, but I also thought that I might be able to manage, too. When my career was over, I thought teams might come to me about managing. My dad always had taught me that if you work hard at your profession, you will be discovered. He believed you created your own opportunities with your work ethic. Unfortunately, he never taught me that sometimes you have to knock to get inside the door. I didn't send out résumés. My feeling was that the baseball world knew who I was, and my record in Venezuela was certainly no secret to anyone in baseball. I ended up with coaching jobs with Oakland, the New York Yankees, and the Chicago White Sox. But no one ever asked me to interview for a managing job.

Even if I had rapped on some doors, would I have been given fair consideration for a manager's job? It's hard to say. When Willie Randolph was hired as the New York Mets manager in November 2004, he was only the twelfth black man to serve as a major-league manager.

My parents taught me not to view the world in racial terms, but my own personal experiences taught me that the baseball world has been slow to embrace that same philosophy.

# Chapter 12

**PREJUDICE AND PRIDE**

**IT SURPRISES A LOT OF PEOPLE WHEN** I tell them I didn't experience true racism until I signed my first professional contract with the Detroit Tigers in 1962.

My initiation to being a black man in America came on my first trip to spring training in Lakeland, Florida. Excited and brimming with confidence, I flew to Tampa and took a Greyhound bus to downtown Lakeland. From there, I tried to hail a taxi for the final leg of my trip to Tiger Town.

The first cab driver rolled down his window and said he couldn't take me.

"Why not?" I asked.

"Because you're black. You have to call Wigs Taxi. They can take you," he said.

To be honest, I began to laugh because I really thought someone was playing a joke on me. That didn't even sound like a legitimate cab company. In Detroit, it was Checker Cab Company or Black and White Cabs, or Yellow Cabs.

"Wigs?" I said, "That sounds like a barbecue place."

Remember, I had played winter ball in Tampa the previous fall after signing with the Tigers. Teammates were always playing tricks on each other, and I'd been warned that in spring training, veterans liked to have fun at the rookies' expense.

The cab driver finally convinced me that he wasn't pulling my leg. But I didn't call Wigs—the designated cab company for black people in Lakeland. Instead, I picked up my duffel bag, slung it over my shoulder, and walked the seven miles from the bus depot to Tiger Town. I can't say for sure why I didn't call Wigs. Maybe I wasn't sure I believed the cabbie. I think I was probably too proud.

Clearly, my life in the Jeffries projects didn't prepare me for what I found in Lakeland. There were black and white folks living in the projects when I was a child. We all got along fine. Certainly, I understood that segregation existed. I thought back to my old coach Ron Thompson, who organized the kids from the projects into a ball team when I was a youngster. There were no integrated teams in the Detroit Federation League that he wanted us to join. League officials apparently suggested to Thompson that our black players should join the all-Black Mohawks team and the white players should join one of the all-white teams. Thompson decided that the players should vote on whether we should split up.

We voted to play together, even though it meant we had to play in a lower recreation league. My hunch is that the vote was unanimous. My parents had really taught me not to see color when it came to getting along with people.

Maybe that's why I was just a little shocked when I arrived at Tiger Town and realized that life down south was different than life up north. It didn't matter whether you were a professional baseball player or not. If you were black, you were going to be treated differently.

At Lakeland, in 1962, black fans still had to sit in special sections of the baseball park. There were separate drinking fountains for black fans and white fans. And even in the Tiger Town dormitories, black players were assigned to sleep on different floors than the white players. When I first joined the team, there were no hotels in Lakeland that would even accept black players, so veterans relied on local families in the area to open up their homes to them for the duration of spring training. That's how I met Charles and Madeline Brooks, a black couple who adopted black ballplayers and made sure we had a place to stay. They're still my friends today.

Knowing that some restaurants in Florida didn't allow black diners in those times, the Tigers would have box lunches for us to eat on the bus rides home after exhibition games. At night, after games and practice in Lakeland, the Tigers would pick up the young players—black and white—at Tiger Town and bus us to town. But the black players were dropped off along the road, and we had to walk another quarter-mile into the black area of Lakeland to find a place to eat. The bus would then take the white players downtown. But if it was a nice night, many of us would walk instead of taking that bus. Maybe that was our form of protest.

When spring training was over in 1962 and the bus took us minor leaguers north to Duluth, we had a hard time finding hotels that would accept black players. I remember our manager Al Lakeman telling the bus driver, "If we can't stay together, you just keep driving straight through." It was such a long drive, Al even took a turn driving the bus himself.

Sometimes in '62, our white players would be at one hotel, and our black players would have to stay at another. That season, I remember playing the Aberdeen Pheasants in South Dakota. We were forced to put six black players in one room while white players were just two to a room. That shouldn't have surprised me because if you were a baseball fan, you knew that society was slow to change when it came to racial issues. Eleven weeks after Jackie Robinson broke the color barrier with Brooklyn in 1947, Larry Doby joined the Cleveland Indians, giving the American League its first black player. But it wasn't until 1958 that the Detroit Tigers signed their first black athlete—third baseman Ozzie Virgil—just a few years before I signed.

On April 22, 1957, the Philadelphia Phillies became the last National League team to integrate when John Irvin Kennedy became their first black player. He played just five major-league games. The Tigers were the next-to-last major-league team to sign a black player. On June 6, 1958, Virgil, acquired from the Giants the previous winter, went 1-for-5 to help Detroit pound the Senators, 11–2, at Griffith Stadium in Washington, D.C.

On June 17, Virgil was 5-for-5 in his Tigers debut at Briggs Stadium, helping beat the Senators, 9–2. Twenty-nine thousand fans gave him a standing ovation—in the same ballpark where former owner Walter Briggs once insisted that the Tigers field an all-white roster.

Briggs died in 1952, but his estate owned the team until 1956, when a group headed by radio pioneer John Fetzer bought the team. According to an article in The Detroit News, the Tigers did apparently invite some black ballplayers to training camp after Briggs' death in 1953, including an 18-year-old outfielder from Detroit Northwestern High School named Grover Moses. Others included an outfielder named Claude Agee and a shortstop named Henry Gaskins. The Tigers also purchased the contract of Arthur Williams, a pitcher who had been very impressive in the California State League. None of them made it to the major leagues. Briggs' influence on the racial makeup of the Tigers roster seemed to last until Fetzer officially took over.

When Virgil debuted with the Tigers, I'd just started at Northwestern High School. It was an important step for the city, but I couldn't help but wonder if Virgil's acquisition would've been more meaningful if he had been a black kid who had learned his baseball on the streets of America. Ozzie was from Monte Cristi in the Dominican Republic, and he'd moved to New York at the age of 13. He was a man of color, but he wasn't truly an African-American. When he made his major-league debut for the New York Giants in 1956, he became the first Dominican to play in the majors. Felipe Alou and Juan Marichal would soon follow.

To me, when I think of the first black ballplayer in Detroit, I think of Jake Wood, who was signed by the Tigers in 1957 out of

Elizabeth, New Jersey. He worked his way through the system to become the starting second baseman in 1961, the season I signed with the organization. The Detroit Tigers won 101 games that season and finished second in the American League, eight games behind the Yankees. Boston's Don Schwall, a 6-foot-6 pitcher, won 15 games that season and was named A.L. rookie of the year. It's hard to believe that Schwall or even fellow rookie Carl Yastrzemski was more important to the Red Sox than Jake was to the contending Tigers that season. The Red Sox were 10 games under .500 that season. Dick Howser also had a good rookie season for the Kansas City Athletics, but they weren't contenders either. Jake played 162 games that season and hit 11 home runs, 17 doubles, and a league-leading 14 triples. He also stole 30 bases, which ranked fourth in the A.L. He scored 96 runs and drove in 69, which was fourth on the team. Jake had 171 hits that season for Detroit. Only Norm Cash and Al Kaline had more. Not even Rocky Colavito had that many.

This was a few years before Lou Brock and Maury Wills reminded the baseball world that speed can dominate a game. If the Tigers would've allowed Jake the freedom that Wills and Brock had, he might've swiped 60 bases. He was as fast as anyone I've ever seen. He would actually make errors because he would run past the ball.

Who can say whether Jake Wood's race cost him any votes for rookie of the year, but it was clear that the American League did not embrace black players as quickly as the National League did. The American League didn't select an African-American as Rookie of the Year until Chicago White Sox outfielder Tommie Agee won the honor in 1966. Minnesota's Tony Oliva, who was from Cuba, was the first minority named A.L. Rookie of the Year in 1964.

By 1966, the National League already had 10 black players named Rookie of the Year, including Jackie Robinson (1947), Willie Mays (1951), and former Negro League stars Sam Jethroe (1950) and Joe Black (1952).

In the winter of 1960, the Tigers acquired Billy Bruton from the Milwaukee Braves to play center field. Chico Fernandez, born in Havana, Cuba, was the team's starting shortstop. So in 1961—the year I signed—the Tigers had three minorities among their eight starting position players.

When I got to Tiger Town in 1962, former Negro League pitcher Sam "Red" Jones was on the team. He'd played for the Cleveland Buckeyes in the Negro Leagues and then signed with the Cleveland Indians in 1951. But he didn't find true success until he joined the National League with the Chicago Cubs in 1955. In his first full season with the Cubs, he pitched a no-hitter. A two-time All-Star, Sam won 21 games for the San Francisco Giants in 1959. He won 18 the following season.

He was 36 years old when he was dealt to the Tigers before the 1962 season, and he still parked a toothpick in his mouth, which had become his trademark over the years. He was also known as "Toothpick Sam."

In my first spring training, Sam had a habit of picking up the black players and driving them over to a local family's house for a cookout. He turned me into a barbecue specialist, and I carried that tradition through the years at Tiger Town.

More importantly, Jones, Bruton, and Jake Wood would tell stories about the Negro Leagues and their experiences as black men in a sport that struggled with integration for years.

Sam was a lighter-skinned black man, and that spring when he was injured, he was hospitalized in the white ward. He told us he didn't want his wife to visit him because he knew when the nurses saw her that he was going to be transferred to the black unit.

But she did go to visit him, and that's exactly what happened. Sam said the quality of care was so inferior in the black ward that he checked himself out. It was a sad commentary on what was happening at that time in American history, but Sam made it a funny story. "It was like I was driving a Rolls Royce and then suddenly I was behind the wheel of a Chevrolet," he said.

The black players who paved the way for me to the major leagues had a much more challenging road to travel than I did, and I had great respect for them. It seemed as if the black players looked out for each other. For example, Jake Wood was quiet and reserved—much like Al Kaline. Jake wouldn't come knocking on your door, but if you approached him, he was always there for you, always willing to put his arm on your shoulder and tell you what you needed to hear.

Once I made it to the majors, I also became friendly with Larry Doby, who was coaching by that time. His stories really made me appreciate the struggle that black athletes endured—like the day Doby was promoted to the Indians in 1947, when some of his new teammates wouldn't even shake his hand. He heard racial taunts from the fans in the stands, and some of them tried to provoke him into lashing out. But Doby wouldn't stoop to their level.

Early in his career, he had to stay at different hotels than his teammates did. And even though Doby was the first black player in the American League—in the same season that Jackie Robinson broke into the National League—I can't help but wonder why Doby never got the same recognition as Robinson. In 1998, Doby was voted into the National Baseball Hall of Fame by the Veteran's Committee.

Sometimes people forget that the Tigers acquired Doby from the Indians and he played briefly for the Tigers at the start of the 1959 season. Later that season, the Tigers sold him to the Chicago White Sox for $30,000.

Based on my conversations with Doby, my understanding is that he believed he was ready for retirement in 1959. But he decided to ask for a trade to the Tigers instead. He wanted the last laugh on the late Walter Briggs. Doby believed what many others did at the time—that the former Tigers owner had vowed the Tigers would never have a black player on their roster.

1959 was also the same year that the Boston Red Sox became the last major-league team to integrate, when Pumpsie Green made his debut on July 21.

When I joined the Tigers in 1962, the civil rights fight was far from over, particularly in the American League. Gates Brown was already on the team when I showed up. He was three years older, and he took me under his wing. Young black players looked for an older black player to help them find their way. My guide was the Gator, who was street-smart and wise beyond his years.

Gates and I had played winter ball together in 1961, and he already had two years of professional baseball under his belt. In 1961, he'd hit .324 with 33 doubles and 15 home runs playing for the Durham Bulls in the Carolina League.

He was just 22 and his chest seemed enormous to me. One day, he turned to me and said, "You have to come up and meet the Gator." He gave me directions to a place he was renting in Tampa. I'll never forget that when I walked up, he was sitting on the porch wearing a silver smoking jacket, a long flowing robe that made him look like a king. He was a king in my eyes.

"Have a seat," he said.

When I plopped down on the steps, he began his line of questioning. "Was that for real, what I read in Jet magazine about you signing for big money—more than $50,000?" I told him that I thought it was but I didn't know for sure because my father and Judge Keith had handled everything. The Gator just whistled.

From that point on, Gates Brown and I became the best of friends. We played together for 13 seasons, and I learned much from him during my career. Going through that period of integration in the American League seemed to make us stronger. Maybe it made us closer. I called Gates all the time. There wasn't a day that passed that I didn't talk to him. In fact, I even introduced him to his wife.

Billy Bruton was a first-class man, and probably the closest thing we had to a civil rights activist on the Tigers in those days. He was supposedly 36 years old when I came to the Tigers in 1962, but the rumor was Billy was actually in his 40s. He was the son-in-law of Judy Johnson, the Hall of Fame Negro League star. Billy knew about the Negro Leagues, and he'd lived through the integration of the National League. He spent eight years in Milwaukee, leading the N.L. in stolen bases three times (1953–'55) and triples twice (1956 and 1960).

As a young black player, I looked up to Billy because he was willing to take a stand. He was appalled that the American League was years behind the National League in terms of racial equality. And he wasn't afraid to say so. "I went through this early in my career with the Braves," he said, "and I'm not going to do it again."

Billy was angry at the lack of hotels willing to accept black players, and he told the Tigers that he wouldn't report to spring training in 1963 if the situation didn't change. Sam Jones stood beside him on that issue. "We'll just meet the team back in Detroit," Billy said. That's when Tigers general manager Jim Campbell went to the city and got officials moving on the construction of a new hotel.

Billy Bruton remained my friend through the years. In 1995, he was on his way to meet me at a family reunion when he suffered a heart attack driving in Delaware. With Billy incapacitated, his car veered off the road and struck a tree. He died at the hospital.

When Charlie Dressen was hired as manager of the Tigers on June 17 1963, the organization brought in an honest man who believed in racial equality. When it came to choosing his ballplayers, Charlie was colorblind. He'd managed Jackie Robinson in Brooklyn, as well as the great Roy Campanella. He later managed Bruton with the Milwaukee Braves. Dressen clearly wanted to give me and Gates Brown the opportunity to play in Detroit. Most Tigers fans have forgotten that Dressen toyed with the idea of moving Al Kaline to center and using Gates in left and me in right field.

Having mastered his craft in the Dodgers organization, guiding the team to back-to-back pennants in 1952 and 1953, Charlie brought a sense of family to the Tigers' organization. He was the one who wanted to bring Tiger Town and the major-league team closer together. He wanted the Tigers' minor leaguers to be closer to the team's major leagues. And he tried to help bridge the gap between the A.L. and N.L.

When Charlie died in 1966, I missed him dearly. I learned so much from him in such a short period of time. He was tough on me, but he did so like a parent trying to get the best out of his child. One way Charlie inspired me was with my battle to keep my weight down. He told me how Campanella had the same problem in Brooklyn, but was able to overcome it. I figured if Campy could do it, so could I.

To motivate his Detroit players—and particularly me—Charlie would also tell the story of George Crowe, the former Negro Leagues player who made it to the majors when he was 31 years old. Crowe started his baseball career with the New York Black Yankees and the New York Cubans in the Negro Leagues in the late 1940s. He had also played in the National Basketball League with the Dayton Gems, as well as with Jackie Robinson on the Los Angeles Red Devils basketball team in 1946–'47.

Crowe was clearly a superior athlete, but he didn't get a chance to play in the majors until the Boston Braves promoted him in 1952. And he didn't get an opportunity to play full-time until Cincinnati gave him the first baseman's job in 1957. At age 36, he belted 31 home runs and drove in 92 runs.

"Sometimes you get stuck in one organization or you just don't get the opportunity," Charlie would say. "So when you're given that chance, you have to take advantage of it because you don't know when you'll get another one."

One day when the Tigers had a day off in New York, Charlie took me to meet Campanella, who owned a liquor store in the area. We spent all afternoon there with Campy. Clearly Charlie was trying to inspire me, and it worked. Charlie was a fiery 150-pound manager who loved the game more than life itself.

Given the young team we had coming up, I wonder how far Dressen could have taken the Tigers had he lived longer. Could we have won two or three pennants? I'll never know. But I do know he was one of the best managers I've ever had. And it seemed to me that the American League would've been a better league if it had brought over more managers like Dressen from the National League.

The A.L. didn't just lag behind the N.L. in race relations. The A.L. trailed the N.L. in many aspects of the game. Most of it had to do with attitude. In the older National League, which many in baseball called "the senior circuit," managers and players seemed to understand that everyone played more aggressively when they enjoyed coming to the ballpark every day.

In 1965, I was named the American League's starting left fielder for the All-Star game in Minneapolis. Shortly after taking my defensive position in the field, Willie Mays homered, Willie Stargell singled, and Joe Torre homered. Bang. Bang. Bang. We were down 3–0 before we had our stirrups on straight. Cleveland Indians players Vic Davalillo and Rocky Colavito were in center and right and I yelled over to them. "Do we have any business playing these guys?"

We did come back to make a game of it before the National League won, 6–5. But it was clear to me that there was a major difference in the two leagues that went beyond talent. It's no coincidence that the National League went 23–2–1 in All-Star games from 1960 to 1982. Back in the early 60s, they played two All-Star games a year, giving the N.L. two chances to wallop us.

At the 1973 All-Star Game at Royals Stadium, I can remember quietly sitting on the bench with my fellow American League teammates watching the N.L. players running around out on the field in the midst of talking to themselves and fans. There was plenty of horseplay when the National Leaguers were on the field.

Cincinnati Reds outfielder Pete Rose spotted us all on the bench, and yelled over to us. "Look at all of you guys getting ready to get your behinds whipped again. You guys are so tight you can't even talk."

Pete was right. The N.L. players always seemed to be having a good time, and we always seemed subdued by comparison. That attitude seemed to flow from the top down. In the A.L., we had rules against talking to fans. We really did. In the N.L., there were no such rules. The National League was people-friendly.

Once time in the late '60s, we were in Chicago to play the White Sox. Gates Brown and I found time to go across town to see our former Tigers teammate Willie Smith, who was then playing for the Cubs. We were sitting in the stands at Wrigley Field, and Cubs players Smith, Ernie Banks, and Ron Santo came into the stands to sit with us before the game. They were shocked when I told them we wouldn't be allowed to do anything like that in the American League.

With that kind of mindset, it's really not surprising that it wasn't until halfway through my career before we had true racial equality in the American League.

As I've often said, I only caught the tail end of the ugly discrimination that black players faced in the major leagues. But it was clear to me early in my career that some people within the Tigers organization still weren't ready for the team to have a black star in its lineup.

Word spread around the team that our opponents had been given a scouting report on how to pitch to me. It detailed my strengths and weaknesses, and it had been sent to them from someone within the Tigers' front office. Mr. Campbell and Charlie Dressen found out about this and were furious. So were some of my teammates. Clearly, not everyone was ready for racial equality in baseball in Detroit in the mid-1960s.

I witnessed enough incidents, and heard enough stories from Billy Bruton, Larry Doby, Sam Jones, Roy Campanella, and others to believe that I owed it to those who came before me, and to those who would come after me, to stand up for civil rights.

When I was playing for Syracuse in the minor leagues, I stood in a line one day just to shake Jackie Robinson's hand. He didn't say a word. And he didn't need to. Just shaking his hand was enough for me. I understood that he had opened the door for so many of us. And when it came time for me to meet him, I just thanked him for all he had done.

I admired the Kennedys for their civil rights views, and I campaigned with presidential candidate Hubert Humphrey in 1968. I protested at the infamous Polk Theatre in Lakeland, Florida, because it refused to admit black people. That actually amused me because when I first joined the Tigers, a young white man who worked around the clubhouse (coincidentally named "Gator") once took me to the Polk after we'd gone fishing. No one said a word when I bought a ticket.

When Dr. Martin Luther King was assassinated on April 4, 1968, it certainly made every black person in America realize that we hadn't changed enough. And the shooting death of Robert Kennedy was another terrible reminder later that spring. In Detroit, we had gone through the riots in 1967 and the following year, the Tigers had helped heal the city by winning the World Series.

But by 1969, it started to bother me that I was the only starting black position player on the team. Every other team in the American League had at least two minority starters—even the Red Sox, who were the last team to integrate. Reggie Smith was in the Boston outfield, and George Scott was at first base. The Baltimore Orioles had four black players out of their starting eight. And the National League was even more integrated, with the Atlanta Braves using six or seven minority players in some games.

Gates Brown only had 14 at-bats in the first month of the '69 season. And starting pitcher Earl Wilson was the only other black player on the team.

My mother and father had taught me not to think in racial terms, to view people for what they stood for rather than for the color of their skin. But it began to gnaw at me that Detroit, a city with a large black population, had only three black players on the team. There were certainly black players in the organization—particularly Les Cain, Wayne Redmond, and Ike Brown—who were capable of playing in the big leagues.

Redmond was a talented player with some pop in his bat. He'd hit 26 home runs at Rocky Mount in the Class A Carolina League in 1968, and showed plenty of promise. But I never thought he received a true opportunity to make the big leagues. Redmond was a minister, and back then, I remember it was suggested that his religion held him back. But would they have said that if he were white?

Just the mere fact that we have to wonder whether race held him back says to me that even by 1969 when we hadn't come far enough yet.

To be honest, I never felt a hint of racism with my Tigers teammates. We were a family, and I believed that most of those guys would've done anything for me, and I would have done anything for them. Gates Brown, Earl Wilson, and I were in the middle of every social event, and none of us ever felt out of place for a minute in our clubhouse or when we were with the guys. General manager Jim Campbell was like a second father to me, and I certainly didn't view him as a racist. But certainly there was a sentiment in baseball, specifically among the black players, that in some organizations a black player had to be much better than a white player to make the team. Ties always went to the white player.

Back when I joined the Tigers, there was an outfielder in our system named Jessie Queen. He was the best hitter I'd ever seen. He was a few years older than I was, and I thought he was a better ballplayer than I was. I never understood why he didn't make it to the big leagues.

"You just pay attention to what you're doing," my dad told me, "and nevermind him. There must be a reason why he hasn't made it."

Was it the color of his skin? I didn't know. Just like I didn't know why the Tigers still didn't have many black players. Near the one-year anniversary of Dr. King's death in April of 1969, those discrimination issues began to dance in my mind. The summer before, while the Tigers were chasing the pennant, African-Americans Tommie Smith and John Carlos won the gold and bronze medals, respectively, in the 200-meter run at the Mexico City Olympics. At the awards ceremony, they bowed their heads and gave the Black Power salute during the national anthem, raising their fists in the air to protest racism in America. Black athletes all over were feeling that more needed to be done. I know I began to feel that way.

By mid-May 1969, I was in a 2-for-24 slump and fans were booing me. I'd struck out 10 times in those 24 at-bats. All of my thoughts, issues, frustrations, and convictions boiled over on May 15, 1969, when I walked out on the Tigers in the middle of a game against the Chicago White Sox at Tiger Stadium. Apparently in the sixth inning, after left-handed sinkerball specialist Tommy John struck me out for the second time, I dropped my bat in the middle of the infield and walked slowly to my position in left field.

When the White Sox had been retired, I went through the dugout straight to the clubhouse, showered, and left the ballpark. Reportedly, Norm Cash and Gates Brown tried to convince me to stay, but I wasn't listening to whatever they had to say.

The reason I say "apparently" is because I really don't remember doing any of that. In fact, a day after it happened, I still didn't remember doing it. It was front-page news in Detroit when I also didn't show up for the team flight to Minneapolis the next day. Manager Mayo Smith suspended me $340 per day based on my salary of $60,000.

Although Detroit had talented sportswriters, no one was able to dig up the true story of my departure because I didn't tell anyone. Everyone focused on my slump, or whether the boos had simply overwhelmed me. Reporters talked to Cash about how he had handled the boos over the years. Some suggested that I was "oversensitive."

Channel 4 reporter Al Ackerman had reported that I was unhappy with Tigers management and that I wanted to be traded. When I heard that, tears welled up in my eyes because I never asked to be traded—never even thought about being traded. This was my city, and I came up with most of the guys on that team. They were like family to me, and I didn't want to leave them.

Maybe the boos stunned me a bit because we had just won the World Series seven months before. And clearly I was disappointed in my performance because I wanted to help the team more than I was. I had hit .285 in 1968, and when I left the team in May of '69, my average was .213.

My buddy Gates Brown was quoted as saying, "I don't think any of us really knew what was going on inside Willie. He seems like a mild, easygoing man, but he keeps things bottled up."

An article in the Detroit Free Press did suggest that there were racial issues bubbling beneath the surface. Managing Editor Frank Angelo wrote:

*"There is one aspect to this attempt to understand the Horton incident which none of his friends wanted to discuss, but which cannot be overlooked. Willie is a Negro. He is fully aware of the civil rights fight.*

*"He is the only Negro who is a Tiger regular outside the pitching staff and being as sensitive as he is, it is also certain that he feels there is even greater pressure on him to succeed.*

*"The fact that living arrangements at Lakeland were not the best as far as he and other Negroes on the team were concerned undoubtedly triggered other thoughts about his role as an athlete and a Negro.*

*Put those personal concerns together with a horrendous batting slump, a desperate desire to win and general overall sensitiveness and you have the makings of the 1969 phase of the Willie Horton story."*

The mere fact that the story still referred to blacks as "Negroes" should illustrate that the civil rights fight was still ongoing in 1969.

Although Angelo's story had elements of the truth, he didn't have the whole story. What Angelo didn't know was that when I had walked away from the team, I had asked for a meeting with owner John Fetzer and GM Jim Campbell to discuss why there weren't more black players on the Tigers' roster.

The two of them listened and acknowledged my points. No promises were made. "You can't change things overnight, Willie," Campbell said. "It takes time."

I was away from the team for four days. When I returned, I told reporters that there were no racial issues. The Free Press quoted me as saying, "I don't want any trouble to come out of this…I believe every man is a man and we can live together. It doesn't have anything to do with racial issues."

It was necessary to say that because I'd received some nasty telegrams. This was nothing new to me. Since I arrived in the major leagues, I heard racial slurs raining down from the outfield stands. I had received hate mail and even death threats. One man was actually arrested for making threats against my family. I never wanted it publicized because I was afraid it would just fuel more trouble. You didn't want to admit to the hate-mongers that they could get to you because that would only encourage them.

That's why I had to say that there weren't any racial issues connected to my departure in 1969. Some of the mail was so hateful that my first wife, Patricia, fainted because of all of the stress. My son, Darryl, found her lying on the floor one day when he got up to go to school.

When I returned to the lineup in Detroit for the first time, 25,990 fans cheered loudly when I was introduced. I received more applause when I singled in my first at-bat. Mickey Lolich fanned 16 batters to break Paul Foytack's 13-year-old strikeout record, and we beat California, 6–3. Soon the focus was back on the pennant race and not on me.

After talking to Campbell, I felt as if a weight had been removed from my shoulders.

A month later, without any fanfare, a 27-year-old black outfielder named Ike Brown was promoted to the Tigers, and he ended up playing parts of six major-league seasons. Before his promotion, Ike had never been given an opportunity to play in the majors.

I can't say for sure whether my discussions with Fetzer and Mr. Campbell played a role in the decision to promote Ike. But I certainly know that I made Mr. Campbell think about the situation. It didn't change overnight, but I could feel a difference.

In August of 1970, infielder Kevin Collins joined the team, and he started rooming with the Gator. I think that was the first instance of a black Tiger and a white Tiger rooming together on the road. In 1972, I started to room with Frank Howard. By then, I don't think anyone gave it a second thought. "Big Daddy" and I were great friends, and he used to help me organize our barbecues in spring training.

As close as we were on that 1968 Tigers team, maybe I should have roomed with Mickey Stanley or Wayne Comer or Jon Warden or one of the other white players. I'm sure it would've been accepted fine, but it never occurred to me that I needed to do that. By 1969, I had started to think it was important that we push away the last traces of racism in the sport.

In my basement at home today, is a montage of newspaper stories and pictures about Hank Aaron and his chase of Babe Ruth's record of 714 home runs. When Aaron was in the midst of that chase in 1973 and 1974, I carried those clippings on every road trip. Everyone in baseball knew what Aaron was going through. The threats he received were undoubtedly scary for his family. But I was proud of Hank, and it made me feel strong to carry those stories.

The black men who played in the major leagues in the 1950s and early 1960s were pioneers in the truest sense of the word. They blazed trails, cut through barricades, and cleared away debris to make a clear path for black players who followed them. Maybe they weren't all great ballplayers, but they were all exceptional men, rich in fortitude and strong of spirit. They had pride in the face of prejudice. And they had the mental toughness and survival skills necessary to play at a time when owners demanded that both uniforms and players be all white. In that era, black players endured taunts, threats, and isolation, just to be part of a group that acted as if it didn't want them. They did it because they loved the game—and because they knew that a black man should have the same right to live his dream as a white man has. These were indeed exceptional men.

By my last full season in Detroit in 1976, there were three black players getting regular playing time—Ron LeFlore, my good friend Alex Johnson, and me—plus three other minorities in the starting lineup—Panamanian Ben Oglivie, Mexican Aurelio Rodriguez, and Puerto Rican Pedro Garcia.

To this day I'm glad I made a stand in 1969. It was payment for the debt I owed to Robinson, Doby, Bruton, Wood, and all of the other black players who put up with the abuse to allow me to wear a major-league uniform.

The strength that I got from those black players wasn't mine to keep. I needed to pass it along. It was a gift I had to share with others. And after I met with Fetzer and Campbell in May of 1969, I felt as if I'd done my part.

# Chapter 13

## MULL DIGGER BECOMES THE ANCIENT MARINER

WHEN I SIGNED WITH THE SEATTLE MARINERS for the 1979 season, I owned a glove and two batting helmets that were five times older than my new team.

The Mariners craved a media-friendly, high-profile player to heighten the team's identity, and I was looking for a team willing to offer a fresh start to a 36-year-old power hitter. We were a perfect match.

Remember, this was only the third season in the Mariners' existence—more than a decade before Ken Griffey Jr., Randy Johnson, and others would arrive in the Northwest. In 1978, the Mariners had lost 104 games and they were drawing fewer than 6,500 fans per game in the Kingdome near the end of the season. Even at the start of the season, only about 11,000 or 12,000 were going to the ballpark. The Mariners didn't have an Al Kaline or a Mickey Mantle or a Hank Aaron in their history, and the public seemed to view my signing as a significant move.

Originally, I'd signed a tryout contract with the Mariners. But when I began to consistently launch the ball with authority during spring training, Mariners' management got anxious to convert my tryout deal to a regular contract.

When I was playing in Venezuela in the previous few months, Pablo Penton kept telling me that my swing looked sweet and powerful. He had armed with me with confidence.

"These are major pitchers down here in Venezuela," Pablo would tell me. "And you're hitting .300 against them. You're going back to the majors and hitting .280 or .285 and 25 home runs."

At the end of the 1978 season, it seemed as if I was on retirement's doorstep. But I got the little boy back in me while I was playing and winning in Venezuela. The Mariners signed an aging veteran, but they got a player who felt reinvigorated. It's not an exaggeration to say that I was in the best shape of my major-league career at age 36. In the photos featuring me in a Mariners uniform, I look almost thin. I showed up at training camp weighing 210 pounds—a full 15 pounds lighter than my usual playing weight with the Detroit Tigers. With Billy Martin's preaching about conditioning, Ben Oglivie's nutritional advice, and my own desire to continue to be an impact player, I was suddenly overflowing with confidence.

The funny thing with the Mariners is that management was worried about me. I was pounding the ball so well, they were afraid I was going to leave at the end of spring training and sign with a contender. The more hits I got, the more the Mariners fretted.

"I just want to concentrate on getting my game together," I told team executives Danny O'Brien and Lou Gorman. "We'll talk about a contract at the end of spring training. I'm not going anywhere."

Mr. O'Brien should've known what kind of man I was because he had been general manager in Texas when the Tigers traded me there in 1977. Seattle had given me a chance to be an everyday ballplayer again, and I felt indebted to them. Loyalty should always be mutual. People who know me well know that I'm loyal to a fault. One of the reasons why I signed with Seattle was that I respected Danny O'Brien.

O'Brien presumably expected the worst when I finally came into his office to negotiate with him. He seemed stunned when I made my contract demand.

"I want a rookie contract," I told him.

"A rookie contract?" he repeated. "What do you mean?"

"I mean, give me what rookies get, and then let's work in some incentive bonuses," I said. "If I hit those bonuses, it'll mean the contract has worked out for both of us."

My agent at the time, Charlie Dye, was against my decision to ask for an incentive-laden contract, but I felt very strongly about it.

O'Brien could not have agreed quicker, and that deal ultimately paid me more in one season than I'd earned in many seasons with Detroit. I reached all of my bonus incentives by the All-Star break, and it turned out to be the most lucrative contract I ever signed.

That season, I would joke with other players about my rookie contract. When the Tigers came to town in June, the Detroit Free Press quoted me as telling Ron LeFlore, "I'm losing money playing. I bet I'm the only one in the majors for 15 years and making $36,000."

The 1968 season probably was the best of my career. My 36 home runs, .285 batting average, and 85 RBIs contributed to a world championship. But 1979 might've been my second-best individual season. For the first time in my career, I played all 162 games, and my 29 home runs were my highest total since '68. My 106 RBI and 180 hits— Seattle franchise records—were also personal highs.

Certainly, some people believe my home run total was aided by the homer-friendly Kingdome in 1979. But I actually hit more home runs on the road than I did in Seattle that year. I did take advantage of the Kingdome's deep alleys for more extra-base hits. Thirteen of my 19 doubles and all five of my triples came in the Kingdome. Over the years, I learned to take advantage of a park's design. If it had lengthy power alleys, I tried to hit the ball in the gaps.

In my first game in Seattle, I had three hits, including a home run, to help beat California, 5–4. From that point on, the Kingdome fans treated me royally. It was like being home in Detroit.

At times, I remember thinking that people in Seattle were almost too nice to me. It was like I could do no wrong there. Even members of the media seemed to treat me that way. No one in Seattle wanted to hold me accountable.

I remember flagging down the late Seattle Times columnist Emmett Watson once, after he wrote some really flattering things about me in the paper. "Thank you very much, Emmett," I said to him. "But when I don't play well, you have to kick me in the butt. That's the way it's supposed to work."

He laughed, but I was serious. When Joe Falls would criticize me in his column in Detroit, it motivated me. I considered Joe a friend, but I understood his job description. I knew it was his job to analyze my performance. And if I didn't measure up, it bothered me. I feel the same way about retired Detroit News columnist Jerry Green. Old-school journalists like Green and Falls didn't write columns simply to stir up controversy. It was their job to hold teams and players accountable, and they were quite serious about their business—as serious as I was about mine.

That's why I worried in Seattle when everyone treated me with almost too much respect. I didn't want a free pass. And I didn't want to get complacent. Fortunately, I didn't.

The Mariners won 67 games that season, and that was actually a respectable number, given that our pitching staff had an average age of about 24 or 25. The team boasted some talented ballplayers. Ruppert Jones was 24 and coming into his own, and Bruce Bochte was a fine hitter. If he hadn't had some injury problems, he might've developed into one of the major leagues' finest hitters. When I initially signed with Seattle, Bruce actually offered to give up No. 23 so I could have my old number. I appreciated the gesture, but I decided to wear No. 53 instead. I picked that number because Dodgers Hall of Famer Don Drysdale had worn it. I'd always had a lot of respect for him, and he was a credit to the game.

The Mariners had a wealth of interesting characters, including Tom Paciorek, who is one of baseball's all-time funniest people. We also had Mario Mendoza, who was to Seattle what Ray Oyler was to the Detroit Tigers in the '60s. Mendoza gobbled up ground balls with amazing accuracy, but he just couldn't hit the breaking ball. Today, a .200 batting average is referred to as "the Mendoza Line." Some say

Paciorek invented that phrase, but he insists it was Bochte. Either way, it was developed during that 1979 season in Seattle.

Mendoza was always fooling around with me—razzing me and playing little pranks, and I was always shooing him away. I called him "The Crazy Mexican." Paciorek has often told the story of sitting next to me while I was sleeping on a spring training bus ride. Apparently I was dreaming, and when I woke up suddenly, I said, "Get away from me, you crazy Mexican!" Mendoza and my old teammates had a good laugh at that one.

In Detroit, I was "Willie The Wonder," and in Seattle I was the "Ancient Mariner." But my teammates called me "Mull Digger." I often used that term because my father did. And so did his father. But I have no idea where it came from. I just assumed it was a mining term down south, but a search for a definition yielded no results while we were working on this book.

But my father and a former Detroit Tiger from Mississippi named Bubba Phillips used that term to describe a hard-working player— someone dependable who came to work and did his job every day. To me, that was a mull digger. And in Seattle, some of the guys even had a jacket made with my nickname "Mull Digger" sewn on the back.

That 1979 season provided me with many wonderful memories, including my 300th career home run. My heart has told me that God has a plan for all of us, and I believe that it was more than coincidence that my 300th came against the Detroit Tigers.

On June 4, 1979, I parked No. 299 into the outfield stands of the Kingdome. Milt Wilcox was on the mound for Detroit, and he threw me a breaking pitch that was outside and so close to the dirt that a sand wedge might've been more useful than a bat. When I connected, I was leaning over the plate with one arm extended. It was more like a golf swing than a baseball swing. The ball flew toward the outfield on a long arc and fell into the left-field stands like a wedge shot landing on the green.

"I don't know how I hit it," I told the Detroit Free Press that night. "I guess I was just meant to hit that pitch." But looking back, maybe it was prejudice that helped me learn to hit a pitch like that. Early in my career, when someone in Detroit's front office was tipping teams on how to pitch to me, I didn't see too many fat pitches. But maybe it was the best thing that could've happened to me because I learned how to hit bad pitches. I learned I had to take what I could get. Late in my career, I hit as many balls as strikes because I would move the plate in my mind by adjusting my body positioning. If you're leaning way over the plate, a ball a foot outside can be right in your power zone.

I was expecting Wilcox to throw me a pitch down and away, and so I moved closer to the plate as he finished his wind-up.

Early in my career, I didn't like to be cheated on my swings. I felt the same way late in my career, too. I tell young players that if you're relaxed and confident at the plate, and your eyes are in control of your strength, then you're in a perfectly balanced position. You're using your inner-strength. You aren't searching for your swing. You have your swing. When you're in that position, you don't hold back. All of my energy went into each swing.

The only exception I made was when I knew my swing wasn't quite right. People who followed my career closely would probably argue that I never choked up on a bat in my life. But that's not accurate. If I was slumping or out of sync, and if we had a runner in scoring position, I would let the bat handle slide down between my fingers a couple of inches. Not even the catcher would notice. I made sure I made contact in those situations. If I wasn't swinging the bat well, I would actually strike out less than if I were on a hitting tear.

In that same game against Detroit, in my next at-bat, Wilcox hit me in the hand with a fastball. I charged the mound, benches emptied, and it took several minutes for umpires to restore order.

"He wasn't trying to hit me," I admitted to the press afterward "But when you're mad, you don't think about that. Besides, I was hurting anyway."

At that point, I showed the media my badly scabbed hand, which had been injured a few days before when I was spiked against the Texas Rangers. Whenever you see someone charge the mound, there's usually an underlying cause.

Back in the mid-'70s when I was still playing for the Tigers, I charged the mound one time after the Angels' Frank Tanana hit me.

To be honest, I wasn't mad at Frank. I was mad at his manager, Dick Williams. As I got to the mound, I kept telling Frank that he shouldn't listen to Williams when he orders him to hit a batter. Then I turned to Williams and told him if it happened again, I was coming after him. I was pretty animated at the time.

People tell me how intimidating I was in those situations, but most of my close friends find that amusing, especially those friends I met after my playing career. Today, people see me as a playful, friendly guy. That was probably true back then, too.

The night after the Wilcox fiasco, it looked as if I'd hit my 300th homer, but my long drive off Tigers reliever John Hiller hit a speaker 132 feet above the Kingdome playing surface in left field. It was one of the most bizarre singles in baseball history. That didn't bother me in the least, though. I remember thinking how Al Kaline had lost a couple of home runs because games were rained out before the fifth inning. One was in 1958 and the other in 1963. He finished his career with 399 home runs. If it weren't for some bad weather, Al would've had 401 official career home runs.

At least I ended up on base. Six years later, A's designated hitter Dave Kingman smashed a ball off Seattle pitcher Dave Geisel that struck a wire hanging from the Kingdome roof. Instead of being a home run, it fell safely into left fielder Phil Bradley's glove for an out.

Somehow, I knew I would hit my 300th the next day against Jack Morris. Before I left for the game, I told Gloria to make sure she had the family in their seats by the start of the first inning. It was Wednesday, June 6, 1979.

The Tigers jumped out to a 3–0 lead against us in the top of the first on a Rusty Staub home run. In the bottom of the inning, I came up to bat against Morris with Ruppert Jones on second base. I dug in and ripped a shot over the left field wall for number 300. It made me proud that I hit it off a quality pitcher like Jack Morris. He had established himself as the Tigers' ace that season. He had that nasty forkball, and even when he was young, you still had to work Morris to get a good pitch to hit.

Rounding the bases, I was crying tears of joy and laughter mixed together. I really didn't know whether I was happy or sad. Mostly, I was confused. Playing against the Tigers was the most difficult part of my playing career. I didn't even like to go on the field with them before the game. I preferred to stay in the trainer's room. If I went out and socialized with the Tigers, I didn't think I would be able to compete against them. The Tigers had raised me. My emotions overwhelmed me that night. The Tigers' players congratulated me, but I couldn't help but think I should've been in their dugout.

The Mariners organization and their fans were first-rate. The night after my 300th, it was Willie Horton Night at the Kingdome, and the team presented me with artwork commemorating the home run. The piece had 300 silver dollars framed in the shape of the number 300.

In that era of baseball, we didn't think much about milestones. But late in a player's career, he begins to ponder them more, and his legacy becomes important to him. Heading into the 1980 season, I was looking forward to my 2,000th hit. Obviously, making that list wasn't going to change the way I saw my career, but the 2,000-hit club did include plenty of outstanding ballplayers, and at the time, it still included a relatively short list of African-American players. I needed just 81 more hits. Based on my 1979 output, I expected to be there by midsummer.

As it turned out, I never got there at all. In spring training of 1980, I ripped open my hand sliding into a base. I didn't think much of it until the wound refused to heal. Doctors diagnosed it as a rare disease that interfered with the healing process. The hand bothered me all season, even forcing me to the disabled list a couple of times.

The situation was so bad that at times, I would pull off my glove and my bandage would be soaked in blood.

When I came off the disabled list in August, I still had a chance to get my 2,000 hits. I needed 20. I had 13. Seattle manager Maury Wills, who'd replaced Darrell Johnson that season, didn't use me immediately. He did start me for several games in a row in September, but then benched me for two games down the stretch and only used me as a pinch-hitter in another game. Right before that, I had nine hits in eight days. I certainly wonder that if I would've played those three games, plus a couple of others earlier in the season, whether I would've made it. I ended my career just seven hits shy of my milestone, tallying 1,993.

Newspaper accounts say that Wills has been clean and sober for many years now, and I'm happy for him because in 1980, his problems were obvious to his players. I sometimes wonder if Maury didn't play me those games because he knew that I knew what was going on in his life. I wanted to help him, but he didn't want my help at that time. I hit .286 that September. It wasn't like I was hurting the team chasing my 2,000 hits.

Did he want me off the team? That was certainly my impression. But I was still surprised when I got a call from the Mariners in December of 1980 to tell me I was part of an 11-man trade with the Texas Rangers. It was an odd situation because I was actually on the Mariners media public relations tour—talking about the upcoming season—when the deal was made. They waited until that was over to tell me I'd been traded.

Seattle traded Rick Honeycutt, Mario Mendoza, Larry Cox, Leon Roberts and me to Texas for Richie Zisk, Rick Auerbach, Ken Clay, Jerry Don Gleaton, Brian Allard, and minor-leaguer Steve Finch. At the time, only four trades in major-league history had involved more players.

At the time, it seemed like a good move for me. I thought the Rangers had a chance to win their division. Looking at their lineup, I saw myself batting cleanup. Battling through my injury with Seattle in 1980, I batted only .221, with eight home runs. But my hand finally healed in the offseason, and I looked forward to working with the kids in the Rangers system. In spring training of 1981, I was hitting the ball well. So I was a bit surprised when the Rangers started playing me less often as we got closer to the regular season.

At that time, my good friend Dennis "Hoggie" Gordon was staying with me at the Rangers' spring training base in Pompano Beach, Florida. I had gotten to know Hoggie when he was running the kitchen in Lakeland at Tiger Town. He had played some Negro League baseball back in his day, and I more or less adopted him as a grandfather for my kids. He even moved to Seattle to live with me for a while. Hoggie knew his baseball, and people liked having him around. The Mariners had even allowed him to sit on the bench with the team, although Hoggie was such a straight-shooter that manager Darrell Johnson didn't always appreciate what he had to say.

One time on the bench, Johnson asked Hoggie what the problem was with the team. "Well," Hoggie said, "you're the problem." He sure didn't pull any punches.

Hoggie watched me bang the ball around the ballpark in spring training for the Rangers in 1981, and he couldn't figure out why I wasn't playing more often.

"Something's wrong here," Hoggie told me. "You have to go find out what's happening."

I told him not to worry. I could still see myself batting fourth, with Al Oliver in front of me. It was going to be a great season.

"I'm tellin' you, something is wrong," Hoggie insisted.

I figured that the Rangers wouldn't have traded for me if they didn't have plans for me. I thought they were just trying to get a good look at the kids on the roster. I was content to put on my army clothes and do my workout every day. I wanted to be ready for Opening Day.

But day after day, my name was missing from the lineup card. Hoggie finally convinced me to go talk to manager Don Zimmer. I called Zimmer "Uncle Popeye" because he really did look like the cartoon character.

When I went to Zimmer to discuss the situation, he raised his hands in the air, and said, "I have nothing to do with this," he said. "You have to talk to Hopalong." That was everyone's nickname for general manager Eddie Robinson.

Robinson was honest with me. And as he ushered me out the door, at least he had some kind words for me. "You did everything we asked of you, Willie," he said. "But we just want to go in another direction."

I couldn't help but wonder...couldn't they have gone "in another direction" earlier in spring training? The real issue I had with the Rangers was that they released me on April 1 when it was too late to catch on with another team. Teams had already finalized their rosters. Of course, I also couldn't help but wonder if Maury Wills was indirectly responsible for my predicament. Maybe the Rangers hadn't wanted me at all, but were simply doing the Mariners a favor by taking me in a trade. Had Seattle simply released me, there would've been a backlash. By trading me, they had least eased the public relations pain.

And there was another issue: At that time in baseball, there seemed to be a push to sweep out older players like me. Even though I didn't find work with another team in 1981, that might've said more about labor issues than about my playing ability. A strike loomed on the horizon, and it came later that season in June. Nine years later in 1990, Major League Baseball was found guilty of collusion for some of its actions in the 1980s. Maybe I was just at the launch point of that line of thinking.

One of the most difficult issues that a professional athlete faces is deciding when to hang the spikes on a nail in the garage.

After the Rangers cut me, I wasn't initially thinking about retirement. I returned to my home in Seattle, believing that someone would call. Injuries happen in baseball, and I'd hit consistently enough in spring training to convince anyone that I could still play. If someone got hurt somewhere in the majors, I felt like I'd be called on to take his place. But the call never came.

Then one day, I heard a baseball broadcast on the radio and I heard the announcer mention Luis Tiant and Rusty Torres. I figured it must've been an exhibition game. But after a minute, I realized that Tiant and Torres were playing with the Portland Beavers of the Pacific Coast League.

A Philadelphia native named David Hersh had bought the team at age 21 and made a name for himself with a variety of promotions, including the signing of former major-leaguers.

I called Hersh and asked him for a tryout. "Can you still hit?" he asked.

I laughed. "I can still hit," I said.

In my tryout, I ripped a few balls beyond the confines of the Portland park and busted out the windows across the street. They signed me on the spot.

The Beavers were a Pittsburgh Pirates farm team, and I thought that if I hit well, the Pirates would call me up. I hit well, but in parts of two seasons with the Beavers, I never got the call. I played against Pirates legend Willie Stargell in an exhibition game, and even he was a bit surprised I was stuck in the minors.

In a last effort to stay in the game, I decided to go to the Mexican League with the hope of attracting attention. I signed with Nuevo Laredo. Maybe I was thinking about 2,000 major-league hits, but mostly I just wanted to continue to play ball.

But it didn't take me long in Mexico to realize it was time to put an end to that chapter of my life. I looked around at the young players on the team, and I realized that if I played there, I'd be taking playing time from a younger player who needed those at-bats to develop. And that's just not what Willie Horton's about.

My son Deryl Lemar was also in southern Mexico, attending a baseball school to get his game together. Not speaking a word of Spanish, he took a bus down all the way there. When he got there, he broke out in hives. He toughed it out four or five days before coming up to rejoin me. Once he got back with me, he asked me if this is really what I wanted to do. I told him to pack up his van because my playing days were over.

From Mexico, we drove to Houston to visit my niece. Then we drove to Florida to pick up my daughter April. Next, we drove to Detroit. Then we drove to visit my son Al at Drake University in Des Moines, Iowa. He had been a high school standout at Redford, and had earned a basketball scholarship to Drake. Then we drove back home to Seattle. It was a beautiful trip with Deryl. Over all of those miles of driving, I was able to make peace with my retirement. I realized how much I needed my family, and I was ready to go home.

# Chapter 14

## YOU CAN GO HOME AGAIN

WHEN THE PHONE RANG AT MY HOME 23 years ago and a voice boomed, "Hey, Roids!" I knew immediately it was one of my 1968 Detroit Tigers teammates. Nobody even knew that nickname except those guys. Only a few seconds of razzing was necessary before I realized it was Jim Price.

"What the heck are doing in Seattle?" he asked. "You belong in Detroit. Get your butt back here. This is your city."

Mostly, Jimmy was giving me the business, but he was serious about believing I should be in Detroit. I explained that I still had kids in school in Seattle, and that it wasn't easy to pack up and move. But he persisted, telling me that I was more "marketable" in Detroit than I was in the Northwest.

"We're putting together a fantasy camp using the 1968 Tigers, and we want you to be involved," Jimmy said.

"Fantasy camp?" I said, "I don't want to go on any cruise."

Jimmy started laughing because he realized I didn't have any idea what he was talking about. When he said "fantasy camp," all I could think of were the old TV shows Fantasy Island and Love Boat.

But once he explained the concept that he and his friend Jerry Lewis had put together, I liked the plan. The idea was to bring together fans and members of the 1968 Tigers for a week of playing baseball. It turned out to be a great idea, and Jim Price's phone call may have altered the course of my life.

In the midst of writing this book, I attended my 22nd consecutive Detroit Tigers Fantasy Camp. In many ways, I probably have benefited more from those camps than the participants. By re-connecting with those Detroit fans, I think it made me realize that at some point, I had to come home again. It makes me misty-eyed when I think about all of the devoted, wonderful fans I've met at these camps.

Unfortunately, I wasn't able to take a direct route back to Motown, but eventually I returned. Billy Martin hired me to coach in Oakland for a couple of seasons. But right after the Tigers won the World Series in 1984, I thought I had an opportunity to come back. I remember calling Gates Brown, who was the Tigers' hitting coach at the time, and laying out my plan to approach the Tigers about becoming their minor-league hitting instructor.

"We could really lay down a strong foundation here," I told Gates. "We can work with each hitter individually, and take him where he needs to go."

Gates seemed excited about the possibility. But after I was given the job, he told me that he was probably going to resign. Gator was offended, maybe even insulted, that the Tigers had only offered him a $2,500 raise after the World Series.

"Don't tell anyone I'm resigning," Gator told me. "But send the Tigers a letter and tell them that if my job ever opens up, you want to be considered for it."

Following Gator's advice, I sent the letter. As soon as Gator's resignation became official, ex-Cincinnati Red Vada Pinson was hired, and the Tigers said they never received my letter. It was a bit odd at the next spring training in 1985 because some players thought I was the major-league hitting coach.

But the situation became stranger still when the New York Yankees called the Tigers to ask permission to talk to me about a coaching position. Martin had been hired to manage the Yankees again, and he wanted me on his staff.

With the season about to start, I had driven through the night to Nashville to coach some of our prospects. Tigers general manager Bill Lajoie woke me up with the news that the Yankees wanted me. Our conversation went something like this:

"That's really a decision I don't want to make," I said. "Maybe I can't make it."

"It seems to me that you can't pass up this opportunity," Lajoie said.

"But it took me so long to get back here, that I really don't want to leave," I said. "I waited too long to get back to Detroit."

"I'll help you make the decision—this is the best opportunity for your future," he said. "You should go."

And that's how I ended up wearing the Yankees' pinstripes. Bill Lajoie helped me reach that conclusion. And I thought he was trying to help me.

That would've been fine with me, except a few years later, people started asking why I wasn't with the Tigers organization. Lajoie essentially told everyone that the Tigers had given me an opportunity before, and I had run out on them. That scarred me deeply because that's just not an accurate portrayal of our phone conversation.

As it turned out, the Yankees situation worked out nicely for me. When I met with owner George Steinbrenner, he asked what my salary had been in Detroit. I told him $25,000. He then asked how much more I had deferred. "None," I said.

He couldn't believe it. He raised my pay to $60,000 per season.

People have mixed opinions about Mr. Steinbrenner. However, I watched him in action. He was five or 10 years ahead of everyone else in terms of his approach to the game.

After a year in New York, Chicago White Sox general manager Ken Harrelson asked permission to talk to me, and he hired me to coach in Chicago. I was at least getting closer to Detroit. And there in the Windy City, I met a rising young executive named Dave Dombrowski, who years later would become my boss in Detroit.

On December 23, 1989, Billy Martin called me and told me that he was going to end up back with the Yankees. "Don't take another job," he told me. "You're going to end up working for me again."

Two days later, he was killed in a car accident.

By then, I'd made up my mind that I really didn't want to work anywhere but Detroit. The fantasy camps had really reminded me that my roots were in this community, with the many fans who'd supported me for so many years. They gave me strength when I played, and they were still giving me strength.

Before the great Yankees legend Joe DiMaggio died in 1999, I was blessed with the opportunity to meet him. He was well up in years, but he knew every ballplayer who came to compete in his Joe DiMaggio Classic exhibition game. And he knew more about my career than I knew about his.

"You should've been able to play your whole career in Detroit," he told me. "That's what's wrong with baseball today. We don't have loyalty."

I've never forgotten what Joe said to me.

Actually, I did return to work in the Detroit area, working first in a job-training program and finally for the City of Detroit as the Police Athletic League (PAL) director.

Detroit mayor Coleman Young had recruited me for PAL through Charlie Primas, who was president of the city housing commission from 1985 to 1994. Primas was a well-known athlete himself, having played for the Harlem Globetrotters.

I was hired as PAL's deputy director, working under former Detroit Lions great Dick "Night Train" Lane.

PAL was struggling a bit when I arrived, but I made it clear to Mayor Young and Charlie that I had tremendous respect for Mr. Lane, and I planned to be extremely loyal to him. As long as Mr. Lane wanted to be there, he was going to be there. In my mind, Night Train

Lane and WJR broadcasting legend J.P. McCarthy were PAL. The organization had been around since the 1967 Detroit riots. Once I showed Mr. Lane how much I respected him, he put me in charge of PAL operations.

He told me that he thought his football mentality had probably gotten in the way. He hadn't been able to get the staffing he needed from Detroit police chief William Hart.

Once I got involved, I made an effort to develop a better relationship with the police. I learned how to do what was necessary to get the staffing I needed. I even went to the shooting range. In fact, by the time I resigned, I was a second deputy chief and executive director of PAL. I had Officer Butler working for me, and Officer Nail and Joe Howard were assigned to me. We put together a career-development program, and with the support of Ford Motor Company, we took that from 9,000 to 22,000.

Again it was the Tigers fantasy camp that helped me. There I met a man named Carl Manoogian, whose brother was a top executive at Ford. Through him, I met others, including Gary Nielsen, and I began to work with Ford's marketing company. They showed me how to develop a budget to help meet my needs at PAL.

When we started, we were hanging on with well over a million-dollar budget. By the end, we had almost a $2 million budget.

Our career development program was based on sports and recreation, but it was really about education. All of the outreach programs in the city, including after-school babysitting—we started those at PAL. People have patterned themselves after us, and I'm very proud of my work with PAL.

I was actually still living in Seattle, but I commuted to Detroit and lived with my in-laws until I could save up enough comp time to go home for a month. They were two wonderful people, and they treated me like a son. It was a difficult home life situation, but my father had taught me long ago that you had to do what's best for your family—and my girls needed to finish school in Seattle.

Thanks to the fantasy camp, I was able to move back to Detroit permanently a few years later. Bobby Milano, owner of Ort Tool and Die in Erie, Michigan, came to the Tigers fantasy camp, and he offered me a job as salesperson. I enjoyed working for Ort. I liked the company, and more importantly, I liked the people.

I didn't have any more thoughts about rejoining the Tigers, especially after an incident one day at Tiger Stadium. I showed up to attend a game, headed to the same gate I'd been going to since I was a kid working in the clubhouse in the 1950s, and was informed I needed to show identification to enter the park. I needed a pass, and I didn't have a pass.

Shortly after that happened, my friends from Windsor, Ontario— photographer George Brooks and Arsene and Bonnie Bondy, were at my house to help me put in a flower garden. We were planting impatiens. I'd met Arsene and Bonnie at Eastern Market, and their family owns a farm in Essex County, Ontario. All of us became the best of friends, and maybe they figured that my spirits needed a boost because they wouldn't accept my contention that my days in baseball were over.

As we were spading up the earth, George planted a seed of hope in my mind. "There's still more good you can bring to the sport of baseball," he told me. "Too many people around here feel like we do about you."

Apparently, Tigers owner Mike Ilitch was among them. And he believed that I needed to be more involved with the Tigers family.

Behind the scenes, many people, including Detroit mayor Dennis Archer and deputy mayor Freman Hendrix, had been lobbying for the Tigers to retire my No. 23. My good friend Dr. Turner had also been pushing in the background, along with City Council member Brenda Scott and council president Maryann Mahaffey. Mr. Ilitch apparently had also decided that it should be done. But not only would they retire my jersey, that honor would also come with a statue in the outfield, which would stand alongside those of Al Kaline, Ty Cobb, Charlie Gehringer, Hank Greenberg, and Hal Newhouser in Comerica Park. Each statue rests atop a granite pedestal and reaches a total height of 13 feet.

When Tigers president John McHale called to tell me the news, I was driving home from Tennessee, on I-75 near Louisville, Kentucky. I had to pull over because I was shaking so bad. Tears filled my eyes, and I started to remember walking down those railroad tracks in Virginia and meeting Larry Munsey. That was about 50 years ago, and can't help but wonder whether I'd be where I am today if I hadn't taken that walk.

Anyone who thinks he can get to the top without help is simply a fool. My list is long. My father. Judge Keith. Ron Thompson. Sam Bishop. Charlie Dressen. I could list a thousand names, and still only be halfway done.

My jersey-retirement ceremony was held at Comerica Park on July 15, 2000, and I needed 400 tickets for all my friends and family. Just as George Brooks had predicted, my baseball career was far from over. Mr. Ilitch brought me into his office several months later and asked me to become a member of a special committee to help turn around the Tigers. Al Kaline was also on the committee, and he told me to see if I liked the job. If I did, I could work full-time.

A year later, I returned to Mr. Ilitch's office, telling him I wanted to do more for the Tigers. I wanted a permanent place in the organization. It was difficult to say goodbye to Bob Milano and Ort, but baseball is my love, and the Tigers are my family.

I think Mr. Ilitch understood that the city is in my soul because he's a native Detroiter himself. He went to Cooley High School and was offered $5,000 to play for the Tigers in 1948, but he turned them down to join the military. He has never been given enough credit for his commitment to Detroit. He could've built Comerica Park in the suburbs. He didn't have to put as much money into the city as he has. But Detroit is also tattooed on his heart, just like it is on mine.

The last five years have almost been as much fun as my playing days. I love being around the guys in the Detroit organization. Craig Monroe reminds me of myself. He's a strong, powerful man with the potential to be an impact player. It's not too late for him. Rondell White has that Al Kaline-style of class. I still can't break him of the habit of calling me "Mr. Horton." And Dmitri Young is like Norm Cash was on our team. He just loves being at the ballpark and having a good time. Cash was a great player who always brought something to the table.

It's been my great fortune to be around bullpen coach Lance Parrish, a quiet man who's never received enough credit for his playing career. He played 19 seasons in the major league and much of his career was spent as one of the A.L.'s best catchers. He was an eight-time All-Star and a three-time Gold Glove winner. To me, he's a Hall of Famer.

I remember sitting on the interview committee when we hired Alan Trammell as manager. After we interviewed him and Bruce Fields, I was ready to hire either one of them. The funny part of that process was that both men essentially had the same coaches picked out in their minds. If Trammell got the job, he wanted Fields. And if Fields got the job, he wanted Trammell. When you have that level of togetherness, you know it's a winning formula.

Bruce has been with this organization for more than 30 years, and I don't think I've met a more knowledgeable baseball man. I'm just worried that some other team is going to poach Bruce away from us. He's going to be a big-league manager someday.

Seeing Trammell and Lou Whitaker as often as I do, I'm reminded that it's simply an injustice that these two aren't in the Hall of Fame. The Hall is about career recognition, and these two were among the best at their positions for many, many years. The fact that they played so well together defensively should strengthen their Hall of Fame candidacy.

In my opinion, there are a couple of other former Tigers who should be in the Hall of Fame. My former teammate Mickey Lolich should be inducted. I've been in the game, or I have watched the game, for more than 45 years, and Mickey is clearly one of the most dominant left-handers I've ever seen.

And former Tigers great Jack Morris has to get into the Hall of Fame. His postseason pitching record speaks for itself.

Speaking of Hall of Famers, I can't say enough about broadcaster Ernie Harwell. Although he didn't play the game, he was as important to me as any player in the clubhouse. During spring training, I would go to his house almost every Sunday for dinner. I would call his wife "Mother Lulu." He's a special man, and he always gives you something to think about when you leave him.

Willie humbly speaks at his Northwestern High
School field dedication.

2004 Northwestern Field dedication with sister
Ruth and family looking on.

Family and friends at Horton home reception.

DETROIT TIGERS FIELDS OF CHAMPIONS

# WILLIE HORTON
## Baseball and Softball Diamonds

**NORTHWESTERN HIGH SCHOOL**
Dedicated August 6, 2004

...rd Mack, Willie, Reggie Chapman, Walt Terrell, and Mavis Chapman.

1968 teammate and friend Earl Wilson.

Willie's friend Mike Relph.

Gloria and Willie share the moment with Dr. Kenneth Burnley.

Willie and Charlie Primas.

Willie shares a laugh with great friend and former teammate Jim Price.

Willie and Tigers team physician Dr. Michael G. Workings.

Denise, Bonnie, and Gloria.

Tigers Vice President of Public Affairs Elaine Lewis speaks at the Northwestern High School field dedication in 2004.

Standing from left, Tigers executive Cliff Russell,
Detroit City Councilman Ken Cockrel Jr., and Tigers
Community Affairs Coordinator Corey Bell share
Willie's Historian Award in November 2004.

Gloria and Willie have deep respect and admiration for Tigers GM
Dave Dombrowski, right. He is a genuine friend and a terrific leader.

Willie's nephews from Tennessee, Sherman, left, and Richard, right.

Mr. Teasley and Willie.

Our Detroit magazine's Dave Mesrey pays tribute on Willie Horton Day.

Niece Lisa Wright presents Willie with an award at the October 2004 reception.

Willie with his father-in-law, Sam Reid. *(Courtesy of Brooks Photo)*

The Unsung Heroes of Sport.

Immortal Investments publisher Michael Reddy,
left, and Willie's agent, Mark Dehem, show off
one of Willie's many awards.

Close friend and attorney Ron Seigel, and Willie, in October 2004.

People also forget that Ray Lane was doing radio when the Tigers won the pennant in 1968. My son Darryl William's first plane trip came when he was four years old, and Ray volunteered to bring him to Lakeland for me.

When my number was retired, it occurred to me that two other Tigers have worn No. 23 as proudly as I did—Kirk Gibson and Steve Kemp. I'm proud that my number was associated with these two men because they both played the game with passion.

Since re-joining the organization as an assistant to Dave Dombrowski, I see we're heading in the right direction. Mr. Ilitch intends to build a winner, and he showed his commitment by signing expensive free agents Ivan "Pudge" Rodriguez and Magglio Ordoñez.

Also, since my return, I've enjoyed being with the Tigers. I've enjoyed working with Jimmy Devellano, who serves as one of Mr. Ilitch's right-hand men for his baseball and hockey teams. I don't think I've ever met anyone who understands the business side of sports like Jimmy does.

Pudge made such an impact on this team in 2004. He talks like a winner and performs like a winner, and his confidence is infectious. When the season was over in 2004, he told everyone, "I'm not used to going home this early. Next year, we're going to be playing in October."

It gave me goose bumps because that's how my teammates and I talked in 1967, the autumn before we won the World Series against the St. Louis Cardinals.

Another friend who has influenced my life significantly in recent years is my agent, Mark Dehem. Given how my previous agent negatively affected my life, it's a real joy now to have an agent who's like a member of the family.

Many years ago, a fellow named Cliff Cooke had asked me why I didn't sign autographs at trading-card shows. "I don't believe in charging for my autograph," I told him. But Cliff said I should be doing those shows because my fans wanted to see me, and he figured out how to structure deals so that fans wouldn't have to pay.

When Cliff died, I assumed my signing days were over. But Mark Dehem said, "Willie, let me take care of you."

And he's done just that. I have trouble saying "no," and Mark has made sure I'm sheltered from having to deal with those situations. He's also taken the load off my wife, Gloria. And frankly, he's been by my side during some tragedies in my life.

Happiness surrounds my life these days, but it's not only because of my return to baseball. I've always been a spiritual person; my parents raised me in a Baptist household, and God has always influenced my life. I have to admit that I strayed from his word at times during my career, but I knew his presence, even if I wasn't a regular at Sunday services.

Gloria had accepted Jesus Christ into her heart a young age, and she would ask me occasionally, "Willie, do you believe in a higher power?"

Of course I did, but it wasn't a discussion I was prepared to have.

But I believe God has a plan for us all, and He guided me to places where I watched my children, one by one, accept Him into their hearts. I knew I was being drawn to Him, too. The signs were all around me.

My three sons, Darryl William, Deryl Lamar, and Al, jointly owned a record label and management company with M.C. Hammer for a while. It was called Bust It, and they lived a lifestyle that involved the rich and famous. But eventually, each of my sons decided that wasn't the kind of lifestyle they wanted to live.

Deryl Lamar became close friends with NFL star Deion Sanders along the way, and in fact, Deryl introduced Deion to his future wife. Deryl also fondly remembers the day he and Deion had an important phone conversation.

"Deion, there's something I want to tell you," Deryl Lamar said.

"No, first there's something I have to tell you," Deion replied. "I've accepted Jesus Christ as my Lord and savior."

Deryl was stunned. "That's what I was going to tell you!"

That's a true story.

At different times, under different circumstances, all of my sons and daughters have been saved.

And what I found out later is that Deryl Lamar, now a deacon at New Light Baptist Church in Detroit, would pray with his mother that I would find my way to God.

God sent a messenger to help me find the right path. My family experienced a series of tragedies that left us mourning. My niece, Mar-Kecia, a student at Western Michigan University, was murdered in 1998. A woman ran her over with a car because she didn't like that my niece had paid attention to a young man. Mar-Kecia had lived with us in Seattle for a time, and it was like losing a daughter. It was a senseless death—almost impossible to discuss without being overwhelmed by the horror of it.

Just three days after Mar-Kecia was killed, my brother Robert, who would call Gloria every day to say hello, strangely didn't call. We were concerned, so Deryl and I went to Robert's house. I held Robert and cried, but we were too late. He had passed away.

On December 8, 2000, my nephew David Griffin died. Gloria's mother, Thelma, also died that year. She was very, very close to us. Each death took a toll on me. Then on December 20, 2001, my brother Ray passed away in Tennessee. Five days later, we were all on the highway on Christmas Day, heading to his funeral. In 2002, we lost our 19-year-old nephew Kenyon. Each death brought us so much pain. But Deryl says the pain was taking me where I needed to be.

In 2003, another nephew named Raymond Tyner—we called him Mr. T—was suffering from cancer, and I had called to see how he was doing. In the midst of that conversation, I mentioned some minor aches and pains I was having.

Mr. T cut me off. "I respect you greatly, Willie, but there's no need for you to complain," he said. "The only thing you should be worried about is your soul."

I tried to talk to him about how he was feeling, and he told me not to worry about him. "You should be worrying about your soul," he said.

His words hit me like a fastball to the ribs.

Mr. T was a spiritual man, and his cancer was in remission. That's why I was stunned a couple of days later when I got a call that he had died of a heart attack.

At his funeral in Dayton, Ohio, I told the congregation what Mr. T had told me two days before he died. I told him he was at peace with his God.

But God's message overwhelmed me eighteen days later when our nephew Durand Ferris was gunned down at a gas station in a case of mistaken identity.

At his funeral at New Light Baptist Church, I could feel God in my heart, and I remember what Reverend Dr. Benjamin Stanley Baker said that day: "Anyone who believes in their heart and wants to confess with their mouth that the Lord Jesus Chris is the Savior should please come forward."

At that moment, I rose from the pew and marched to the front of the church.

Reverend Baker asked if I had words to say. "It's time," I said. "The Lord has always put his hands on me, and has been right there for me. I do believe in my heart, and I am confessing with my mouth. He has always held my hand and now it's time for me to hold His."

Deryl Lamar says that Gloria cried when I went to the front of the church. My daughter Pam was actually in charge of taking down the names of new members, and she hadn't looked up to see it was me who had come down the aisle. Reverend Baker said to her, "You have someone else to sign up."

When she turned and realized I was a new church member, you could feel the joy in her heart.

Deryl Lamar's son, Deryl Jr., also accepted Christ that day. And when Darryl William was told of my acceptance of the Lord, he broke down over the phone.

Despite the tragedies that my family endured in the last five years, I've found a peace in my life. I'm closer to my team, closer to my family, and closer to my God. My life seems complete.

# Chapter 15

## THE HOTEL HORTON

MY PARENTS' FIRST HOME IN DETROIT had one bedroom, a sitting room, a kitchen, and a shared bathroom. But there always seemed to be plenty of room for friends and family.

These days, we hold family reunions once a year. But back then it seemed as if we had family reunions every weekend. All of Lillian Horton's children came to see her often, and no one ever considered paying for a hotel room. Family sometimes would visit from down south, and some would bunk at my sister Faye's home, or over at my sister Virginia's. When I was young, my cousins were so involved in my life that they seemed like brothers and sisters to me. And my mother was always bringing home someone for supper. Even if you didn't have much, my mother believed that you did what you could for those who had less than you.

When I close my eyes, I can still see Papa looking out the window, shaking his head and laughing. "Who's Sis bringing home for supper tonight," he would say.

It was chicken or fish every Friday night, bologna and crackers on Saturday, and a special meal on Sunday.

Family was important to my mother and father, and that belief rubbed off on their youngest child. When I think about my baseball career and my life, the family atmosphere has always been a central theme.

The Detroit Tigers became like a second family to me, and Jim Campbell was like a second father to me when my own dad passed away. When I think about my first few years in organized baseball, black ballplayers like Billy Bruton, Sam Jones, Gates Brown, Jake Wood, and others made me feel like I'd joined another family. In the early 1960s, it still was a struggle for blacks to make it to the major leagues. But you knew you weren't in it alone. Black players looked after one another. They helped each other make the climb to the top.

Down in Lakeland, Florida, Charles and Madeline Brooks made black ballplayers had a place to live when no hotels would accept them. Madeline worked for the NAACP, and the Brookses didn't just talk the talk. They walked the walk.

And when I barbecued every spring for players and fans down in spring training, it was undoubtedly inspired by my need to feel surrounded by "family."

My former Tigers teammates remain close to me to this day. Some have passed on, including a few who died far too young. Joe Sparma, Norm Cash, and Ray Oyler all died very young. Sadly, we've also lost Earl Wilson, Eddie Mathews, Don McMahon, and John Wyatt. I keep in touch with many others, including Jon Warden, who appears these days on the ESPN2 TV show *Cold Pizza*. Jon and I talk regularly, and when I had health problems one winter in Florida, he stepped up to help me. I'll never forget his kindness.

In addition his work in the Tigers radio broadcast booth, Jim Price still operates the team fantasy camps. I always suspected he'd make a name for himself. Al Kaline and I work together now with the Tigers, and we remain close. And the Gator and I still talk several times a week. So when the 1968 Tigers gather for a reunion, it always feels like family.

I'm proud of my own family, and I thank my wife, Gloria, for how my children turned out. George Brooks calls her "the matriarch" of our family. My daughter Pam says Gloria's "The Rock" of the family. Gloria really is the backbone of our family.

Although, both of us had children before we were married to each other, we decided that we weren't going to use the word "stepchild." All of my children are Hortons. And we raised them and loved them like they were Hortons. Gloria was the perfect person to raise this family. And I never worried when I was on the road because Gloria was always in control.

Gloria was my perfect match because she could both support me and guide me at the same time. Late in my career, when I had doubts about whether I should still be playing, she would tell me, "Willie, you can still play—and you love to play, so you keep on playing."

She's always been a strong woman, and she wasn't afraid to tell me when I was about to make a mistake. "Willie," she would say, "when you're wrong, you're wrong. And you are wrong here."

Remember, she had managed Club 23, and she had good business sense. I really needed to listen to her more than I did. Sometimes, people would ask me to get involved in financial deals, and she would say, "Willie, not all of these people are your friends."

Her patience with me was almost unbelievable. When people would come up and ask me for an autograph at an inopportune moment, she could've said, "Willie, this isn't the right time." She could've made it an issue out of it. I saw other baseball wives do that. But Gloria understood that I wanted to treat the fans like kin. So she let me be me, and I'm thankful for that.

When I traveled with the team, she always kept me informed about what was happening with our children. They were always surprised that I already would know the scores of their games when they called me. But Gloria always tried to keep me involved in the parenting process, even if I wasn't home. She kept me informed, although now my daughters joke that one of Gloria's talents was making me feel like I had some input, even when the decision had already been made.

"Go ahead and do it, but don't tell your father," she would say to the kids. "Let me talk to him." We all laugh about that now because it's the kind of maneuvering that has to be done when you have a father who's traveling more than 100 days a year.

People probably believe that it was me who got my children involved in sports. But during my career, Gloria was more involved with the kids' athletics—and she was well-qualified. She also went to Northwestern High School in Detroit, where she played basketball and field hockey. She also worked with a teacher named Miss Nelson to try to convince school board officials to launch a girls track program at Northwestern. It wasn't started in time for Gloria to join, and it's too bad because she probably would have been an outstanding track athlete.

Even today, she knows more about basketball than I do. When we were living in Seattle, she worked at the Sheraton Hotel, managing a restaurant. She convinced the hotel to sponsor a men's recreation basketball team, and she coached the team to the championship. The trophy is still on display in the hotel. She was extremely serious about the team, calling our sons occasionally for advice because they also knew the game. When the boys were young, Gloria was often in the driveway playing hoops with them.

The funny aspect about my relationship with my wife is that she wasn't even sure she even liked me when we were teenagers. We both attended Northwestern High School, and we knew each other well, even though we didn't date. She wrote for the school newspaper. Her brother Sam Reid and I were good friends, and he used to get in trouble at home for coming home late. Gloria used to blame me for that.

Years later when I invited her to go to a party with me, she said she wasn't even sure she wanted anything to do with me. More than three decades later, we're blessed with nineteen grandchildren.

My father's parenting style was firm and confrontational. My mother's style was soft and caring. Hopefully, my children see my style as a combination of the two. I wanted to be softer with my children than my dad was with me, but I felt I had to give them some tough-love lessons. You have to push your children to be the best they can be.

Deryl Lamar has thanked me for the tough-love approach I took with him after he was diagnosed with scoliosis. He had a curved spine, and doctors recommended risky surgery to insert a metal rod to straighten it. Deryl was a second baseman with pro potential, and doctors told us that he would likely not be an athlete after the operation. They told us that it would be a year before he would even be able to walk again.

"Don't you worry about that," I told the doctors, already believing in my mind that we were going to get Deryl moving long before that.

Just a teenager at the time, Deryl wasn't even sure he wanted to endure that level of rehabilitation. But he also didn't want to endure the pain of scoliosis.

"Son," I told him, "you have to take chances in life. You have to have the surgery. You have to believe that it's going to work out."

Doctors warned us that "it was a 50-50 proposition," and if there were any complications with the surgery, the damage could be severe. They were already concerned about his flexibility. They really did effectively rule out his hopes for pro baseball.

"Son, don't let another man tell you what you can or can't do," I told Deryl. "If you work hard, anything can happen."

My father had said those same words to me many years before.

After the surgery, he was in a full body cast. We would go into his room and lift him three times a day. After a few months, his spirits were down, but Gloria and I weren't having any of that. We told him it was time to get up out of bed and rejoin life. We bought him a weight bench and an exercise bike, and I worked out with him.

In just five months, he was walking again. And after nine months, Deryl could dunk a basketball.

His rehabilitation went so well that he actually went to an Oakland A's tryout camp in Medford, Oregon, a year later. He ran well and looked terrific, but his bat speed wasn't where it needed to be. He survived the first cut, but didn't get through the second.

I thought I'd need to console Deryl, but he told me he'd be fine.

"This wasn't about baseball," Deryl said. "This was about the commitment you had in me. It was about what we accomplished when people told us we couldn't do it."

Today, Deryl Lamar is president of Willie Horton, Inc.

When my boys went off to school, my only request was that they continue to communicate with one another and remain close. They all promised they would, and they've lived up to that promise. Darryl William is a regional manager for (Polo) Ralph Lauren and lives just outside Atlanta. Al lives in Las Vegas. Even though they no longer work together, they remain very close.

Darryl William had tremendous talent, and maybe he could've been a major-league outfielder. I remember when he was in the minors in the New York Yankees chain, Bucky Dent would call and ask me to speak to Darryl about working harder. Darryl was invited to the Detroit Tigers' spring training camp once, and he also spent a couple of seasons in the Chicago White Sox farm system.

He was a terrific all-around athlete at St. Benedictine High School in Detroit. He was 6-foot-2, over 200 pounds, and had a 38-inch vertical jump, which also came in handy on the basketball court. He averaged 27.5 points per game as a junior at St. Benedictine, which made him one of the top 10 scorers in the state. He averaged 24 or 25 points a game as a senior and finished with more than 1,500 career points at St. Benedictine. He played one season at Navajo Junior College in Arizona, but was injured during there. He also ended up playing one season of football at Saginaw Valley State University.

Al is 6-foot-4 and he had a strong basketball career at Redford High School. For years, he held the school record of 38 points in a game before it finally fell a few years ago. When he played there, my daughter Gail was the team's mascot. Al later played at El Camino

Junior College and then Drake, but his college career was undermined by two knee surgeries. He ended up in the military, before settling into the entertainment business.

My daughter April lives in Florida, and my other three daughters have settled in Michigan. Terri, who went to Oregon State, works for the Detroit Board of Education. In college, she was an exchange student in Paris. Pamela attended Clark Atlanta University and now works in public relations in metro Detroit. Gail is back in school. My wife says Gail is a lot like me—tough and stern in her approach. When she played soccer back in Seattle, they called her "Thunderfoot" because she could kick with authority. Gloria coached Gail in softball, and she once walked into someone swinging a bat. Gail's face was swelling dramatically, but she wouldn't let Gloria take her out of the game. She was a tough athlete.

One funny story about Pam is that—believe it or not—she married a man named Darryl. So when you count our two grandsons, we now have five men named Darryl or Deryl in our immediate family. I joke that it's like boxer George Foreman naming all of his boys "George."

Today, Gloria and I are raising our 14-year-old grandson Dominique, and that again reminds me of my life growing up in the projects. My mother helped raise her grandkids like they were her own children. As I've said before, my nephews seemed more like siblings to me. And in the Horton family, everyone helps raise the children.

The older members of the family talked about that recently when my nephew Michael passed away. Michael, of course, was one of the youngsters in the car in 1965 when my parents were killed in that car crash. Joe, the other youngster in the car, he died years ago.

Of the five Horton family members in that car on New Year's Day 40 years ago, only my brother Billy is still alive—and he is reclusive. We believe he's having flashbacks about the accident. He is retired, but doesn't socialize much any more.

At Michael's funeral, I told the congregation: "Michael was a nephew, but he was raised like he was my brother, and I disciplined him like he was my son. And in the end, he was my friend."

173

At the funeral, I told Michael's mother, Faye, that she had been like a mother to me back in the days when I spent nights with her in the projects. I would eat at Mama and Papa's house, but I would sleep at her place in the projects. Really, all of my brothers and sisters were like parents to me. Even my late brothers-in-law, George and Ken, were also parental figures to me. George was married to Helen, and Ken was married to Frankie.

In the Horton family, my brothers and sisters always did what they could to help. My brother Joe went into the service to help the family, and I always believe that Billy's decision to go into the service helped me get through school because he was helping support the family.

Today, I draw my strength from my family, and it gives me great pleasure to talk to them all the time. It's not hard to believe that all of my daughters have taught me—and maybe even humbled me—many times. One of the turning points of my life came when my daughter Pam, then 13, confronted me about all the days I'd spent away from home as a baseball player. At the time, I was playing for the Portland Beavers, the Triple-A affiliate of the Pittsburgh Pirates. Pam and I were driving to the store one day when she got very upset with me.

"You don't even know me!" she said.

"What are you talking about?" I said. "I know you very well."

I initially thought that this was just a teenage rebellion issue, but I knew I had to be careful here. But that wasn't it at all. She was just trying to tell me that I needed to think more about spending time with my family. And I decided she was right. Maybe I had taken my family for granted.

Branch Rickey III headed up the Pirates organization then, and I got his permission to take Pam on the next road trip, which included stops in Arizona and New Mexico. Just to show how baseball is one big family, I should explain that Branch Rickey III is the grandson of Branch Rickey, who, in 1945, signed Jackie Robinson to his first pro contract with the Brooklyn Dodgers.

My trip with Pam was a memorable event, and it included one funny episode that's become a staple of Horton family storytelling.

Having just been paid, I stopped at a store in Arizona to make a quick purchase. I asked Pam to wait in the car. I removed the money I needed from my wallet and threw the wallet back into the car and told Pam to hold onto it.

Being young, Pam became impatient and eventually came into the store to find me. "Where's my wallet?" I asked.

The mortified look on her face told me she had left it in the car.

The problem was that it was a very hot day, the windows were down, and someone walking by the car had larceny in their heart that day. When we got back to the car, the wallet was gone. Pam started crying, figuring her dad would erupt like a volcano.

"It's only money," I said. "Nothing bad happened here. We can always get more money."

Pam has often told that story, and maybe it'll be passed down through the generations. Maybe all of our descendants will embrace that philosophy that there should never be heartache over money.

While I might have some good parenting stories here, I would never suggest that my retirement from baseball went smoothly.

As I sorted through the emotional issues of leaving the game, there were some difficult times in my home. I'd been a professional ballplayer for almost two decades, and I really didn't know who I was outside the lines. When it became clear that the end was near, I started to think that I was letting my family down. Who knows, maybe deep down, I believed I was letting my father down, too. I felt as if I could still play, so why couldn't I catch on with another team?

Even hitting 29 home runs for the Mariners in 1979 couldn't save me from the hardship of saying goodbye to a sport that was so intertwined with my life that it was hard to know who was beneath all those statistics.

Today, I'm told that I'm a national hero in Venezuela for winning the Caribbean World Series in 1979. There's even a bust of me at the stadium in Valencia. But when I returned to the city to manage and play in 1980, it didn't go as well. We had different players, and more importantly, there was a different attitude in management.

When we struggled for a few games, I was called into the office. They told me that either I was going, or we were going to change some players. I said I wasn't going, and so I was fired.

Players were upset. Gloria was crying, and I was agitated. Then Deryl Lamar overheard the team's traveling secretary bad-mouthing me to the media. Deryl's temper got the best of him, and he attacked the secretary. I had to pull him off. I knew there would be trouble after that—and there was.

We wanted to leave Venezuela the next day, but there were suggestions that Deryl would be arrested unless money was paid. I don't know who received the money or why, but no one was arresting my son for standing up for his father. I paid what needed to be paid, and didn't ask any questions.

If I would've listened to Gloria more, I probably would've had more money when I retired. But much of my financial difficulty was caused by a former agent who led me to believe that my finances were in order— but they were not. Several other major-leaguers were victimized by his actions, and all of us ended up with back taxes owed to the Internal Revenue Service.

When I appeared before the judge, I accepted responsibility because it was my fault for not overseeing my own finances. In the end, it was Gloria who was able to get us square with the IRS.

My troubles were weighing heavy on mind when I retired, and I told my wife to take the girls and move back to Detroit while I sorted through the issues. Maybe I just needed to be alone. But I ended up spending much of my time with a friend named Jim Brown. He was an outdoorsman and a spiritual man, and he made realize that life was really just beginning for me.

"You don't have to be rich and play baseball to enjoy life," he said. "Your job now is just to raise your family."

He really just brought me back to my southern roots and made me to realize what was important in my life. Jim was a man who had suffered catastrophic injuries as a teenager when he was hit by a train, but he persevered to become a man of exceptional character. He believed strongly in the man upstairs. And when my No. 23 was retired in Detroit, he and his wife drove all the way across the country to be there.

Although I would soon get involved in coaching, I had to find some immediate work, and I ended up working on a maintenance crew at the *Seattle Post-Intelligencer*. When some of the executives saw me sweeping the floors, they offered me a job in the office. But I stayed where I was.

Deryl Lamar was working with me, and one night when I was scrubbing toilets, he told me, "Dad, you shouldn't have to do this kind of work."

"Son," I said, "my dad taught me long ago that what's important in life is that you do whatever you need to do to support your family. If you have to wash dishes, you wash dishes. If you have to sweep floors, you sweep floors. And that's what I'm going to do."

By taking that job, I actually felt better about who I was. And only then was I ready to move on to coaching.

At 63, I still have much I want to do in the world of baseball. It's hard to describe how good it makes me feel when the young players ask me for advice and talk to me about their game.

I still want to do more with the children, which is why I still work with the Boys and Girls Club in Lakeland and Mulberry, Florida, and in the Tigers' operation in Lakeland. One of my other goals is to help resurrect baseball in the city of Detroit. Inner-city baseball seems to be dying all over the United States, and it's a shame because there are more Willie Hortons in the projects waiting for an opportunity.

To me, there's a three-fold problem that needs to be addressed. First, we need to place more emphasis on developing neighborhood leagues. People spend too much emphasis on travel baseball. That's fine, but it's the local leagues where the process starts. Second, we must offer more training for coaches. There are men and women out there willing to coach, but they need to be taught how to coach effectively. Finally, we have to restore the hunger in the African-American players. Today, Latin American players have that hunger. They see baseball as their ticket to a better life, and they work hard at becoming better players.

Better fields will also help. We played on quality fields when I was a youngster. That's why I was very proud that Northwestern High School honored me, dedicating new softball and baseball fields in 2004. They were paid for by a $127,000 grant from the Baseball Tomorrow Fund.

I had trouble finding the right words at the ceremony, but this is what I said: "It's about people—my whole life is about people, my whole career was about the fans. The city, the park, and the school—we and this family and our community have to become a partnership for all this to work."

BTF executive director Cathy Bradley attended the dedication ceremony, along with my Tigers buddies Tigers Dmitri Young and Rondell White, Tigers general manager Dave Dombrowski, Major League Baseball's Vice President of Community Affairs Tom Brasuell, and Tigers Vice President of Public Affairs and Strategic Planning Elaine Lewis.

There's a sense of contentment in my life these days. I call Deryl Lamar every day, and when I ask him, "What's the word today?" he knows I'm not making small talk. I want to know his take on the Scriptures.

People write new chapters in their lives every day, and I'm writing some beautiful chapters these days. I was in an automobile accident in 2003 and ended up with a hip replacement. But honestly, that just seems like a minor inconvenience. I like where my life is at, and I'm surprised every day about where it takes me.

In 2004, Gloria and I attended Major League Baseball's All-Star game in Houston, and while we were there, Dave Winfield's wife spent an hour telling me how much I meant to her husband. He actually thought I was in the Hall of Fame. I can't tell you how touched I was by that.

Likewise, I was surprised when Deryl Lamar told me that famed boxing promoter Emanuel Steward once told him that my boxing ability was exceptional enough that I could've challenged for the heavyweight championship of the world, had I pursued it.

"Your dad was Mike Tyson before there was Mike Tyson," Steward told Deryl. "He was called, 'One Punch Willie' because he would knock out grown men when he was 15 years old."

Most days, I'm on the phone at least once with my sister Ruth, and she's the most amazing woman you'll ever meet. She's lost two husbands, children, and endured cancer. But she's the most positive woman I've ever met in my life.

One of my hobbies is watching vintage black-and-white Western movies, particularly the old Roy Rogers classics. Apparently the love of those films runs in my family.

One time, my friend Arsene Bondy traveled down south with me. While we were at a hotel in Tennessee, I found one of those movies on TV and settled into watching it. We left the hotel in the middle of the movie to visit my brother Ray and his wife Pinkie. When we got to their house, Ray was watching the same movie.

Arsene started laughing, but he was really amused when Ray and I started to watch it together.

When Ray said, "Hey, Willie, look! He's behind the bush—he's going to get 'em," I thought Arsene was going to die laughing.

I'm also more open in my old age, maybe because I don't get to the phone fast enough. Every year, someone has invited me to go on some cruise, but Gloria beat me to the phone and agreed to join the Stan Bahnsen cruise. "You turned down every one of those, but we're going on this one," she said.

The truth is I had a very good time, and we might go again.

However, what I spend most of my time on these days is my family. We decided in 2003 that we would all meet for Thanksgiving at Darryl William's beautiful new home in Jonesboro, Georgia. I was trying to figure out what hotels we were all going to stay at when one of my kids said to me, "Dad, we won't need any hotels. We're all staying at Darryl William's house."

All seven of my children and their families spread out on air mattresses and sleeping bags all over the house, and everyone was together for the holiday. It was just like being at my parents' house fifty years ago. It didn't seem like it was overcrowded either. It just reminded my wife of what her mother's house was like when everyone came to visit her just before she died. Nobody went to a hotel. "You couldn't walk without stepping on someone," Gloria says.

Before Thanksgiving dinner, we decided that everyone at the table was going to be able to say why they were thankful on that fine day. And we vowed that we would gather together every year at Thanksgiving.

My father didn't often hold conversations with me. He didn't much care about my opinion. But I remember having a couple of discussions with Papa after I worked out at a park across the street from the family home on Edison. I would run laps around the park, and when I stopped for a breather, I'd sit on the bench next to Papa. That's when he used to tell me stories about all of his children.

"They're all my kids, and I claim them all," he told me. "But there are probably only four or five of them I would sign my name for."

I've always wondered whether I was one of those four or five.

Papa never told me he was proud of me. That wasn't his way. But I always believed that he was proud of me as a baseball player, and I like to believe if he saw my kids sleeping all over Darryl William's house, he would've been proud of how Gloria and I raised our children. I've signed for all seven of my kids, and it made me feel good to be able to do that. Today, we're raising our grandson Dominique. He's 14 years old and has been with us since birth.

It just goes to show that for the Hortons, it's family that matters most.

# ◈◈ Willie Horton Timeline ◈◈

- **October 18, 1942**: Willie Wattison Horton, the 21st child of Lillian and Clinton Horton, is born in Arno, Virginia, where his father works in the coal mine.

- **June 9, 1959**: As a sophomore at Northwestern High School, Willie hits an opposite-field home run that travels more than 450 feet and lands on the roof, striking the light standard in right-center field. The mammoth home run during the Public School League Championship game against Cass Tech is considered one of the greatest sports accomplishments in state high school history.

- **August 7, 1961**: With several teams bidding for his services, Willie signs with his hometown Detroit Tigers. Horton's cash bonus is more than $50,000 and may have been as much as $70,000. The Tigers also buy a house for the Horton family on Edison Street.

- **September 10, 1963**: At D.C. Stadium in Washington, Horton is inserted as a pinch-hitter for Hank Aguirre in the fourth inning and singles to center in his first major league at-bat against pitcher Jim Hannan.

- **September 14, 1963**: In his second major league at-bat, and his first at Tiger Stadium, Horton launches a pinch-hit, eighth-inning, two-run homer off future Hall of Famer Robin Roberts to send the game into extra innings. The Tigers eventually win the game, 3–2, on a Gus Triandos home run in the tenth.

- **January 1, 1965**: A traffic accident on I-94, east of Battle Creek, Michigan, claims the lives of Willie's parents, Clinton and Lillian Horton. Clinton, 67, dies instantly, and Lillian dies a day later in Albion Hospital. Willie's brother Billy is also injured severely in the crash, but recovers. Two nephews also survive the crash. Willie is playing winter ball in Puerto Rico at the time of the crash. Although he immediately heads home, inclement weather prevents Willie from reaching Albion before his mother dies.

- **May 11-18, 1965**: Willie goes on a hitting rampage on a road trip to Washington and Boston. Over an eight-game period, Willie has seven multiple hit games. In that span, he hits six home runs and drives in 18 runs. He hits .615 (20-for-32) in that span. In back-to-back games at Fenway Park, he hits two home runs and drives in five runs in each game.

- **July 13, 1965**: At Minnesota, Horton, 22, makes his Major All-Star debut as the starting left fielder for the American League in a 6–5 loss to the National League. Willie is 0-for-3 with a walk in the game. It's the first of four All-Star appearances. He makes two putouts in the game.

- **October 3, 1965**: In the third inning of a game against the Washington Senators, Willie moves from left field to third base. It's the only time he will play there in his career. The first ball he faces is a grounder by Frank Howard and Willie makes the play to retire Howard. He finishes with two assists and no errors.

- **May 14–21, 1967**: In a week's span, Willie clouts seven home runs, including three in a four-game series against the New York Yankees.

- **October 1, 1967**: Willie's Tigers lose the pennant on the final day of the season, falling 8–5 to the California Angels. After the loss, Detroit players vow that they'll be ready to win in 1968. Two days later, Horton has surgery to repair a tear in his Achilles tendon, which had been bothering him all season. He played the entire season with a small, soft cast on his foot.

- **July 7, 1968**: Willie hits a three-run homer to help Detroit sweep the Oakland A's in a doubleheader. The Tigers take a nine-and-a-half-game lead into the All-Star break.

- **September 17, 1968**: Don Wert singles in Al Kaline for the winning run as the Detroit Tigers defeat the New York Yankees 2-1 to clinch the American League pennant and give Willie his first opportunity for World Series competition. It's Detroit's first trip to the Fall Classic since 1945.

- **September 3–29, 1968**: Willie hits safely in 14 of the final 15 games to finish fourth in the American League batting race with a .285 average. Boston's Carl Yastrzemski wins the AL with a .301 average, and he's the only .300 hitter in the AL that season. Willie's 36 home runs rank second to Washington's Frank Howard, who wins the title with 44.

- **October 7, 1968**. Tiger Stadium. Trailing three games to one and teetering on the brink of elimination, the Tigers rally to beat the St. Louis Cardinals in the pivotal Game 5 of the World Series. The turning point comes in the fifth inning, with Detroit trailing 3–2. With Lou Brock on second base, Cardinals second baseman

Julian Javier lines a single to left. As Brock dashes for home, Willie fields the ball on one hop and comes up throwing. Brock hasn't slid into home plate all season, and this time's no different. He comes in standing up. Willie's throw is right on the money, and by less than an inch, Brock is out. The Tigers rally to win, 5–3, and as everyone knows, they take the Series in seven.

- **May 15, 1969**: Willie leaves the Detroit bench during a 2–1 win against Chicago and goes AWOL for four days. Three days later, he meets with general manager Jim Campbell and owner John Fetzer to explain his disappointment that the Tigers haven't brought more black players to the team.

- **June 21, 1969**: Willie Horton hits two homers, one a grand slam, and drives in six runs to power the Tigers to a 9–5 win over the visiting Senators. Mickey Lolich is on the mound to raise his record to 8–1.

- **July 18, 1969**: Willie makes 11 putouts, tying the 69-year-old major league record of putouts by a left fielder. The mark was originally established by Dick Harley in 1898, and tied by Topsy Harley in 1901 and again by Paul Lehner in 1950.

- **September 13, 1969**: Willie hits his third grand slam of the season, but the Senators win 11–6 to eliminate the Tigers from postseason consideration. Willie believes the Tigers should have won in both 1967 and 1969.

- **June 9, 1970**: Willie clubs three home runs, including a grand slam, knocking in seven runs in an 8–3 win over Milwaukee.

- **June 1-30, 1970**: Willie hits .340 for the month, with 36 hits, including nine home runs and 26 RBIs.

- **July 14, 1970**: At Riverfront Stadium in Cincinnati, Horton collects two hits, walks once, and scores a run for the American League in a 5–4 loss to the NL in the All-Star game.

- **April 17, 1971**: At Detroit, Willie is 5-for-6 with a grand slam, a solo shot, and six RBIs. And the Tigers need it all, topping Boston in 10 innings, 10–9. With two outs and the bases loaded in the bottom of the tenth, Willie singles in the winning run.

- **August 27, 1971**: Willie is struck in the eye by a pitch from Chicago's Rich Hinton and sidelined for 28 games. Hinton, in his first major league start, leaves the game immediately after the errant toss. Although Willie tries to call Hinton to thank him for yelling a warning, they don't speak to each other for eight years, when they're teammates in Seattle. Willie tells Hinton that he might have saved Willie's career, or perhaps his life, by yelling that he lost control of the pitch.

- **August 27, 1972**: Willie delivers an eleventh inning, two-run homer to beat Minnesota, 5–3, in the opener of a doubleheader.
- **April 19, 1973**: Al Kaline, 38, steals home on a double steal with Willie. The Tigers defeat Boston 11–7.
- **April 14, 1974**: In the eighth inning of Detroit's 1–0 triumph over Boston, Willie mortally wounds a pigeon with a foul pop-up directly over home plate at Fenway Park. The pigeon lands at the feet of catcher Bob Montgomery. On the next pitch, Willie singles to left.
- **October 5, 1975**: The Associated Press names Willie the American League's Designated Hitter of the Year. Orlando Cepeda and Tommy Davis had won the award the two previous seasons.
- **April 19–25, 1976**: After homering in three consecutive days and driving in ten runs, Willie is named American League Player of the Week. During that span, he also drove in at least one run in ten consecutive games.
- **April 12, 1977**: At manager Ralph Houk's urging, Detroit trades Willie, a popular 15-year Tigers veteran, to Texas for pitcher Steve Foucault, who had been the Rangers' top reliever the season before. Houk claims that Willie wouldn't accept a part-time role, but Willie maintains that Houk never even discussed his role. At the time, Horton was anticipating reduced playing time and looking forward to mentoring Steve Kemp.
- **May 5, 1977**: Playing his first game back at Tiger Stadium as a member of the Texas Rangers, Willie goes 4-for-6 with a double and two runs in a 13–0 Rangers victory.
- **February 28, 1978**: The Rangers trade Willie, along with David Clyde, to the Cleveland Indians for Tom Buskey and John Lowenstein. Willie wears jersey No. 23 in Cleveland.
- **July 3, 1978**: The Indians release Willie.
- **July 13, 1978**: Willie signs as a free agent with the Oakland Athletics. Again, he wears No. 23.
- **August 15, 1978**: Willie is traded to the Toronto Blue Jays for designated hitter Rico Carty. The irony is that Willie had lobbied A's owner Charley Finley to trade for Carty because he felt the team had a chance to contend for the Western Division title. In

Toronto, Willie wears jersey No. 48, the same jersey he wore when he began his career with the Tigers.

- **November 4, 1978**: After playing for the Valencia Magallanes in the Venezuelan League, Willie is asked to replace Cookie Rojas as manager. He takes the club, which was in the midst of a 10-game losing streak, to a league championship and Caribbean World Series title. It's the country's first Caribbean World Series crown since 1970.
- **January 27, 1979**: Willie signs as a free agent with the Seattle Mariners. He wears No. 53. Originally, he accepts a tryout contract, and then in spring training accepts a rookie contract with incentives. He reaches all of those incentives by the All-Star break and ends up making six or seven times the money he made in his best season with Detroit.
- **May 2–18, 1979**: At age 37, Willie uncorks a 15-game hitting streak for the Mariners, going 23-for-58 with a .396 average. And right before this hot spell, Willie owned a nine-game streak. Overall, he hits safely in 24 of 25 games.
- **June 5, 1979**: In Seattle, Willie connects on what should have been his 300th home run, but his drive off Detroit left-hander John Hiller smashes into a speaker hanging from the left-center field roof of the Kingdome. Willie settles for a single. Coincidentally, Butch Hobson hit the same speaker on April 25, but managed a triple out of it.
- **June 6, 1979**: This time, Willie does deliver his 300th, off Tigers right-hander Jack Morris, in Seattle's 4–3 triumph. The next day, the Mariners hold Willie Horton Day at the Kingdome.
- **August 25, 1979**: Willie smacks two home runs off Dan Petry, including his ninth career grand slam, to give Seattle an 8–4 win over Detroit. It's the 30th time in his career he's delivered two home runs in a game. Willie also doubles and drives in five runs.
- **September 21, 1979**: With a two-run homer in the eighth inning, Willie becomes the first Mariner to drive in a hundred runs in a single season.
- **October 3, 1979**: The Sporting News names Willie their Comeback Player of the Year after he records career highs in runs (81), hits (180), RBIs (106), and at-bats (646). He is also named AL Designated Hitter of the Season for the second time.
- **August 1, 1980**: Willie and Gloria Horton are married by Reverend Cornell Talley at New Light Baptist Church in Detroit.

- **September 25, 1980**: Willie's last career home run is a ninth-inning blast off Danny Darwin that ties up a game and sends it into extra innings. The Mariners win 7-6 in 11 innings. In his final September as a major leaguer, Willie bats .286 with three homers and 10 RBIs in 10 games.
- **October 5, 1980**: Batting cleanup, Willie plays the last major league game of his career. In the fourth inning, he's hit by a pitch from Don Kainer. It's the 58th time in his career Willie's been hit by a pitch. His last career hit came two days before when he singled twice off Texas pitcher Doc Medich.
- **December 12, 1980**: Seattle trades Rick Honeycutt, Mario Mendoza, Larry Cox, Leon Roberts and Willie to the Texas Rangers for Richie Zisk, Rick Auerbach, Ken Clay, Jerry Don Gleaton, Brian Allard and Steve Finch. Willie was the player to be named later. At the time, only four trades in major league history had involved more players.
- **April 1, 1981**: Willie is shocked to be released by the Texas Rangers right before the start of the season. He had expected to be Texas' cleanup hitter, batting behind Al Oliver.
- **May 4, 1981**: Willie signs with the Portland Beavers, the AAA affiliate of the Pittsburgh Pirates. His teammates include Luis Tiant and Rusty Torres.
- **Spring training, 1985**: The Detroit Tigers sign Willie as a minor league hitting instructor. However, just before the start of the season, the New York Yankees ask permission to talk to Willie about becoming one of Billy Martin's coaches. Willie accepts the job with New York.
- **Spring Training, 1986**: Chicago White Sox general manager Ken Harrelson hires Willie as a coach. Willie works two years for the organization.
- **July 15, 2000**: The Tigers retire Willie Horton's No. 23. He joins Charlie Gehringer (No. 2), Hank Greenberg (No. 5), Al Kaline (No. 6), and Hal Newhouser (No. 16) as the only Tigers to have their numbers taken out of circulation. Every major league team has also retired No. 42 to honor Jackie Robinson's contributions as the first black player. A statue of Willie is also unveiled. He joins Gehringer, Greenberg, Kaline, Newhouser, and Ty Cobb as players who have statues dedicated to them at Comerica Park.
- **June 19, 2001**: Tigers owner Mike Ilitch names himself, along with Willie, Al Kaline, general manager Randy Smith, and

manager Phil Garner to a special committee to re-energize the franchise. Willie's title is Special Assistant to Baseball Operations. It's a part-time position, but a year later, Willie resigns from Ort Tool and Die in Erie, Michigan, to work full-time with the Tigers.

- **August 2004**: Mike Reddy of Immortal Investments Publishing and Willie's agent, Mark Dehem, meet with Willie to formulate a plan for Willie's autobiography, *The People's Champion*. It is agreed that renowned sportswriter Kevin M. Allen will write the book to document for the thousands of Willie Horton fans his life in and out of baseball.

- **August 14, 2004**: The "Willie Horton Fields" are dedicated at Northwestern High School. They will be used for both softball and baseball.

- **October 18, 2004**: This date, Willie's 62nd birthday, is proclaimed Willie Horton Day in the state of Michigan, thanks to legislation introduced by state Majority Floor Leader Randy Richardville of Monroe. It is an annual event.

**From Willie's speech at Northwestern High:** *"I really don't have the words to say what this day means to Willie Horton. But I can say it's about people. My whole life is about people, and my whole career was about the fans. Our community, the city, the park and the school has to form a partnership for all of this to work. As parents, we have a responsibility to provide for our kids and grandchildren. We did that today."*

# ◆◇ Statistics ◇◆

On July 15, 2000, Willie was immortalized with the highest honor in Tigers history: retirement of his No. 23 and the unveiling of his statue, just the sixth in the team's Walk of Fame.

## WILLIE HORTON
*(Inscribed on his statue)*
WILLIE HORTON
*"Willie the Wonder"*
Born: October 18, 1942 (Arno, Virginia)
*Detroit Tigers (OF, DH) 1963-77/ Texas Rangers, Cleveland Indians, Toronto Blue Jays (DH, OF) 1978/ Seattle Mariners (DH) 1979-1980*
A hometown hero whose accomplishments on and off the field are a credit to the city of Detroit

### ACHIEVEMENTS AND HONORS

- Raised in a Detroit housing project and overcame adversity to become a Tiger hometown hero
- Was a baseball star for Detroit's Northwestern High School and played Detroit Sandlot baseball
- Was instrumental in helping crush the violence that erupted during the 1967 riots in Detroit
- Batted .326 his first season with the Tigers
- Had 100 or more RBI in 1965 (104) and 1966 (100)
- Threw out Lou Brock at home plate in the pivotal game five of the 1968 World Series
- Led the team in home runs 1968 (36), 1969 (28) and 1975 (25)
- Hit 325 career home runs, 1,163 RBI, and had a .273 lifetime batting average
- Was elected to four All Star teams as a Tiger
- Had his uniform number 23 retired July 15, 2000

*Sculptors: Julie & Omri R. Amrany    Co-sculptor: Gary Tillery    Dedicated: July 15, 2000*

# ❖❖ SUMMARY ❖❖

### A SUMMARY OF THE SPORTSMAN AND HUMANITARIAN

On and off the field, Willie Horton is a Detroit hero whose major league accomplishments are legendary and a credit to the city of Detroit and to Major League Baseball.

### HIGHLIGHTS

- On October 28, 2003, the Michigan legislature passed a bill designating every October 18th (beginning October 18, 2004) as "Willie Horton Day." Willie is just the fourth person in Michigan history to be given a day; the last one was Rosa Parks.
- The Winter 2003 edition of *Corp* magazine named Willie one of "Michigan's Most Powerful African-American Leaders."
- October 16, 2002, Willie was inducted into the CATCH 2002 Hall of Fame. CATCH is an organization dedicated to improving the quality of life for pediatric patients at Children's & Henry Ford hospitals.
- In January 2002, Willie was named special assistant to Tigers president Dave Dombrowski, where he still serves in an advisory role today.
- On June 18, 2001, Detroit Tigers owner Mike Ilitch announced the formation of the Tigers Baseball Committee, which included Willie and Al Kaline. In addition, Willie was appointed as Assistant to Baseball Operations.
- On May 2, 2001, in gratitude for Willie's concern for the state's youth, Virginia governor James S. Gilmore III designated the coming weekend "Hometown Hero Weekend of Appalachia, Virginia." And the governor of Tennessee announced that Willie would be inducted into the Tennessee state Hall of Fame.
- In May 2000, the Tri-Cities of Tennessee and Virginia established the first annual Willie Horton "Baseball for Kids" Benefit Weekend.

189

- On August 5, 2000, Willie was inducted into the Syracuse SkyChiefs Baseball Club Hall of Fame.
- On July 15, 2000, the Detroit Tigers immortalized Willie by retiring his jersey, No. 23, and by unveiling a statue of him at brand-new Comerica Park.
- In 1999, Willie was named No. 69 in the Detroit Free Press "Century of Champions Top 100."
- In 1992, Willie was elected to the International Afro-American Sports Hall of Fame and Gallery.
- In 1987, Willie was elected to the Michigan Sports Hall of Fame.
- In 1979, Willie became just the forty-third player in major league history to hit 300 home runs.
- When he left the Tigers in 1977, Willie ranked fourth in team history with 262 home runs, and tenth with 886 RBIs.
- In 1975, local sportswriters named Willie "Tiger of the Year."
- In both 1975 *and* 1979, Willie was named Comeback Player and Designated Hitter of the Year.
- In the crucial Game 5 of the 1968 World Series, Willie made the key play, throwing out St. Louis's Lou Brock at home plate to keep the Tigers' hopes alive. In the epic seven-game series, Willie batted .304 with one home run and three RBIs. His heroics helped spur Detroit to its first championship since 1945.
- In five different seasons, Willie drove in 90 or more RBIs.
- Willie ranked among the top five American League RBI leaders in 1965, 1966, and 1968.
- Willie drove in 100 RBIs for Detroit in 1965 and 1966. And thirteen years later at age 36, Willie did it again for Seattle.
- Willie played in 2,028 major league games.
- Willie had 325 career home runs, one of the American League's most powerful hitters of his era.
- Willie's lifetime statistics include a .273 average, 1,993 base hits, 1,163 RBIs, and .457 slugging percentage.
- In 1972, Willie tied a 30-year-old major league record with 12 putouts in a game against the Cleveland Indians. The record still stands today.

- Willie was just the second player in Tigers history to post back-to-back 100 RBIs seasons in his first two years.
- Willie was selected to the All-Star team seven times. Due to injuries, he played in only four.
- Willie contributed significantly to each team with his exceptional ability to provide key hits, RBIs and home runs.

Willie suffered several injuries throughout his career, but he showed great resilience, displaying production and power while amassing nearly 2,000 career hits. Willie could do more than hit with power, though. He was a skilled batsman who could hit to all fields—his three seasons over .300 attest to that.

### MAJOR LEAGUE PLAYING CAREER

| | | |
|---|---|---|
| 1963–1977 | Detroit Tigers | LF/DH |
| 1977 | Texas Rangers | LF/DH |
| 1978 | Cleveland Indians | DH |
| | Oakland Athletics | |
| | Toronto Blue Jays | |
| 1979–1981 | Seattle Mariners | DH |

(LF = Left Fielder / DH = Designated Hitter)

### MANAGING/COACHING CAREER

**Valencia, Venezuela Baseball Team, Winter 1977–'78**
- Player/manager
  *Note:* Under Willie, Valencia won the Caribbean World Series. In 1978–'79, the team finished in second place.

**Oakland A's, 1983–'84**
- Roving organizational hitting coach

**Detroit Tigers, 1985**
- Roving organizational hitting coach
  *Note:* Spring Training/and only one month of 1985 season

**New York Yankees, 1985**
- First Base/Hitting coach

*Note:* After the first month of the season, Billy Martin was hired as Yankees manager and hired Willie for this position.

### Chicago White Sox, 1986
- Hitting coach/Organizational consultant
- Player development coach

  *Note:* Promoted by Chicago White Sox vice president/ general manager Ken Harrelson.

### ADDITIONAL AWARDS AND RECOGNITIONS

| | |
|---|---|
| 2004 | Honored by Michigan governor Jennifer Granholm with the first annual statewide Willie Horton Day October 18. |
| 1998 | Received "Father of the Year" award from Michigan state senator Jackie Vaughn III. |
| 1997–1998 | Continued to support our active military community as a guest speaker at various installations in the Unites States and abroad. For his support, Willie was inducted into the Military Hall of Fame. |
| 1997 | Was one of the former major league players selected as "Ambassadors of Baseball European Tour Team" at Spain's Naval Station Rota. |
| 1996 | Inducted as an honorary member of the U.S. Army Infantry Training Brigade at Fort Benning, Georgia, for presentation titled "Liberty and Justice for All." |
| 1996 | Received New Light Baptist Church Men's Day Award, serving as keynote speaker. |
| 1994–1998 | Worked with the Foundation Fighting Blindness. |
| 1994 | Received the Father Vincent Welch Award (Tiger Citizen of the Year) for outstanding contributions to youth in the area. |
| 1993 | Received the Unsung Hero of Sport award. |

| | |
|---|---|
| May 1993 | Awarded a special proclamation from Michigan senators for participation in the National Amateur All-Star Baseball Tournament. |
| March 1993 | Advisory Committee member, Skillman Sports, Recreation and Youth Development (Skillman Foundation). |
| 1992–1993 | J.C. Penney Golden Rule Award Panel Member. |
| 1992–1998 | Award presented by the Knights of Columbus for his participation at St. Christine's Soup Kitchen. |
| 1991 | One of the former major league players selected to represent the "Ambassadors of Baseball World Tour Team." While in Japan, Taiwan, and Korea, Willie acted as Ambassador of Goodwill, visiting hospitals, schools, and military bases between scheduled exhibition games. Received one of Seoul, South Korea's highest goodwill awards presented by the Premier. |
| 1990 | Served on the board of directors of Bishop Borgess Catholic School. |
| 1990 | Award of participation in Father & Son Banquet at Beth Eden Baptist Church. |
| 1985 | Worked with the Wayne County Executive Office as a youth adviser. |
| 1979 | Received *Seattle Post-Intelligencer* Sports Star of the Year award in Seattle, Washington. |
| 1979 | Seattle mayor Charles Royer proclaimed June 9, 1979, as Willie Horton Day, as Willie became just the 43rd player in major league history to hit 300 home runs. |
| 1977 | Received Spirit of Detroit award from Detroit City Council. |
| 1975 | Received award on Detroit Tiger Recognition Day, signed by mayor Coleman A. Young. |
| 1972 | Willie was awarded a special proclamation for donating sports equipment and assisting a clinic, |

|      | which helped youngsters develop their natural ability in the state of Michigan. |
|------|------|
| 1970 | Willie received an award from the Michigan Heart Association for "seeing what needed to be done and doing it, thereby quite probably saving the life of his teammate Al Kaline." Unconscious after a collision in the outfield, Kaline was turning blue and his jaw was locked. Willie rushed over and forced open Kaline's jaw, allowing air to reach his lungs. "Speed in applying this first step in cardiopulmonary resuscitation is all important," says the award. And indeed, Willie's quick thinking helped save Kaline's life. |
| 1967 | Was instrumental in helping quell the violence that erupted during the 1967 riots in Detroit. |
| 1964–Present | Willie has served as a member of the Detroit Branch of the Lions Club. He is a mentor for blind youth and gives motivational presentations to clubs throughout the Midwest. He promotes, supports, and is actively involved in the United Way, and in the Boys and Girls Clubs of America. He also continues to support our active military community as a guest speaker at various installations in the United States and abroad. |

# A SPECIAL TRIBUTE

**Mike Ilitch**

WHEN I THINK OF WILLIE HORTON, I think of power. He was muscular when he played for the Detroit Tigers in the 1960s and 1970s, and baseball didn't have too many big guys in those days. Willie hit the ball hard. He was a confident hitter, and he was a competitive athlete. You could tell he was serious about his baseball. He looked intimidating.

What you couldn't tell from his baseball demeanor was that he is one of the softest-hearted people you're ever going to meet.

Since he re-joined the Tigers organization, he has given us a big lift. He always has a smile on his face. He spreads goodness and warmth.

When he and I talked about his desire to return to baseball, I was impressed with his sincerity. But I had no idea what a hard worker he is and how much compassion he has for people.

Once he began working for the Tigers, he became totally involved. He visited every minor league team and was particularly sensitive to players from other countries. He talked to them about eating right. He made sure they had enough money. He made sure they weren't getting too lonely. He was like a big daddy to them. Willie couldn't help himself. He said he was going to lose some weight so he could swing the bat more easily when he was working with the kids, and he did.

He's had a lot of bad breaks in his life. Recently, he was forced to have a hip operation. I spoke to one of the doctors, who told me, "Mr. Ilitch, I don't know how Willie took the pain he was living with."

But Willie just brightens up the room when he walks in, and he never has anything bad to say about anyone. Everyone in the organization loves and respects him.

As a graduate of Cooley High School in Detroit, I'm very proud that Willie was a local guy who made it big. I could relate to him because I played amateur baseball on the same diamonds he did. Diamonds 1 and 3 at Northwestern were great diamonds.

Willie has close ties to the city. Through his involvement with the Police Athletic League (PAL), he has worked with many youngsters in the city. He can walk into the mayor's office. He can walk into any office in Detroit and command respect. People will sit down and listen to him. If he has something he wants done, it'll get done.
We're all very impressed with Willie.

He's just grateful to be alive, to be part of society, to be a husband and a grandfather. And he's grateful to be associated with the Tigers.

The black community loves Willie, but to me, he represents success for all people. He has played a significant role for a lot of years in the city, and I felt he was under the radar screen in Detroit.

Early on, I considered retiring his number and giving him a statue. My only reservation was that he wasn't a Hall of Famer. The others we had honored were, and I wondered how other important Detroit Tigers would feel.

Some folks did lobby for Willie to have a statue, but in the end, I sat by myself, evaluated the situation, and concluded it was time to honor a hometown hero. And his numbers weren't too shabby either. In fact, they're quite good.

And my concerns about what the other Detroit Tigers heroes would think about Willie's number being retired were all for naught. Most of them showed up to see Willie honored. You can read how people are feeling by studying their faces, and I could tell that the former Tigers were all happy for Willie that day.

*Mike Ilitch*
*Detroit Tigers Owner*

# ◆◆ TRIBUTES ◆◆

**WHEN WILLIE WAS PLAYING BASEBALL AT** Northwestern High School, I received a call from his coach Sam Bishop, who had been my coach when I ran track there. At the time, I was practicing law in the Tobin Building in Detroit, and Sam and I had become friends. He was one of the finest men I've known.

"I have a young man who's hitting the ball across Grand River," said Sam. "I think he has great potential to be a major league player. I wonder if you'd come by and see him."

I went to Northwestern, met Willie, and watched him hit balls all over the place. I also went to meet his parents, who lived in a dingy place on Forest. At the time, Willie was starting to get scouted. The Tigers were very interested, as were the Red Sox and Yankees. Willie was underage, and his parents asked me to become his guardian, as well as his attorney. I went into Judge Ira Kaufman's probate court and took care of that.

Boston wanted Willie because the Red Sox had that short left-field fence in Fenway Park. The Yankees were a concern to us because Yankee Stadium was pretty rough on right-handed hitters. Center field was pretty deep there. The Yankees' right field porch was better for left-handed hitters. That's why Willie and I decided, with his mother and father's consent, to go with the Tigers.

I have a picture in my office that shows Judge Kaufman with us when we signed Willie's contract at Tiger Stadium. Tigers general manager Jim Campbell and I became good friends, and he used to tell me, "You started all of this agent stuff." I don't know whether I was the first agent or not.

Willie didn't even have a coat to wear to sign the contract. I gave him my coat that I was wearing. After Willie signed, I took him back to my house. I was living in Virginia Park. I said. "Willie, God gave you the ability to play ball. He didn't give it to me. He gave it to you. You can utilize this and become a great ballplayer and a great human being, or you can throw it away. You have that ability, no question about it. I want you to use it to become a good citizen."

197

Back then, he was very far removed. I can't describe the atmosphere he came from. One anecdote that I've told with Willie present is about the time his parents called me to say that Willie was driving without a license. When he returned home, his parents called and I came right over.

"Your Mom and Dad told me you were driving without a license," I said.

"Well, Mr. Keith," he replied. "I have a driver's license."

He handed me a driver's license with another man's name and picture on it. He didn't understand the licensing process. He just thought you needed any driver's license. He was that far removed. I called the chief of police, and Willie took the test and got his license.

After he signed his contract, Willie wanted to buy a home for his mother. They picked out one on Edison Street in Detroit, and when reporters asked him about it, they wanted to know where the house was located. "It's in the suburbs," Willie said.

That section of the city *was* a suburb compared to where Willie came from.

The most difficult time I had with Willie came when his mother and father were killed in an automobile accident. He didn't want to go back to winter ball. He said he was not going to play baseball because he was too depressed. He spent one weekend at my house, and I told him, "Look, your mother and father would want you to play baseball and make them proud."

Willie's dad was very proud of his son. He used to go into the bleachers in center field and let everyone know that. Sam Bishop was proud of Willie, too. And I'm thankful that he asked me to help Willie because Willie changed my life, too. He has always been kind and gracious to me, giving me a bat from every All-Star game he was in, plus one from the World Series.

When the Tigers put Willie's statue in Comerica Park I gave a recitation of what he meant me. I have so much respect and admiration for Tigers owner Mike Ilitch. He has a lot of conviction. He wanted Willie's statue up there because of what he means to Detroit. Now Willie is part of the family.

When the riots broke out, Willie was there. When the Detroit Tigers beat St. Louis to win the World Series in 1968, Willie threw the ball to get [Lou] Brock. That turned the series around. I remember walking out on Michigan Avenue after we won that World Series, and I've never seen so much love and affection between the suburbs and the city of Detroit. They were all proud of the Detroit Tigers.

When Willie comes to my chambers to see me, people all over the federal building come down. You hear people saying, "Willie Horton is here." Marshals, agents…everyone comes down to meet him. He still has that humble way of acting. I'm sure his mother and father must be delighted as they look down on him.

*Judge Damon Keith*
*U.S. Court of Appeals for the Sixth Circuit*

WHEN YOU MENTION THE DETROIT TIGERS, THE two names you hear are Willie Horton and Al Kaline. Willie knows the game, and he's big in the community. When you have that combination, it can't be overlooked. Unfortunately, in this game, it's been overlooked a little too long. But guys like Rondell White, Craig Monroe and me — we'd bend over backward for Willie. When I spoke to some inner-city kids recently, I wore a Willie Horton throwback jersey. When you talk to the kids, you don't want to wear a suit. You want to wear something they can relate to. And I wanted to represent Willie. When he tells me that I remind him of Norm Cash, I take that as a compliment because I'm a baseball fan and a student of the game. And I know Norm Cash was dear to Willie.

*Dmitri Young*
*Detroit Tigers Player*

THE DETROIT TIGERS' TRADITION IS ONE OF THE better ones in baseball. Arguably, there are teams ahead of us, but the Tigers are in the upper tier. So to have Willie around to be a sounding board means a lot to this organization. He's from the city and he was a great player. It's huge to have him here.

*Alan Trammell*
*Detroit Tigers Manager*

WILLIE IS A GREAT GUY AND A HUMBLE MAN, considering all that he's been through in his life. He cares about young players and he wants to see them succeed. He's a family man, and he's very sincere about that.

*Rondell White*
*Detroit Tigers Outfielder*


WILLIE IS PROBABLY THE MOST COMMUNITY-oriented guy we've seen come through the Detroit Tigers organization. Since he was a rookie at Henley Field in 1961, Willie has adopted Lakeland as his second home. He's worked with kids groups and has been willing to do whatever the Boys and Girls Club of Lakeland need for support. I've known Willie for 31 years, and he has been just phenomenal.

Willie was very influential in the development, layout, and construction of the Tigertown complex—the minor league operations behind Joker Marchant Stadium.

He's very well-known to many different groups in Lakeland. And when I need someone from the Tigers to be an ambassador, I go to Willie. When he walks into Lakeland City Hall, everyone in the building knows him.

In fact, one of the suites at the ballpark is named "The Willie Horton Suite," and there's even a special hitting-instruction area at the minor league field named after him. It was designed on the basis of his training methodology. It takes into account how Willie used to train—by hitting tires. He was the first major leaguer that anyone had heard of who hung tires on poles, and hit them to develop arm strength. And he is truly one-of-a-kind.

*Bill Tinsley*
*Director of Lakeland (Florida) Parks and Recreation*


THE DETROIT TIGERS DON'T GO AFTER THE Canadian fan the way they used to in the 1960s when Willie played. He has dreamed of getting the Canadian base to come back to Tigers games. For no charge, he has done the parade at Tecumseh, Ontario, for the last four years. He would like to spread it to Leamington and different areas in

Canada. He comes in and talks to people. He's about people and family.

When I went to the Detroit Tigers fantasy camp, Willie could have hung out with anyone he wanted. But he spent a lot of time with me because he likes my family. He likes my wife, Bonnie. He likes that I have kids involved in sports. And he loves my mom, too. Willie's been to our family produce farm in River Canard, and my mom has made him a big dinner. She's a 75-year-old widow. My dad died in 1975, and so Mom raised nine kids on a little vegetable farm.

Willie loves our family situation. All of my mom's children are still in Essex County, Ontario, and we're all connected. We rarely talk about baseball. But it doesn't matter to Willie. He has this analytical mind. He wants to know how everything is done step-by-step. He wants to go in the greenhouse and see how you start the plans and how you pick and how you pack. He wants to know. Once, I saw Willie spend half an hour talking to someone about how the guy made his special fried chicken.

*Arsene Bondy*
*Friend*

THE DETROIT POLICE ATHLETIC LEAGUE (PAL) WAS **BOUNCED AMONG THE THREE** automobile companies. General Motors was making the change to Ford when I got involved. Bob Rewey was executive vice president of Worldwide Marketing and Sales for Ford, and he was asked to oversee Ford's involvement. He had me go down and see what it was about.

Bob became president of PAL. And I became the assistant to the president. I told Bob that this isn't your usual charity. First, when you assume the position, you assume fiscal responsibility. You aren't just president for show and tell. It's a real honest-to-goodness operation.

At the time, PAL was struggling. The late WJR radio personality J.P. McCarthy had adopted PAL and was doing the PAL golf tournament. Even thought J.P. was very active, the money was starting to dwindle. Fundraising had deteriorated—probably making $250,000. Dick "Night Train" Lane was the head of PAL, and Willie was his assistant. With Ford in the leadership, Bob said he would like to restore PAL to what it once was. Then Night Train retired, and Willie took over full directorship. We said, "Let us help you." We started to put in a structure, and to Willie's credit, he embraced the whole process. That meant realigning some officers and leadership working with Detroit mayor Coleman Young at the time. It also meant taking a more direct role as a corporation in what was essentially a very valuable charity to the city of Detroit because of the number of kids it reached.

After the first year, it was time to move it to the next automobile company. But Bob took a look at it and said, "I don't think we've made enough progress." To make a long story short, we kept leadership of PAL for six or seven years. It took that long before we thought it was stable enough to pass along to General Motors. We took it to $1.25 million and that's probably where it is now.

Willie was very supportive and receptive to what we wanted to do. We started to have more discussions with J.P. about maybe moving the golf tournament. We had people working with Willie almost on a daily basis.

Willie was there through all the changes made to the program. His passion for the kids is infectious. And once you get involved with Willie, you can't say "no." He becomes the driving force because of the heart and emotion exuded by the children.

You can imagine he was already entrenched when we came in and made these suggestions. He could have rejected it, but his attitude was "What can we do for the kids?" If it was good for the kids, it was good for Willie.

Willie has much the same attitude toward mentoring the kids that Judge Damon Keith does. I always tell Judge Keith that he passed on those tendencies very, very well.

We produced a six-minute film all about Detroit to be featured at the Imax Theatre. It's basically about the people of Detroit. And we have a segment in there that shows Willie coaching kids on the field. We have Judge Keith in the background. It's a way of showing how that mentoring torch has been passed along. He is just a great individual. And you know that you have been hugged by him. It's not half-hearted. It's genuine and impassioned. It's Willie telling you, "I like you, and you are a great friend."

*Gary Nielsen*
*Former Ford Executive*
*Worked with Willie in the PAL Program*

BORN INTO THE TIGERS FAMILY, I GREW UP WITH Mr. Kaline's kids and Gates Brown's kids, and I have so many memories of running around Tiger Stadium at eight and nine years old. I can remember running around one minute, and then hearing that my dad had won the game with a ninth inning home run the next minute.

When I see my dad's teammates now, the kind of looks they give me are priceless because I grew up around them.

Remember, initially it was a little difficult for me, because I had to share my father with the entire world. It really felt like that at times. That was difficult because sometimes I just wanted him to be Dad. And when he remarried, it was like I had to share him all over again with another family. And that wasn't easy for me. But he made it easy for me to understand what family was about. My stepmother, Gloria, has been nothing but a mother to me. In fact, we don't even use the terms "stepmother" or "stepchildren" because of what my dad learned from his parents—you treat everyone like family.

What I've learned from my father has nothing to do with sports. He has taught me the true meaning of family and hw to make everyone feel loved. Even at 41, I have so much respect for my father because I know what he went through in his career. And I'm humbled in his presence.

I really respect what he's done over the years. I didn't always understand it as a young man at 13 or 14 years old, but maybe I wasn't supposed to understand it. He and my mother were divorced. And when you're 14 and reading about it in *Jet* magazine, it's tough. As I got older, I really, really understood and respected what my father did and how he did it.

*Darryl William Horton*
*Willie's Son*

# ❖❖ CHARITIES ❖❖

**IN 2002, WILLIE HORTON** established the Willie Horton Foundation. It's a charitable organization committed to helping children and the elderly. Since it started, it has provided 2,000 backpacks and school supplies to inner-city children. It has also provided support for the youth program at the New Light Baptist Church in Detroit. The foundation also has recently announced it will adopt a kindergarten class, and it will provide assistance and guidance for that class until those students graduate from high school.

Willie is a Lifetime NAACP member and has been involved with the following charities:

- Boys and Girls Club of Lakeland and Mulberry, Florida
- Red Cross Blood Donor Champion and Spokesperson 2004–2005
- Youth Sports and Recreation Commission
- Don Boscoe Hall
- Think Detroit
- Lions Club
- Canadian Charities
- Joe DiMaggio Classic in Hollywood
- Tecumseh, Ontario, Little League
- Baseball Assistance Team (BAT)
- Major League Alumni
- South Central Community of Kingsport

# ❖❖ PHOTO CREDITS ❖❖

**THANKS TO THE MANY PHOTO CONTRIBUTORS** who helped make this book possible.

- Cover photo courtesy of Photo Visions/Dennis J. Slagle

- Photos of Northwestern High School Field dedication, Willie Horton Day October 18, and No. 23 Celebration courtesy of George Brooks

- Various photos of Willie courtesy of Bill Eisner

- Various photos of Willie as a player courtesy of the Detroit Tigers

- Special photos of Willie courtesy of Mark Dehem

- Photos of the Horton statue and plaque courtesy of Bright Imaging Group

- Other photos courtesy of those noted

- Photos scanned by David Story of Story Technologies LLC

# A MESSAGE FROM THE PUBLISHER

We are very proud to present the extraordinary story of the legendary Willie Horton in *The People's Champion*. Kevin Allen has artfully crafted the remarkable life of one of Detroit's all time favorite sport's heroes. We are supremely grateful to Willie and his lovely wife, Gloria. Also, we appreciate the Horton family, Mark Dehem and their other special friends for their unique input and participation. Immortal Investments is honored to present *The People's Champion*. It will inspire readers now and in future generations. God Bless!

*Michael J. Reddy*
*Publisher*

Immortal Investments Publishing produces timeless books that move, inspire, and spotlight the best of the human spirit manifested by extraordinary human achievement.

Please review and order our other outstanding titles by visiting **www.immortalinvestments.com** or by calling **1-800-475-2066.**

Please let us know if you have suggestions for other exceptional books or have comments about *The People's Champion.*

***This publishing venture is revolutionary in that this book like all other Immortal Investment titles is not distributed to bookstores. It is available exclusively through Immortal Investments Publishing.

To bring Willie Horton to your event for a personal book signing please contact www.immortalinvestments.com.

## Order your signed copy by
## Willie Horton today!
## 1-800-475-2066.
## NOT SOLD IN BOOKSTORES

Immortal Investmants Publishing
35122 W. Michigan Ave. Wayne, MI 48184

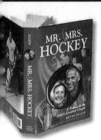

# boji books PRESENTS...

# The Athlete Connection
### Your Personal Connection to Professional Athletes

## Mark S. Dehem
## *Willie Horton's Personal Agent*

*Turn Your Next Event Into a Sports Spectacular. Book a Celebrity!*

*Current Athletes, Legends of the Game, Local Heroes and National Celebrities.*

## The Athlete Connection
*Bringing You the Very Best in Sports Appearances.*

## Best Wishes to the Horton Family.
## From Mark and Karen Dehem

46933 Breckenridge
Macomb, MI 48044

Office (586) 532-8415
Fax (586) 532-8416